The Hardball Times Baseball Annual 2017

Featuring contributions by FanGraphs & THT staff writers:

Emma Baccellieri • Carson Cistulli • Adam Dorhauer
Patrick Dubuque • August Fagerstrom • Stacey Gotsulias
Brad Johnson • David Kagan • Corinne Landrey
Joon Lee • Eric Longenhagen • Chris Mitchell
Jack Moore • John Paschal • Kate Preusser
Alex Remington • Eno Sarris • Gerald Schifman
Alexandra Simon • Jeff Sullivan • Shane Tourtellotte
Steve Treder • Neil Weinberg • Sarah Wexler
Stacie Wheeler • Jeff Zimmerman

With additional contributions by guest writers:
Rob Arthur • Dan Epstein
Sara Nović • Mike Petriello

Produced by Paul Swydan
Edited by Joe Distelheim, Jason Linden,
Dustin Nosler & Greg Simons
Graphics edited by Sean Dolinar

D1445746

The Hardball Times Baseball Annual 2017

A FanGraphs production

New content daily at hardballtimes.com and fangraphs.com

Edited by Joe Distelheim, Jason Linden, Dustin Nosler, Greg Simons and Paul Swydan
Graphics edited by Sean Dolinar
Stats developed by FanGraphs
Cover design by Travis Howell
Cover photo by Flickr user Mr.512 - *flickr.com/photos/mr512/6962726837*
Typesetting by Paul Swydan

Copyright © 2016 The Hardball Times

Published by FanGraphs and The Hardball Times

ISBN-13: 978-1540448262
ISBN-10: 1540448266
Printed by CreateSpace

What's Inside

The 2016 Season

Commentary

History

Analysis

Et Cetera

Welcome to Our Book

Hi everybody! Thank you so much for picking up our book. This is the 13th edition of *The Hardball Times Baseball Annual*. Some might call that bad luck, but as I was born on a 13th, I've never really shared in the fear of that number. In fact, I can confidently say that in my time with this book—this is my fifth year working on it—that it has never been better.

The *Annual* remains the sum of many authors coming together for one goal—to provide the reader with a fantastic group of baseball essays to help ease your pain as another glorious season fades to black. The book has four sections. In the first, which covers the 2016 season, we stuck with the moments-based examination of each division's race.

By this point in the year, you have read, seen or otherwise digested plenty about the overall themes of 2016 for your favorite team, so in the spirit of zigging where others zag, we think it's instructive to look back at the times when the balance of the division races really tipped. For some, it was as early as April. Other divisions took until September. And we aren't just arbitrarily picking these out, we are informed by the division odds at our sister site, FanGraphs.

Commentary starts like it always does, with our Year in Frivolity. John Paschal once again finds the hilarious moments we forgot happened. One tradition that didn't make it into the book this year, however, was our GM in a Box. It was initially in the mix, but it was cut late in the planning stages. It could return next year though. There are several executives who are ripe for their turn under the microscope.

When I sat down to write this introduction last year, I knew very clearly which pieces I wanted to highlight. I do not feel the same way this year. Perhaps I have become overly sentimental, but I feel as though every piece in the book this year has a claim to being, if not the best, then certainly in the top five. The book is a little leaner this year, which is in part due to a couple fewer pieces, and also partly because last year's book contained six pieces that were at least 14 pages long. This year's edition contains only two such pieces, and they are authored by Carson Cistulli and Adam Dorhauer, who are two of the quickest reads around. I think you will find this leaner, meaner edition makes for a better reading experience overall.

One thing that is important to us, both on the site and in the book, is to have new voices in the mix. With this year's book, we have struck a good balance. Nearly half of this year's authors—14 by my count—have never written for the *Annual* before. Reading the same people year after year can become stale, and so we take great pleasure in being able to constantly find new voices to challenge and enlighten us.

You really are going to love this book, and I should stop writing and let you get to it. It's full of thoughtful commentary both specific (Jeff Sullivan on catcher framing,

Jack Moore on amphematimines) and abstract (August Fagerstrom on a beat writer's rooting interests, Sara Nović on why literary writers love baseball). It has unique looks back through baseball history—did you know there was a thing called the Babe Ruth Crown? Or that the 1957 Kansas City A's didn't have a single pitcher qualify for the ERA title? Or that the Rolling Stones played *six* shows at Shea Stadium in October 1989? Finally, there is incisive analysis. Rob Arthur created a new defensive metric that improves upon industry-standard Ultimate Zone Rating. Gerald Schifman tells us concretely how much Hope and Faith each season now holds (hint: more than it used to). Mike Petriello returns to break down the importance of a catcher's arm strength using Statcast. And there is so much more—I am overjoyed with the analysis section this year.

Before I let you go, I need to thank a few people. Our team here at THT works so well together, and that cohesion is the main reason we are able to keep turning this book out with such a small staff every year. Joe Distelheim, Jason Linden, Dustin Nosler and Greg Simons remain an editing force to be reckoned with, as well as a great sounding board and are just genuinely awesome people.

Sean Dolinar also came back to help us with the graphics. Any graph you see in the book this year was produced by Sean, and as such the graphs and charts within are all cut from the same cloth, which is tremendous. It is also a first, and required a lot of work on Sean's part, work that he made look easy. My old friend Travis Howell also came back to handle the book's cover design. This is our second year with a more picturesque design, and I couldn't be happier with it.

Thanks also to The Alchemist's *Rapper's Best Friend 3*, which is great editing music.

Of course, I wouldn't be able to take this on without the extreme patience of my wife, Summer, and my children, Jasmine and Xander. They deserve the ultimate thanks for allowing me the time I need to help turn 29 disparate pieces into an actual book.

As always, I need to take the time to thank both Dave Studeman and David Appelman for trusting me with the challenge of producing this book each year. It has been a couple of year since Studes walked off into the sunset, but I always try to keep his ideals for the book in mind. I wouldn't be able to do so without the freedom given to me by David Appelman to turn out the book I think our readers will enjoy the most. It is refreshing not to be micro-managed, and I am well aware that being in such a position makes me very privileged. And finally, you, dear and faithful reader, for supporting us, both here and online. What we do is possible only because of you.

May your manager never force feed you nerve tonic. May the pitcher hang you a slider. May the dogpile rise up to meet you. May your flags fly forever.

Happy Baseball,
Paul Swydan

The 2016 Season

The American League East View

by Stacey Gotsulias

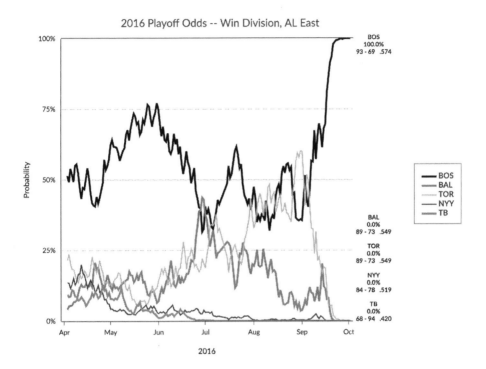

2016 Playoff Odds -- Win Division, AL East

Compared to the latter half of the 1990s and most of the 2000s, the American League East in the 2010s has been mutable. No team has won the division two years in a row, and every single team has won it at least once. The 2016 season was no different. The winner of the division race, the Boston Red Sox, went from worst to first for the second time in the last seven seasons. The last time they followed an atrocious season with an excellent one was 2013, when they went all the way and won their eighth World Series championship.

Before the 2016 season began, most were choosing either the defending AL East champion Toronto Blue Jays to repeat or the Red Sox to pull off another rise from the ashes. It was assumed it would be a two-team race and that the other teams in the division—Baltimore, New York and Tampa Bay—would be battling to avoid the AL East basement. That's not exactly what happened. While the two favorites were in it to the end, the division wouldn't actually be won until the last week of the season, and a couple of the teams that were dismissed as having no shot before the season started, Baltimore and New York, were better than predicted. While Boston won the division, Baltimore tied Toronto for the two Wild Card spots, and New York remained in that race until the last week of the season. The only team in the division that never had a chance of winning the division was Tampa Bay. Its highest mark was a scant 13 percent chance on April 26. Tampa finished the season 68-94 and 20 games out of first place. Baltimore and Toronto finished four games out, and New York finished nine back.

The three series that most impacted the AL East race, according to FanGraphs' division odds, occurred in September, all within days of one another. This was representative of the the AL East becoming a division that can count on competition from nearly all comers.

Sept. 5-7: Blue Jays Swept Out of Yankee Stadium

The Blue Jays came into this series with renewed optimism. After dropping 20 percent in the division odds over the two days prior, the Blue Jays had gained some momentum back with a 5-3 victory over the Rays. The corresponding gain in their division odds was Toronto's biggest jump (10.9 percent) in the division race odds thus far in 2016. It restored their overall division odds to 51.8 percent. That wasn't as great as they had been following Sept. 1, when they stood at 60.2 percent—the only day of the season that they climbed over 60 percent—but it was enough to give them the best odds in the division.

The Blue Jays were now 77-59 overall and were one game up in the division race over the Red Sox, who had just lost a 1-0 game to Oakland. What's more, they had won the game without production from their top three studs. While much of the focus throughout 2016 was on impending free agents José Bautista and Edwin Encarnación, as well as reigning AL Most Valuable Player Josh Donaldson, the Sunday afternoon win had been fueled by down-batting-order hitters Russell Martin (two-run homer), Troy Tulowitzki (2-for-4, run scored) and Devon Travis (2-for-4, two-run single).

The Jays were hoping that all cylinders would be clicking as they headed into Yankee Stadium that Monday afternoon looking to repeat their performance from Aug. 15-17 when they had last faced the Yankees. In that series in Rogers Centre, Toronto had won two out of three, dropping just a 1-0 decision in the series opener.

The first game of the early September series pitted Toronto's R.A. Dickey against New York's ace Masahiro Tanaka for a Labor Day afternoon game. On paper the edge went to New York. Dickey has fallen very far and very fast since his 2012 Cy Young campaign, while Tanaka quietly built a Cy Young campaign of his own in 2016. The 27-year-old righty tallied a 3.07 ERA built on his famously stingy walk rate—he walked only 4.5 percent of the batters he faced in 2016, third-lowest in the AL and fifth-lowest in all of baseball among qualified pitchers.

Starting pitching narrative be damned, it was the Blue Jays who got on the board first against Tanaka in the top half of the first inning. Travis singled home Bautista, who had led off the game with a double. But true to form, Tanaka limited the damage, and his teammates gave him a lead in the bottom of the first thanks to a two-run home run off the bat of Jacoby Ellsbury, righting the ship and the narrative.

New York would score again in the third and fourth innings, while Toronto's bats were shut down until the seventh. Tanaka was removed from the game after his 105th pitch, and Toronto plated two runs against a couple of rookie relievers, but that's all the Jays would get. The Yankees won the first game of the series, 5-3.

The following night was the biggest game of the series for New York and, to that point, one of the most important of its season. While Toronto was leading the division, the Yankees found themselves only 4.5 games back with a chance to gain some ground on everyone ahead of them in the Wild Card race, the Blue Jays included.

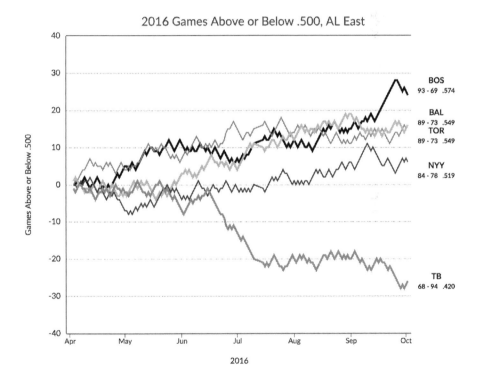

Fans of both teams couldn't have asked for a better game. It was sweaty and nerve-wracking until the very last moment, when Yankees left fielder Brett Gardner jumped up against the wall and came back down with the ball nearly popping out of his glove. That ball was a bases-loaded fly ball off the bat of Justin Smoak. If it had been hit just a few inches higher, it would have been a grand slam to put the Blue Jays up, 10-7. Instead, the Yankees pulled out the 7-6 victory. With the loss, the Blue Jays' division odds had dropped 10.9 percent in the series' first two games, down to 40.8 percent. By that point, the Yankees' division odds were toast, but this was the start of a week-long spike in their overall playoff odds.

On the last night of the series, three Yankees pitchers—Bryan Mitchell, Luis Severino and Tyler Clippard—combined to throw a five-hit shutout. The Yankees' two runs that night came off the bats of Starlin Castro, who hit a solo home run, and Brian McCann, with an RBI single, both in the third inning off Jays starter Marcus Stroman.

While the Jays entered the series with 51.8 percent division odds, they exited them with 32.7 percent division odds. It marked the last time their division odds were over the 40 percent mark, and they lost ground to both the Orioles and Red Sox. And this wasn't even the worst series for the Blue Jays. That would start just two days later back home in Toronto.

Sept. 9-11: Toronto Fails to Make Up Ground

The Blue Jays welcomed the now-first-place Red Sox to Rogers Centre for a three-game weekend set on Sept. 9. Thanks to the Blue Jays getting swept in New York and a cream puff West Coast road trip for Boston, the Red Sox were up on Toronto by a game in the standings.

> ### 10 Things You Should Remember About the 2016 AL East
>
> 1. David Ortiz saved one of his best seasons for last. He hit .315/.401/.620 with 38 HR and a career-high 48 doubles, while playing in his most games since 2006. New York's Álex Rodríguez and Mark Teixeira also retired during or following the season.
>
> 2. Yankees' rookie Gary Sánchez hit .299/.376/.657 with 20 homers in 53 games after his early-August promotion. Sanchez hit his 20th homer in his 51st career game, tying Wally Berger of the 1930 Boston Braves for fastest ever to 20 homers.
>
> 3. The Red Sox enjoyed a coming out party for their Killer B's—Mookie Betts, Jackie Bradley, Xander Bogaerts and rookie Andrew Benintendi. Betts' 31 homers and .318/.363/.534 got him MVP attention.
>
> 4. The Rays' Chris Archer had two distinctly different halves. In 19 first-half starts, batters hit .256/.330/.437 off him, compared to .215/.260/.360 in 14 second-half starts.

The first game of the series was an unmitigated disaster for the Blue Jays. Giving up a combined five runs in the first four innings wasn't the worst part; that didn't occur until the seventh, when they gave up six runs.

Marco Estrada started the game and was relieved by Aaron Loup in the third, who was relieved by Danny Barnes to start the fourth, who was relieved by Brett Cecil to start the sixth, who was relieved by Scott Feldman to end the sixth. Feldman started the seventh by surrendering a home run to Xander Bogaerts and a double to David

Ortiz. Mookie Betts got on base courtesy of a Devon Travis error that advanced Ortiz to third with no outs. With Hanley Ramirez at the plate, Betts stole second on the first pitch, and Ramirez hit a home run on the second to make it 9-2, Red Sox.

Feldman was relieved by Ryan Tepera, who allowed a Travis Shaw single. Tepera mercifully got Sandy Leon to pop out for the first out of the inning. The next batter, Jackie Bradley Jr., doubled on the first pitch, and Shaw advanced to third. Tepera retired Brock Holt, and it looked like maybe the Jays could get out of the inning without further damage. But Dustin Pedroia hit a single that scored Bradley and Shaw to make it 11-2, Sox. Bogaerts, who started the barrage, grounded out to short to end the inning.

5. Orioles closer Zach Britton had a season for the ages. In 69 games, he tallied a 0.54 ERA, 1.94 FIP and 2.09 xFIP and a record 80.0 GB%.

6. Orioles slugger Mark Trumbo hit a career-high 47 home runs, which led the majors, and more than doubled his 2015 output (22).

7. In his second season as Derek Jeter's replacement, Didi Gregorius set a career high with 20 homers, more than doubling the nine he hit in 2015.

8. The Orioles easily led the majors in homers, with 253, while the Blue Jays easily led the AL in bases on balls, with 632, and the Rays easily led the AL in strikeouts, with 1,482.

9. The Yankees traded away Andrew Miller, Carlos Beltran and Aroldis Chapman in July, but "Baby Bombers" like Sanchez, Tyler Austin and Aaron Judge kept them in the playoff hunt until the end.

10. Brad Miller became just the sixth Rays player to hit 30 homers in a season, and he and Evan Longoria became the third pair to do it in the same season.

The Blue Jays would add a run in the bottom of the eighth on an error, and the Red Sox would add two more runs in the top of the ninth. The Sox won, 13-3, and Toronto found itself two games behind in the division race.

The next day was comparatively quiet, and the Blue Jays redeemed themselves by winning, 3-2, to pull back to within one game of first place. J.A. Happ picked up his 18th win of the season, holding the Red Sox to two runs on four hits and a walk in six innings. For the Jays, Melvin Upton Jr. hit a two-run homer in the second inning off Red Sox starter Eduardo Rodriguez, and Bautista knocked an RBI single in the third. Pedroia hit a solo home run in the sixth, and Bradley hit a sacrifice fly in the seventh to get the Sox to within one run, but Joaquin Benot, Jason Grilli and Roberto Osuna each pitched an inning of scoreless relief to secure the win for Toronto.

The Red Sox's chances to win the division fell from 67.4 percent to 57.2 after the loss—it was their largest one-day drop in division odds for the season. Toronto's chances jumped from 23.8 percent to 31.6. Unfortunately for the Jays, any bit of momentum they may have had evaporated the very next day, when the Red Sox all but ended Toronto's run toward the division title. A slugfest ended with the Red

Sox victorious, 11-8. Every member of the Red Sox except Shaw reached base at least once, and seven of the other eight Red Sox hitters (Hanley Ramirez excepted) reached base at least twice. Bradley Jr., Ramirez and Ortiz all homered, with Bradley's and Ortiz's being of the three-run variety, which helped off-set the two homers Edwin Encarnación hit, as well as the grand slam Troy Tulowitzki hit.

Tulowitzki's slam in particular looked like it turned the tide for the Blue Jays. Red Sox starter Clay Buchholz was barely holding it together. A single sandwiched between two walks loaded the bases in the bottom of the third, and then Buchholz walked Russell Martin to force in a run and cut his lead to 4-2, before Tulowitzki crushed a ball into the left-field seats to put Toronto ahead, 6-4. Alas, the lead didn't last long. Xander Bogaerts drove in two runs with a single in the next frame, knocking out Aaron Sanchez and ushering in a battle of the bullpens that the Sox would win, 5-3.

With the victory, Boston's division odds rose once again to 65.3 percent, essentially mirroring its odds at the start of the series. The same was true for Toronto. Nominally, the Blue Jays were still alive in the division race, but they had squandered their best remaining chance to conquer the Red Sox. Boston's division odds never would fall below 61 percent the rest of the season. As for the Blue Jays, the loss dropped them to a 21.6 percent odds. The two teams would meet again from Sept. 30-Oct. 1, but by that point the Red Sox had the division sewn up, and the Blue Jays were fighting to maintain their grasp on a Wild Card berth.

Sept. 15-18: The Hanley Ramirez Show

A few days later, on Sept. 15, the Red Sox began a four-game series with the Yankees in Fenway Park. They had just finished losing two of a three-game set with Baltimore. Heading into the first game of the Yankees series, the Red Sox's division odds were at 61.4 percent, and they were one game ahead of Baltimore (20.3 percent) and two games up on Toronto, whose odds had dropped to 17.0 percent. The Yankees' division odds stood at 0.7 percent, but while their division hopes were dead, their Wild Card hopes were still flickering. As they built a 5-0 lead and carried it into the eighth inning, that flame was still burning. It would soon be snuffed out.

The Sox put a run on the board and entered the bottom of the ninth down, 5-1. Yankees manager Joe Girardi started the inning with Tommy Layne, who struck out leadoff hitter Aaron Hill. That's when things got crazy. With a four-run lead and two outs remaining, the Yankees' win expectancy stood at 98.1 percent. But then right-hander Blake Parker hit pinch-hitter Chris Young, and Girardi turned to closer Dellin Betances. What seemed like overkill would soon not be enough. Betances was uncharacteristically rattled, and ended up giving up a walk, two singles and a three-run walk-off homer to Hanley Ramirez. The Red Sox won, 7-5, and saw their chances to win the division jump to 68.1 percent. Following the season, in an article for The Hardball Times, The Baseball Gauge creator Dan Hirsch noted that Ramirez's blast was the most impactful play of the regular season according to his championship WPA (cWPA) statistic. (cWPA combines WPA with a value that measures importance of that game on the team's probability of winning the World Series.)

The next night the Red Sox were in control most of the game. The Yankees cut the lead to 3-2 in the top of the fifth, but the Red Sox scored two runs in both the sixth and seventh to put the game out of reach. They won the next day, too, 6-5, and thanks to losses by Baltimore and Toronto, their division odds jumped up to 80.9 percent, an increase of 11.3 percentage points. It was their biggest one-day jump of the season.

The Red Sox finished off the four-game sweep on Sunday night, Sept. 18, in front of a national television audience. The Yankees pulled out to a 4-0 lead, but two more homers from Ramirez—a three-run shot off of CC Sabathia in the fifth and a solo shot off of Tyler Clippard in the seventh—started and finished a five-run Red Sox comeback. Boston's division odds sat at 86.5 percent following the win.

The next day, the Sox won in Baltimore to vault those odds over 90 percent, and then won their next five games for good measure to really put the division to bed. On Sept. 28, the Red Sox captured their first AL East Division title since 2013. In a weird twist, they won the division on a night they lost a game, against the Yankees in the Bronx. The soon-to-be-retired Mark Teixeira capped off a five-run bottom of the ninth for the Bombers with a walk-off grand slam, forcing the Red Sox to celebrate their second division title of the 2010s in the visiting clubhouse instead of on the Yankee Stadium diamond.

The American League Central View

by Emma Baccellieri

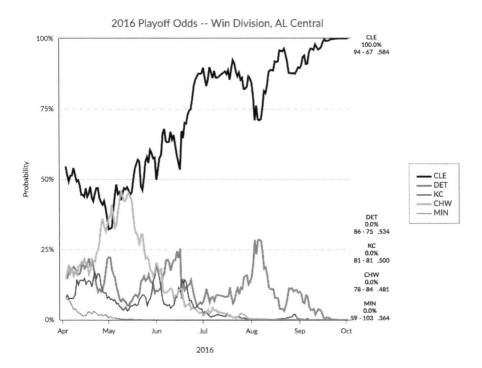

2016 Playoff Odds -- Win Division, AL Central

Preseason predictions for the 2016 American League Central looked, by and large, pretty similar to those filed in 2015. Cleveland were once again early favorites, the Minnesota Twins were once again thought to be very bad, the Kansas City Royals were once again expected to be average in the way projection systems suggested they really were at their core.

There was just one difference—while all of those predictions had faltered in 2015, they came true in 2016. There was no surprising Twins team sticking around for the Wild Card race this year, no projection-busting Royals cruising to a title, and no luke-warm Cleveland summer failing to honor the expectations of a March *Sports Illustrated* cover. Instead, the division's teams ended up falling more or less in line with what had been expected of them, and for the third straight year, the AL Central was repre-sented in the World Series. This time, though, it was preseason darling Cleveland and

---

not astonishing Kansas City that was responsible. But while the ultimate outcome of the AL Central was relatively straightforward, the path it took to get there was not. The Chicago White Sox glided through a win-filled spring that propelled them to the top of the division early, only to disintegrate and tumble down the standings well before the All-Star break. The Detroit Tigers enjoyed a late surge that briefly threatened to disrupt things. And though Cleveland never relinquished the division's top spot once they took hold of it in mid-June, their success came despite a serious set of injuries. Here, the three series that did the most to seal the division's fate.

May 17-19: The White Sox Begin to Slip

The White Sox opened the season with back-to-back wins, and for the next six weeks they kept winning. By mid-May, they had not only a six-game lead in the division but also a comfortable hold on the best record in the AL. Those wins, however, were far more encouraging when viewed as the sum of their parts than when any individual components were broken out and examined.

Chicago's pitching, anchored by ace Chris Sale, Jose Quintana and Carlos Rodon, had been expected to outshine its hitting in 2016—just as had been the case the year prior. Early in the season, the White Sox rotation fulfilled its half of the deal, leading to win after win. But there's only so long a pitching staff can atone for the sins of an offense that collectively hit 16 percent worse than league average (84 wRC+), as the White Sox had in April. And while Chicago's pitching generally was sharp in that time frame, the peripherals around the strong results didn't look so great. A 2.72 team ERA covered a 3.41 FIP and a 4.10 xFIP. The White Sox didn't have to wait too long to get the regression those numbers hinted at.

The team showed the first signs of stumbling on a mid-May road trip during which the White Sox went 2-4 against the Texas Rangers and New York Yankees. That dropped their record to 24-14, and while it didn't do much to hurt their comfortable division lead, it knocked them from their spot as the AL's best team. Returning home to face the cellar-dwelling Astros seemed a strong opportunity for the White Sox to regroup and return to their winning ways. Instead, it brought only more losing and the beginning of what became a summer-long struggle.

First in the series was an extra-innings loss full of missed opportunities—failing to score after Houston starter Dallas Keuchel walked the bases loaded, leaving the winning run stranded on third in the bottom of the ninth, and striking out with a man on second to cut short final hopes of a rally. The result was a 6-5 loss in 11 innings. Then came a second defeat, this one showing the regression the pitching staff seemingly had been destined for.

Mat Latos, signed late in the offseason to a relatively cheap one-year contract, had been quick to make his value known in April—getting out to a 5-0 record despite a low strikeout rate and a high walk rate to match. But his 2.62 ERA for those six starts was backed by a 4.52 FIP and 5.14 xFIP, and his results soon caught up with those peripherals, kicking into gear with this start against the Astros. Latos couldn't make it out of the sixth inning, giving up five runs on 11 hits. Though the bullpen made sure things didn't get worse from there, the damage was done, and the outcome was a 5-3 loss.

The White Sox won the final game against Houston to avoid a sweep, but with exactly the sort of difficult-to-replicate victory that had defined their hot start. Sale threw a complete-game near-shutout—marred only by a solo home run in the eighth inning—with nine strikeouts and no walks. Chicago's bats managed to back up his sharp performance, but just barely, and the 2-1 victory snapped the team's losing streak at four. The series dropped their AL Central lead to two and a half games, the slimmest it had been since the opening weeks of the season, and their odds of winning the division fell from 42.3 percent to 30.7 percent.

Things didn't get any better from there. The White Sox lost eight of its next 10, handing over the top spot in the division in the process, and they never regained it. Their summer was as cold as their winter was hot, and the result was the fourth consecutive losing season for the South Siders.

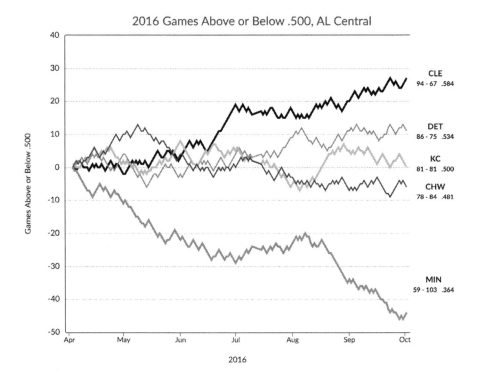

June 17-19 (and Beyond): Cleveland takes off

Though Cleveland entered the season as favorites, that prediction soon began to lose its shine. The outfield was an odd patchwork of backup talent, with both Michael Brantley (shoulder injury) and Abraham Almonte (drug suspension) forced onto the sidelines. The team's rotation, expected to be among baseball's best, had gotten off to a slow start—stumbling out to a 4.05 ERA in March and April with peripherals that indicated about the same. But the month of May saw some improvement as Cleveland pulled itself to the .500 mark, with the pitching beginning to click into the success that had been expected of it and the offense doing enough to back it up.

Cleveland headed into the month of June behind both the White Sox and the Royals, three games out of the division's top spot. They headed into July not just in first place, but with a seven-game cushion.

Such a fate, however, seemed unlikely midway through June. Starting the month with a six-game winning streak (that coincided with the collapse of the White Sox) put Cleveland atop the standings for the first time in 2016. But after suffering a three-game sweep at the hands of Kansas City, Cleveland's lead was gone, and they were left tied for the division's top spot on June 15.

That was the last day Cleveland had to share first place in the AL Central. For the rest of the year, it was theirs and theirs alone—beginning with a sweep of the White Sox that showed Cleveland playing at its most dramatic.

In the series' opening game, a strong performance by starter Trevor Bauer looked as if it might go to waste. With nine strikeouts in seven innings of work, he allowed just one run, but Cleveland's offense was only able to match it with the same. After Bauer was pulled, things started getting exciting—Cleveland pulled ahead in the eighth, only for closer Cody Allen to allow the White Sox to tie things in the next frame. In the bottom of the ninth, though, Carlos Santana made sure there would be no need for extras. The designated hitter walked it off with a solo shot—one of Cleveland's best-in-baseball 11 walk-off victories for the year—and sparked another another winning streak for Cleveland.

The next game had much less drama and far more power. After an explosive five-run first inning, Cleveland easily romped to a 13-2 victory—led by rookie Tyler Naquin, who went 3-for-3 and knocked in four runs, part of a month in which he'd hit .338/.434/.785 to briefly earn a surprise spot in the Rookie of the Year conversation. And for the final game of the series, Cleveland put together one more walk-off win, this time in extra innings. Responsible for the winning run? Left fielder Jose Ramirez, converted from his middle infield background to fill Cleveland's outfield void and finding the best offense of his career. (Shortly after, as Almonte returned from his drug suspension, Ramirez would convert more or less full-time back to third base, where he continued to hit well.)

That three-game sweep took Cleveland's chances of winning the division from 53.4 percent to 68.9. And their winning didn't stop there. Those three victories were the beginning of a 14-game streak, by far the longest of any team in 2016 and a franchise record. June ended as their winningest month since August 1954, a year where the team had gone to the World Series with the highest winning percentage in baseball history. And the June 2016 version didn't look too far off from that—the month saw their pitchers as the best in baseball, with a 2.42 ERA and 3.39 FIP, and their success was only more pronounced during the winning streak. Cleveland's starters were dominant enough in those two weeks that the bullpen pitched just 24 collective innings in 14 games.

By the time Cleveland recorded their next loss, after 14 victories that included everything from blowouts to a 19-inning nailbiter, they had upped their division odds to 89.7 percent. They didn't look back from there, en route to their winningest season and first division title since 2007.

Aug. 8-10: TheTigers Blow their Last Shot

After the All-Star break, only one team came close to challenging Cleveland's grip on first place. Not Chicago, which had slipped below the .500 mark and would not climb back above it; not Kansas City, which similarly had racked up losses since briefly tying Cleveland atop the standings in June. Instead, it was Detroit, which had lingered in the middle of the pack all year before riding its longest win streak of the season into the beginning of August. Detroit's hot spell aligned with a cooler period for Cleveland, and the result was the Tigers pulling within two games of their hold on the AL Central's top spot.

---

10 Things You Should Remember About the 2016 AL Central

1. Minnesota's Brian Dozier had a career year, with 42 homers and a .278 ISO, in one of the strongest displays of power ever by a second baseman.

2. After acquiring Andrew Miller at the deadline, Cleveland manager Terry Francona was creative with his usage, with Miller entering the game as early as the fifth, or whenever leverage was highest.

3. The White Sox season came with some weird spots of drama, including Adam LaRoche suddenly retiring after his teenage son's constant presence in the clubhouse became a team issue and Chris Sale delaying a game by cutting up an entire team set of throwback uniforms he didn't like.

4. Danny Duffy returned to the starter's role for the Royals and had his best year yet, highlighted by a 25.7 percent strikeout rate.

5. Cleveland's Francisco Lindor not only avoided a sophomore slump, but he *improved* on his dazzling

---

After a homestand during which they extended that winning streak to eight games and won seven of nine in total (the winning streak started before the homestand), the Tigers headed out to Seattle to face the Mariners and try to encroach a little more on Cleveland's lead. It didn't go so well.

First came a shutout at the hands of Hisashi Iwakuma, a 3-0 loss in which the Tigers struggled to make contact, let alone score. The series' second game seemed to start out as something far more encouraging. Detroit had jumped out with a first-inning lead it protected well, and headed to the eighth inning ahead, 4-1. But with two outs in the bottom of the eighth, Detroit reliever Justin Wilson gave up a three-run shot, and suddenly the game was tied and headed to extras.

There was little in the way of missed opportunities or close calls for either team until the top of the 14th, when the Tigers had a chance to send everyone home for the night—loading the bases with one out and the heart of their lineup due at the plate. The Mariners were scraping the bottom of their barrel in terms of bullpen options. But the scoring threat went nowhere, with Miguel Cabrera flying out to end the inning and stranding all three runners. The very next inning brought another chance for Detroit, as Víctor Martínez led off the top of the 15th with a solo shot to break the tie. All the Tigers needed to do for the victory was get the bullpen through the bottom of the frame safely…a task handed to Francisco Rodriguez, who couldn't handle it. The Mariners scored twice and walked off with the win.

The following day brought similar misery for Detroit, albeit not nearly in so dramatic a fashion, with the bullpen coughing up two runs in the bottom of the eighth to turn a 1-1 tie into a 3-1 loss. The series' shades of heartbreak were varied—shutout, walk-off, garden-variety depressing loss—but each one had led to defeat. The Tigers had been swept, and their chances of winning the division had shrunk too. They were still only three and a half games back of Cleveland, but their gap only grew from there, and Detroit never got so close to first place again. Before the series with the Mariners, the Tigers' division odds sat at 28.5 percent. After it, they had fallen to 18.8, and from there they only kept falling.

Effectively, it was enough to take the Tigers out of the division race, but the chances for a Wild Card spot kept baseball in Detroit meaningful for the rest of the season. While they managed enough wins to stay in the playoff conversation until the very last week of the season, the Tigers couldn't quite put together enough to

---

rookie year—continuing to awe with his ultra-smooth, highlight-ready defense as part of a 6.3 WAR season, best among AL shortstops.

6. Kansas City faded from the division race early, but stayed in the Wild Card race with a 16 wins in a 21-game August stretch in which the Royals had the AL's best run prevention.

7. Detroit rookie Michael Fulmer had five starts with eight strikeouts or more, a 3.06 ERA and 3.0 WAR.

8. Justin Verlander had his best season since 2012, with a career-best 28.1 percent strikeout rate.

9. Todd Frazier hit 40 homers in his White Sox debut, but the team's best player was Adam Eaton, whose 6.0 WAR was a career best and fourth-best among all major league outfielders.

10. The Twins' Byron Buxton followed his poor 2015 debut with a poor first half of 2016 (58 wRC+), but improved in the second half (114 wRC+), and he recorded the fastest inside-the-park home run of the season while playing tantalizing defense.

make their way into the postseason. Despite their near-$200 million payroll—with stronger seasons than had been seen in years from their players with the two biggest contracts in Justin Verlander and Miguel Cabrera—they were left on the outside of the playoffs looking in for the second year in a row.

October (and November) for the AL Central meant baseball only for Cleveland, favorite at the outset and on through to the end.

The American League West View

by Kate Preusser

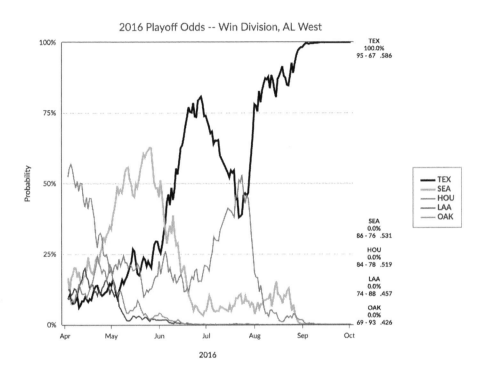

2016 Playoff Odds -- Win Division, AL West

In 1883-1884, William Randolph Hearst was in his sophomore year at Harvard, and he was miserable. He had a cold he couldn't shake despite his most valiant attempts to coax, torture or asphyxiate it out of existence. He dismissed the winning baseball team he played on as "decidedly amateur." He was struggling to make even a gentleman's C in his classes. Worst of all, he was terrifically homesick for his home state of California, writing in a letter to his mother:

> *"I hate this weak, pretty New England scenery with its gentle rolling hills, its pea green foliage, its vistas, tame enough to begin with but totally disfigured by houses and parts which could not be told apart save for its respective inhabitants. I hate it as I do a weak, pretty face without force or character. I long to see our own woods, the jagged rocks and towering mountains, the majestic pines, the grand impressive scenery of the 'far west.'"*

Other divisions in baseball have playoff graphs that look like the gentle rolling hills Hearst so despised. The AL West's, fittingly, echoes the landscape that surrounds the coastal California location of Hearst Castle. The Athletics and Angels fall into the Pacific relatively quickly, while the Astros, Rangers, and Mariners weave in and out of contention like the precipitous heights and hairpin turns of Highway 1 through Big Sur.

The Rangers' playoff hopes climbed steadily through the season, outside of one significant dip in July during which the baseball gods had a conference call debating whether allowing one team to win so many one-run games was deeply funny or just cruel. The Astros, early favorites to win the division thanks to their stable of young talent, swooned early, stormed back in late June and July, then saw their division odds fall from almost 45 percent on July 28 to just 3.9 percent 11 days later. (There's a Tal's Hill joke to be made here, but by the time this comes out, Tal's Hill will be consigned to the scrapheap of Astros memorabilia, along with a Colt .45s jersey and the shag carpeting from Roy Hofheinz's Astrodome apartment.)

The Mariners were maybe the most quixotic of all, alternating between stretches of fire-breathing play and dismal plateaus that would have made young Hearst reach for a book of matches. This was a team that scored the fifth-most runs per game in baseball this year and that on June 2 mounted the largest comeback in club history against its hated rival, the San Diego Padres; this was also a club swept by the struggling Minnesota Twins at home.

The only teams that kept things uninteresting were Anaheim, where Billy Eppler continues frantic Google searches with keywords like "how close human cloning," and Oakland, whose starting rotation immediately went into a synchronized death spiral that earned top marks from the Russian judges. When Wallace Stegner wrote that "one cannot be pessimistic about the West...the native home of hope," he probably wasn't thinking about the California-based AL teams. Overall, however, the AL West's playoff picture this year mostly resembled a Hearst dreamscape, all outrageous crag and jagged peaks, fissures that briefly knit together before spinning away into the untamed expanse of the offseason.

June 14-23: The Seattle Mariners and the Terrible, Horrible, No Good, Very Bad Road Trip

In his office, my dad the engineer has an instruction from the Strawberry Short-cake dollhouse he built me that he's saved since 1984. Step 24 reads, "STOP! Take a short break and admire what you have accomplished so far. Then look back through the preceding 23 steps and make sure you have checked off each step because after steps 25 and 26 you will probably not be able to fix anything that you've done wrong."

It's good advice and something the Seattle Mariners would have been well-served to remember in 2016. Although the team started strong and ended the season vying for a Wild Card spot, playing meaningful October baseball in Safeco—that Halley's comet of Seattle sports events—the Mariners, like Shakespearean heroes in polyester pants, could not overcome their fatal flaw: They skipped Step 24, losing key games in June that altered the course of their season.

The Jerry Dipoto era dawned veneer-bright in Seattle. After a shaky 2-6 start, the Mariners briskly righted the ship, getting back to .500 ball by the end of April and going 17-11 in May, ending the month with about a 50 percent shot of winning the West. But as soon as the calendar flipped to June, the Mariners fell earthward, going just 10-18. Granted, their June schedule was punishing—just two days off on either end of a long road trip that saw them traveling from Seattle to Texas to Tampa Bay to Boston to Detroit before going back home to Seattle. In that trip they went 2-8, including a six-game losing streak punctuated with a four-game sweep in Detroit.

The Mariners began that road trip on June 14 with a 23 percent shot of winning the division; they would end it at just five percent. It's difficult to isolate a single most miserable moment from that long trek, but the final loss of the Detroit series, an extra-inning defeat that pushed the Mariners back under .500, was both numerically and spiritually damaging. It was, in fact, their third walk-off loss of the trip, and demonstrated just how close 2-8 was to being 5-5.

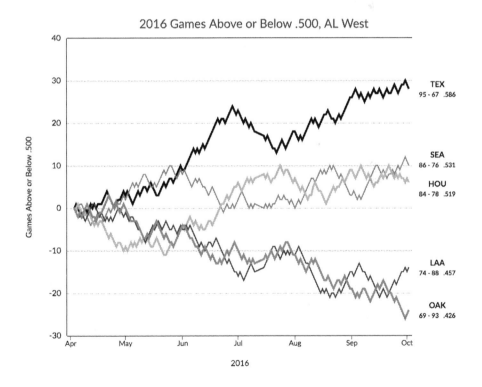

After a spate of injuries beset the pitching staff, local boy Adrian Sampson was set to make a spot start in that series and road trip finale on June 23. He threw four warm-up pitches before he felt a twinge in his elbow. He would not throw another pitch in 2016. On came Vidal Nuño, who mostly spent 2016 being the kid in class the teacher never calls on. He scraped through 3.1 innings, giving up four runs. Recent Double-A call-up Edwin Díaz, who would be the team's closer by the end of the season, chipped in with an inning and two-thirds, and the team also got scoreless inning contributions from Nick Vincent, Joaquín Benoit (later traded to Toronto for Drew Storen), and the then-recently reacquired Tom Wilhelmsen, who was awful with the Rangers but solid with the Mariners, proving you can go home again.

While the bullpen, which was a strong point for Seattle in 2016 even as it featured a revolving cast of characters, held the Tigers scoreless, the Mariners' hitters rallied to tie the game and push it into extras. The Mariners managed to get utilityman Shawn O'Malley to third base in the top of the 10th with just one out, but they were unable to score him. In the bottom of the inning, the Tigers also got a runner to third, and Steve Cishek politely threw a wild pitch to end the game.

Cishek would serve as the team's closer for one more month before being replaced by the young fireballer Díaz, who would go on to collect 18 saves while wielding a 40 percent strikeout rate and a 2.04 FIP. Díaz's ascension helped spur the team to a 34-23 record over the final two months of the season and put the Mariners into contention for the second Wild Card spot, but they were unable to fully recover from the June swoon. Never skip Step 24.

---

10 Things You Should Remember About the 2016 AL West

1. For the A's, then may soon be now, as prospects Sean Manaea, Zach Neal, Ryon Healy, Bruce Maxwell and Franklin Barreto all had neat seasons.

2. The A's traded impending free agents Rich Hill and Josh Reddick for three highly ranked Dodgers pitching prospects, including Jharel Cotton, who posted a 5.75 K/BB ratio in his brief MLB debut.

3. After the Astros gave up and DFA'd Carlos Gomez, the Rangers called five-second rule and he then hit .284/.362/.543 for Texas after hitting, uh, way worse than that in Houston.

4. The Rangers made Ian Desmond an outfielder, and it kind of worked. He postead a 3.5 UZR in left field, but a -4.9 UZR in center.

5. Mike Trout somehow got even better, lowering his strikeout rate and taking more walks than ever. He led the AL in WAR for a fifth straight year, the first player to do that since Babe Ruth.

July 28-31: The Royals Play Prince Charming

The 2016 Rangers season was the ending of a silent movie, looped end-to-end over the summer months: Despite being strapped to a conveyor belt facing the buzz-saw of season-ending injuries and possible one-run losses again and again, somehow

---

the team was able to jam the gears and escape, each time leaving more distance between itself and the rest of the division.

The only time Texas' lead was in jeopardy was a long, miserable month of July. At the conclusion of June 28, the Rangers had an 80.7 percent chance of winning the AL West, but by July 28, that number had plummeted to 46.7 percent. On June 29, a 9-7 loss to the Yankees snapped a four-game winning streak during which they outscored opponents 32-12 and kicked off a losing streak during which they went 7-17 and were outscored by opponents, 158-100.

On July 22, the Rangers' playoff odds had shrunk to just 38 percent, the lowest since early in June, while the surging Astros improved to a 51.2 percent chance, as they climbed to just 2.5 games back of the division-leading Rangers, with the Mariners close behind at 5.5 back.

However, a get-right series sweep against the Royals to close out July got the Rangers' season back on track, and they proceeded to steamroll the rest of the division throughout August, earning a series win against the Astros and sweeping the Athletics and Mariners.

In the opening game of the series against Kansas City on July 28, the Rangers needed their ace, Cole Hamels, to turn around the direction of the season, and Hamels responded, throwing eight innings of two-run ball during which he walked one batter and struck out 12. The Rangers' bats could muster only three runs off Yordano Ventura, who also went eight innings and actually surrendered two fewer hits than Hamels, but as all three of those hits were solo homers, including two from human paper towel mascot Mike Moreland, the Rangers emerged victorious despite a shaky performance from closer Sam Dyson.

The next day, the Rangers put up three runs in the first inning against Edinson Volquez on their way to an 8-3 romp that again featured a multi-home run game from a Rangers hitter—Rougned Odor this time, hitting Nos. 20 and 21 on his way to a 33-homer season, more than double the number of dingers he put up in 2015.

6. Jose Altuve also was MVP-caliber. His .338 average won the AL batting title, his 150 wRC+ ranked eighth in the majors, his 6.7 WAR, sixth, and he posted career bests in homers (24) and ISO (.194).

7. Robinson Canó hit a career-high 39 home runs—10 more than he hit in 2010—and became the first player in history to record 30 doubles in his first 11 seasons. And he was still an asset in the field.

8. The Astros paid $47.5 million to land Cuban defector Yulieski Gourriel. After 61 minor league plate appearances, the 32-year-old was promoted to Houston and hit .262/.292/.385 in 137 PA.

9. New Seattle GM Jerry Dipoto looks like a nice guy, but "Trader Jerry" also earned a rep for being the guy at your aunt's yard sale who offers to "take that big, ugly old table off your hands" before you've looked it up on the Antiques Roadshow site.

10. Five Angels pitchers had season-ending surgery, Matt Shoemaker took a 105-mph comebacker to the head and Tim Lincecum posted a 9.16 ERA.

In the third game of the series, Texas defeated KC with another one-run victory. This one featured a strong performance from the mercurial Martín Perez, who went seven innings and gave up a solitary first-inning run. To be fair, the Royals helped out Perez, grounding into double plays in three consecutive innings to eliminate any whiff of danger.

The Rangers completed the sweep with journeyman Lucas Harrell starting on the hill. Texas had acquired Harrell from the Braves just four days before, and he would win his first start for Texas before dissolving back into irrelevance. Harrell allowed three runs across six innings but was backed up by a strong bullpen performance, while the Rangers batters managed to touch up KC starter Dillon Gee for four runs en route to a 5-3 victory.

The following day, the Rangers' odds of winning the division rose 10.5 percentage points on to 78 percent, on the strength of three acquisitions—catcher Jonathan Lucroy, outfielder/designated hitter Carlos Beltran and relief pitcher Jeremy Jeffress. The club never looked back on its way to an AL-leading record of 95-67.

The Rangers, after being utterly snakebitten by injuries over the previous two seasons, finally enjoyed a year in which only one player, Prince Fielder, was lost to major injury, in his case career-ending. Luck also was on the Rangers' side in one-run games, in which they posted a historic winning percentage: their mark of 36-11 (.766) represents the best record in one-run games in the modern baseball era, narrowly edging out the previous record holder, the 2012 Baltimore Orioles (.763). The Rangers almost lost a one-run game in their final game of the season when they went to extra innings with Tampa Bay, which would have pushed their record down to 36-12 (.750), but the Rays were able to score *two* in the top of the 10th, preserving the record. Baseball: always the weirdest cousin at the family picnic.

The Rangers' luck in one-run games, coupled with their AL-leading winning record of .586—outperforming their Pythagorean projection by 81 points—despite a run differential of just plus-eight, led many to label their success "unsustainable" or "pure luck" or "the old magics." But the Rangers weren't just lucky; they were also good at the times it mattered most.

In "close and late" situations, Adrián Beltré led all batters with a .385 average, and the team as a whole led the majors in slugging percentage (.450) and OPS (.795), and was tied for the lead in home runs (35). Credit also belongs to the front office, which made key moves at the trade deadline to acquire Yankees slugger Carlos Beltran to replace Fielder. The Rangers also landed top trade target Jonathan Lucroy, shoring up a position that had provided just 0.4 WAR over the season—and without surrendering youngsters Joey Gallo, Jurickson Profar or Nomar Mazara. Old magics, indeed.

Unfortunately, the Rangers' magic ran out when they needed it most, facing the Toronto Blue Jays in the ALDS. The Blue Jays swept the Rangers, outscoring them

22-10 to push the Rangers into a negative run differential for the year including the postseason.

July 29-31: Rangers Offer Division to Astros On a Platter; Astros Prefer Coney Dog Out of the Garbage

While the Rangers were getting their mojo back like the protagonist in act two of a Lifetime movie, the Astros, after a tepid July, were starting to see their season slip away. Houston had stumbled out of the gate in 2016, ending the first month of play in unfamiliar territory: last place in the AL West. The Astros rebounded with a strong June, going 18-8, but lost two of three games the lone time that month they faced a division opponent.

The Rangers' prolonged July slump opened the door for the Astros to leap forward in the division, and a series sweep against the Angels toward the end of the month finally gave the Astros some momentum, punctuated by a decisive 13-3 win against Anaheim that raised their division odds to 52.7 percent. This success, however, would be short-lived.

After losing a series at home against the Yankees, the Astros traveled to Detroit, where they were swept by their fellow Wild Card hopefuls from July 29-31. Swept might be putting it kindly, as the Tigers demolished the Astros' pitching staff to the tune of 28 runs in three games, with starters Collin McHugh and Dallas Keuchel allowing 15 of them. In turn, the Astros' high-flying youth force managed only eight runs over the three games and stranded 20 runners, while striking out 26 times.

The losses pushed their chances for the division from 45.7 percent on July 27 to 18.2 percent by the beginning of August, and they would fail to post a winning record in September, eliminating their chances at even a Wild Card bid.

How did the Astros, a popular pick to win the AL West and last year's Wild Card victors, underachieve so spectacularly? Starting off at 7-17 was a hole the Astros couldn't ever climb out of, especially considering the history book-smashing Rangers. Jose Altuve was the Astros' Dobby, desperately cramming gillyweed into his teammates' mouths, but even with Altuve, Carlos Correa and George Springer, plus good returns from Luis Valbuena, Evan Gattis (who hit a career-high 32 homers) and rookie Alex Bregman, it wasn't enough.

The starting pitching was mostly injury-ravaged or middling, and although the bullpen generally performed well, instability at the closer position troubled the team all season. The series against the Tigers is a nightmarish compendium of the Astros' woes in 2016.

Of the eight runs scored by the Astros in the series, Altuve and Correa accounted for half of them. The starting pitching was the true weak point, though, in this series as in the season. Keuchel, just one year removed from his Cy Young season, saw his strikeouts tumble back to his career average in 2016. In 2015, batters hit just .233 against Keuchel's sinker; in 2016, that number jumped to .302, with a .453 slugging percentage—a 150-point increase from 2015. As a result, Keuchel relied more on his cutter, which he struggled to command, leaving too many pitches over the plate for hitters to punish (.315 batting average against).

On July 31 against the Tigers, Keuchel gave up seven runs on as many hits over five innings, and his outing actually was better than the series opener, a 14-6 shellacking in which McHugh, whose FIP has ticked steadily upwards over the past three years, couldn't make it out of the second inning, giving up eight runs. The Astros actually had a chance to win the middle game of the series, thanks to a respectable performance from Mike Fiers, and carried a 2-1 lead into the bottom of the ninth, when Will Harris blew the save.

The Astros were tortured all season by uncertainty at the closer role. Luke Gregerson opened the season as the closer but tied his 2015 season high for blown saves in just his first 25 appearances, causing A.J. Hinch to install the ever-popular "closer by committee." The Astros had handed over a thick fistful of prospects to the Phillies to acquire the services of Ken Giles, but Giles' career-worst April (6.75 FIP) cast a pallor over the beginning of his tenure in Houston.

Meanwhile, unheralded reliever Harris at one point pitched 26 scoreless innings and put up 1.8 WAR for the season, relying almost exclusively on two pitches, a cutter and a curveball. But after a dominant first half, Harris fell back to earth in July. After not giving up a single extra-base hit over the first three months of the season, he gave up four doubles in July. By the beginning of August, Hinch would appoint Giles the closer, but the move came too late to salvage the Astros' playoff hopes.

The National League East View

by Alex Remington

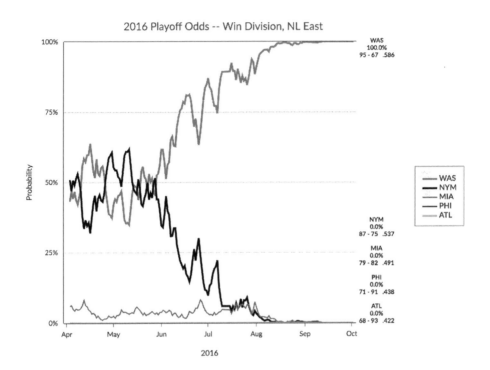

2016 Playoff Odds -- Win Division, NL East

Until Sept. 25, the narrative of the 2016 National League East race was pretty much written. The Nationals led for almost the entire year after fending off an early challenge from the Mets, the Braves and Phillies were predictably bad, and the Mets proved better than the Marlins as the two teams vied for a Wild Card spot. It was more or less what the 2015 season was supposed to look like—before an unexpected Nationals collapse and Mets offensive explosion delivered the division to New York.

And then...everything changed. In the early hours of the morning on Sept. 25, a boat on which José Fernández was a passenger crashed at full speed into rocks in Miami Harbor. He and two friends were killed in the accident, which was tragically reminiscent of the boat crash that killed Cleveland's Steve Olin and Tim Crews in 1993.

It was difficult to come to terms with the enormity of the loss. Fernández was one of the best pitchers and most incandescent stars in baseball, and he had just turned 24. He came to the United States from Cuba when he was just 15 after three failed attempts and a brief prison term for being caught. At one point on his successful fourth journey, his mother was swept overboard by a wave, and he immediately, instinctively, swam out to save her, needing 15 minutes to navigate the 60 feet back to the boat, so treacherous were the waves.

Shortly after that harrowing day, their craft arrived in Mexico. They then took a bus to Texas, and eventually to Tampa, where he went to high school. Four years later, he was taken with the 14th pick in the 2011 draft. Two years after that, in 2013, he was the NL Rookie of the Year and finished third in the Cy Young Award voting, and he had what must have been the brightest smile in baseball. It's hard to accept that he's gone. But his memory will last far longer than that of any game played in the East this season.

April 11: Nationals Get a Big Boost Early

Just as in 2015, the division race was mostly a two-team fight between the Nationals and Mets. Still, the Marlins mounted a spirited charge in the late summer and held onto second place for much of August, a game or two ahead of the frustrated Mets, who finally charged back into second place to claim a Wild Card spot down the stretch.

From the Mets' perspective, the fight with the Nationals was zero-sum. Every Nationals win reduced the Mets' chances, and vice versa. As a result, from the perspective of NL East division odds, one of the most consequential games of the year occurred just one week into the season.

The Nationals were stronger out of the gate than the Mets. They won three of their first four games going into April 11, while the Mets took a 2-3 record into the evening. Both teams were at home, and both were facing weaker intradivisional rivals: the Nats sent Max Scherzer to face the Braves and their latest retread pickup, Bud Norris, while the Mets tapped Steven Matz to battle the Marlins and Jarred Cosart.

In his second season since inking a $210 million contract, Scherzer was once again among the best pitchers in baseball. Since 2013, only Clayton Kershaw has been worth more wins above replacement (WAR). But on that day, going through the order for the first time, he simply didn't have it, as A.J. Pierzynski and Nick Markakis both knocked two-run doubles to give the Braves a 4-3 lead through two innings. From that point on, though, Scherzer held the line, and Norris simply couldn't, as the Nationals offense eked out single runs in the third, fifth, and seventh innings.

The eventual 6-4 victory marked the Nationals' third victory over the Braves in their first five games of the season, and it marked a theme for the season, as Washington went 15-4 against Atlanta.

(That tied the Nationals for the major league-best record in a season series. In all, five teams managed a 15-4 record against one of their opponents: the Cubs against the Reds, the Tigers and Royals against the star-crossed Twins, the Rangers against the Astros, and the Nats against the Braves. All but the Royals made the postseason, perhaps because they went 66-77 against teams that weren't the Twins.)

Meanwhile, at Citi Field, the wheels were coming off. Matz pitched around an infield single in the first, but the Marlins batted around in the second, aided mightily by Matz issuing walks to the first two men he faced. He then gave up four singles, a stolen base, and a homer. He finally got yanked with two outs in the second and seven runs in. The Mets scored three in the fourth, but the outcome was never seriously in question after that, as they lost, 10-3.

At the end of the day, the Nats were 4-1 and up two games in the division, while the Mets were 2-4. The Marlins' victory put them at 2-3. The Nationals' win dropped the hapless Braves to 0-6, and the Phillies dropped their contest with the Padres to fall to 2-5. Despite the lackluster competition in Philadelphia and Atlanta, the Mets struggled all year to distance themselves from the .500 mark, just as the Nationals had in 2015.

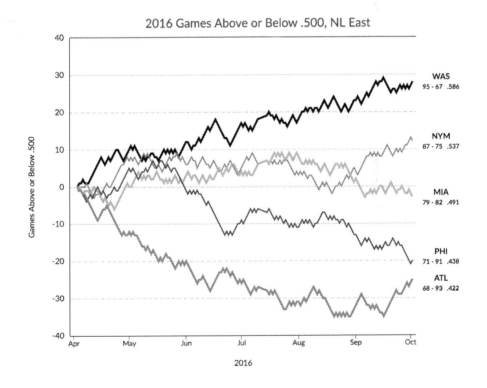

Entering play on April 11, the Nationals had a 48 percent chance of winning the division, and the Mets had a 47 percent chance. After the game, the Nats' chances had increased to 56 percent, and the Mets' chances declined to 38 percent. The 17.2 percentage point swing was the second-largest one-day swing in the division's odds for the entire season.

June 7: Double(header) Trouble for the Mets

After struggling a bit out of the gate, the Mets caught fire later in April, and they ended the month 15-7, just a half-game behind the Nationals' 16-7 mark. May saw both teams tread water, as the Nats went 16-14, just a tick better than the Mets' 14-15.

After a mutual off day on Monday, June 6, the Nationals squared off against the White Sox, while the Mets readied themselves for a road double-header against the Pirates. The Mets were in second place, just two games behind the Nationals.

The Nationals sent young Joe Ross to the mound, just a couple of weeks removed from his 23rd birthday. The talented younger brother of Tyson Ross, Joe came to the Nationals from the Padres in the same deal that brought them Trea Turner, the rookie center fielder who catalyzed their second-half offense.

Ross undoubtedly has a bright future, and he sparkled on many other summer evenings before an injury shortened his season, but this wasn't his night. Fortunately for the Nats, his opposite number, Mat Latos, didn't have it, either. (For that matter, he basically didn't have it all year.) The two of them swapped crooked numbers in the bottom of the first and both halves of the second, and after two innings the White Sox were ahead, 5-2.

Then the Nats scored eight unanswered runs. A two-run homer from Anthony Rendon and a two-run double from Bryce Harper erased the lead and gave the Nats their first go-ahead run, and a four-run sixth made it a laugher. Todd Frazier kicked a ground ball and Matt Albers uncorked a wild pitch, and after a double and a sac

> ### 10 Things You Should Remember About the 2016 NL East
>
> 1. Dansby Swanson and Trea Turner made their MLB debuts. Atlanta's Swanson hit .302 and was solid overall, while the Nationals' Turner hit 13 homers, stole 33 bases, and learned center field on the fly.
> 2. With the Marlins in his 16th MLB season, 42-year-old Ichiro Suzuki notched his 3,000th hit, and 19-year vet Bartolo Colón of the Mets hit his first career homer two weeks before his 43rd birthday.
> 3. After hitting .328/.391/.724 in the 2015 playoffs with the Mets, Daniel Murphy signed a modest deal with the Nationals and kept mashing, hitting .347/.390/.595 and posting a career year at age 31.
> 4. Atlanta's Freddie Freeman was second in the majors in intentional walks. But he crushed the good pitches he got, setting career highs with 34 homers and a .267 ISO (previous highs: 23, .196).
> 5. Giancarlo Stanton had his worst season, which included an August groin strain that cost him a

fly—which would have been the third out if not for the boot—the Nats padded their lead further with a bases-loaded walk. Only two of those runs were earned, but the score stood at 10-5, and the damage was done.

The Mets still had a chance to gain a half-game in the standings if they could sweep the Bucs. In the four o'clock game, they once again gave the ball to Matz, and the young southpaw was much better this time around, if a bit inefficient. He yielded just two runs in five innings while notching eight strikeouts against only two walks. But he gave up eight hits and threw 101 pitches, of which just 58 were strikes. Still, a good effort.

Gallingly, it wasn't nearly enough, because the Mets were mesmerized by an old comrade—Jon Niese, whom they'd traded to the Pirates in the offseason for Neil Walker. Niese, a seventh-round draft pick in 2005, had spent 10 years in the Mets system and had been a Mets rotation mainstay for six years. So it's likely he had a very detailed scouting book on his former teammates. He scattered four hits in seven innings and departed after throwing just 91 pitches. Each bullpen gave up a run, and the Pirates hung on for a 3-1 win.

It was just about the best start of Niese's season, one of only three times he went seven innings, and basically the last good thing he did all year. After that brilliant afternoon, he had a 7.74 ERA in his final 17 games of the season. Overall in 2016, he made 20 starts, and only seven were quality starts. The Pirates were so disappointed with his performance against teams other than the Mets that they traded him back to New York on Aug. 1 for Antonio Bastardo and cash. The Mets promptly put him in the bullpen, and in six appearances with his old team, he gave up 14 runs in 11 innings.

In the second game, the Mets sent Jacob deGrom up against Juan Nicasio, the fiery former Rockies starter who had been a Dodgers reliever in 2015. Nicasio, who had a very up-and-down year, carried a 4.75 ERA into the evening matchup. deGrom, the fireballing former Rookie of the Year, had lost a tick off his fastball but appeared just

---

month and deflated Miami's playoff hopes. He has played just 193 games in the last two years.

6. The Marlins' best position player was Christian Yelich, whose 21 homers more than doubled his previous best, while his strikeout rate stayed essentially flat, and his 130 wRC+ easily led the team.

7. Former Rule 5 pick Odubel Herrera excelled again for Philadelphia, adding walks and power while cutting down his strikeouts. He plays well in center field despite having been an infielder in the minors.

8. Phillies starters Aaron Nola (age 23, 73 FIP-), Vincent Velasquez (24, 94), and Jerad Eickhoff (25, 99) look like rotation mainstays, and Zach Eflin and Jake Thompson (both 22) graduated.

9. Mets starters Zack Wheeler, Steven Matz, Jacob deGrom and Matt Harvey all either underwent surgery or suffered injury rehab setbacks.

10. The Mets' Noah Syndergaard struck out 10 Giants in seven shutout innings in the Wild Card game, with a 99-mph fastball and an unfair 91-mph slider.

as nasty as ever, with a 2.62 ERA on the season and 24 strikeouts in 19 innings over his previous three starts.

He was filthy against the Pirates, too, striking out nine men in six innings and walking no one, but he suffered from some unfortunate cluster luck: Though he gave up just six hits on the day, three came in the second inning as the Pirates scored two, and three more came in the fifth as the Pirates scored again. Had the baseball gods scattered his hits a bit more evenly, his night would have looked a lot better.

Nicasio was even more unhittable, striking out four of the first six men he saw and seven overall in five innings, allowing only allowed three hits. Fortunately for the Mets, all of their hits came in the fifth inning, too, so they were able to put their name on the board and scratch across a single run, making the score 3-1.

The bullpens ensured that the score remained there for the rest of the night. New York was now 31-26, and Washington was 35-23, 3.5 games up. The Nats were still within reach, but the Mets had blown a key opportunity.

Entering play on June 7, the Nats had a 57 percent chance of winning the division, and the Mets had a 38 percent chance. After the games, the Nats' chances stood at 65 percent; the Mets' odds had dropped to 31 percent.

July 8: You Shall Not Pass!

In general, it's rhetorically lazy to label an early-July series as "must-win," but as the Mets planned to welcome the Nationals to Citi Field on July 7, it wasn't hard to do the math. The Nats were coming to town for a four-game set that would close out the first half of the season, and the Mets were four games back in the division. If the Mets swept, they would be tied for the division lead, but if Washington did the sweeping, New York would be eight games back, an extraordinarily difficult amount of ground to make up. So if these games weren't exactly must-win, they were something awfully close.

The Mets won the first game, on July 7. But the next night, July 8, remained crucial. Going into play, the Nationals had a 75 percent chance of winning the division, and the Mets had a 22 percent chance.

These two teams had played each other nine times already, and the advantage had come and gone: The Mets had dropped two of three at Citi Field in mid-May, then won two of three in Washington a week later. Then, in late June, the Nats hosted the Mets and swept them. Six more games were scheduled between the teams in September, three in D.C. and three in Queens.

The Mets were not at full strength. Nominal staff ace Matt Harvey, who had struggled all year, threw his last game of the year on Independence Day. Shortly after that, he underwent rib surgery and was shut down for the rest of the campaign. Meanwhile, Zack Wheeler, whom the Mets had hoped to welcome back to the field after he had missed all of 2015, suffered one setback after another. Wheeler managed all of one minor league inning in 2016 before being shut down for good.

So as they welcomed their division rivals to town, the Mets were trotting out a rotation that included Logan Verrett and ageless wonder Bartolo Colón to complement DeGrom, Matz and Noah Syndergaard.

In the first game against the Nationals, Colón faced off against highly-touted rookie Lucas Giolito, who had made his major league debut just a week before. Colón didn't have his best stuff, giving up an RBI double to former Mets infielder Daniel Murphy in the first inning, then yielding three home runs in the space of four batters in the top of the fourth, as Harper, Clint Robinson and Rendon took turns silencing the crowd.

But Giolito couldn't hang onto his advantage, and after getting through three innings with just one run in, he hit a wall in the fourth inning, as the Mets batters finally gave the Citi Field Home Run Apple a reason to rise. After Travis d'Arnaud and Jose Reyes hit solo shots, Curtis Granderson hit a double, and the rattled Giolito balked him to third. The young hurler then gave up an RBI double to Yoenis Céspedes and finally walked Neil Walker before Nationals manager Dusty Baker mercifully yanked him. But the Nats bullpen provided no relief. The Mets won, 9-7, and they were just three games back.

So, the next night, the Mets sent their best pitcher, Syndergaard, up against Stephen Strasburg, whom the Nats had graced with a $175 million extension two months earlier.

The game didn't go as the Mets had hoped. Robinson hit a two-run homer in the second, and Murphy knocked in a third run with a double. Then Mets manager Terry Collins double-switched Syndergaard out of the game in the fifth inning with a 3-0 deficit. After the game, Collins explained that Syndergaard had a dead arm: "[His] stuff went away…but he said there's no pain." The Mets bullpen kept it there, and Asdrubal Cabrera got one run back with a home run to lead off the bottom of the fifth. But that was the last bit of scoring in the game, and the loss dropped the Mets back to 47-39, once again four games back of the 52-36 Nationals.

The Nats' victory increased their odds of winning the division to 83 percent, and dropped the Mets' chances to 13 percent. The 17.5 percent swing was the division's largest of the season.

The Mets proceeded to lose the next two games in the series, too, as Max Scherzer beat Verrett, and Gio Gonzalez outdueled Matz in the finale, with the Nationals winning, 3-2. That dropped the Mets to six games behind the Nationals. After splitting a doubleheader on July 26, they clawed their way to being only 4.5 games back, but they then immediately dropped four games in a row. New York never got any closer to the division lead.

The National League Central View

by Alexandra Simon

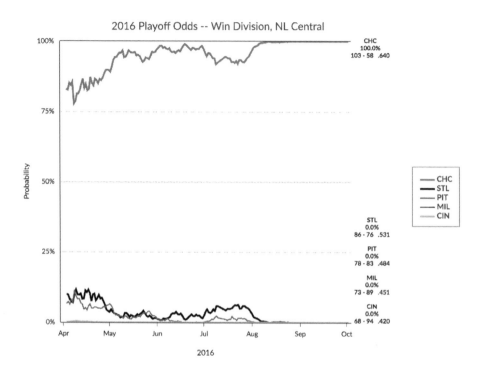

2016 Playoff Odds -- Win Division, NL Central

The young Cubs were unable to solve the Mets or their dominant pitching staff in the 2015 National League Championship Series, but pretty much the entire free world pegged them as NL Central favorites heading into 2016.

The 2015 Cubs saw the emergence of third baseman Kris Bryant as a true force at the plate, while other top prospects like Javier Baez, Addison Russell and Kyle Schwarber also burst onto the scene and immediately contributed to the team. They were paired with young star Anthony Rizzo, and a whole host of off-season acquisitions—Jason Heyward, Ben Zobrist, John Lackey, as well as the unexpected return of Dexter Fowler (who nearly signed with the Baltimore Orioles in free agency before returning to Chicago). They even traded away a popular player in Starlin Castro, signaling that they were no longer content to wait for "next year."

While the Cubs were busy bolstering their roster, the rest of the division largely sat on its collective hands. When St. Louis failed to retain Heyward and traded Jon Jay, it meant the Cardinals would be asking a lot of youngsters Stephen Piscotty and Randal Grichuk. While those two players acquitted themselves well in 2016, and new acquisitions Jedd Gyorko and Seung Hwan Oh were important members of the team, it soon became clear that the Cardinals just weren't in Chicago's class. Given how well constructed Chicago was, the Cardinals (and Pirates) had little margin for error, but unfortunately for them, they erred quite frequently.

April 18: Major Swings End Early

Heading into this game, the Cubs boasted the best team ERA in the majors and were tied for the best starters' ERA at 2.18. They were also owners of the best record in baseball at this point in the season, at 10-3. The Cubs were off to their best 13-game start since 1970. The Cardinals entered the day at 7-6, three games behind the division-leading Cubs. The Cubs were looking to make a statement early against a bitter rival.

The Cubs sent fifth starter Jason Hammel to the mound against the Cardinals' oft-injured Jaime Garcia. Garcia had made just 20 starts during the 2015 season, and made only 36 total starts from 2012 through 2015. Keeping Garcia healthy for a full season for the first time since 2011 would be key in the Cardinals' quest to reach the postseason for a sixth year in a row, especially with Lance Lynn out for the season after undergoing Tommy John surgery.

Hammel, who had been traded away from the Cubs in a blockbuster deal just a few years earlier before returning to the organization, entered the game sporting a sparkling 0.75 ERA in 12 innings. Garcia, for his part, was coming off a one-hit, 13-strikeout complete game shutout in his previous outing. The game promised to be a low-scoring contest, and low-scoring it was.

Leadoff man Dexter Fowler set the tone with a walk to start the game, and ended up reaching base three times. Ben Zobrist, one of the Cubs' free-agent signings, reached base twice and scored a run. The trio of Jason Heyward, Kris Bryant and Anthony Rizzo reached base only twice behind Fowler, combining to go 1-for-12 with a bunt single (Bryant) and a walk (Rizzo). But even with all the Cubs' big bats mostly silenced, they got some offense from an unexpected source.

Hammel drove in the only runs he would need in the fourth inning. After a Jorge Soler walk, and singles from Zobrist and Miguel Montero, Addison Russell struck out, but Hammel delivered a two-run single to give the Cubs a 2-1 lead. Hammel also pitched masterfully, striking out six Cardinals over six innings, the only run scoring on a triple by Yadier Molina.

In the bottom of the fourth, that lead would be quickly tested. A single and double put runners on second and third with one out, before Molina lifted a fly ball to Heyward in right. The Cubs' free-agent acquisition unleashed a cannon from right field to gun down Matt Holliday at the plate to preserve a 2-1 lead. Heyward's throw proved to be important as the Cubs ended up winning by that 2-1 margin. After the game, manager Joe Maddon said, "A lot of momentum came back to us in that moment." Alas, Heyward would go 0-for-5 at the plate for the second time in the young season, foreshadowing a season in which he did little with the lumber but was still able to contribute thanks to his defense.

The Cardinals weren't without their chances against Hammel, but ran themselves into outs and were unable to cash in on the few chances they got. They also left the potential tying run in scoring position in the ninth, when Hector Rondon struck out Jedd Gyorko to end the game.

With this victory in the books, the Cubs benefited from a 7.3 percent division odds swing in their favor, and set the tone for the rest of the season. The Cubs were a force to be reckoned with; even if you found a way to shut down the Cubs' offensive core, they could still find ways to win.

As you have read in the other division chapters in this book, it is common for there to be double digit percentage point swings on a daily basis—sometimes even into September—but after this day's 7.3 percent swing (plus 4.3 percent for the Cubs, minus 3.0 percent for the Cardinals), the NL Central division odds wouldn't see a daily swing of greater than five percent for the rest of the season.

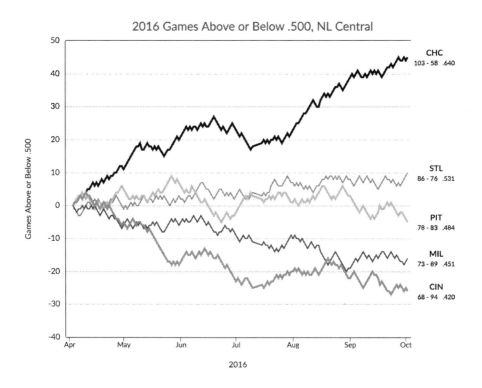

2016 Games Above or Below .500, NL Central

May 3: The Jake Arrieta Show

On May 3, the Chicago Cubs found themselves 18-6, four games up on the Pirates and six up on the Cardinals. Chicago was coming off of a 7-2 win over Pittsburgh in a rematch of the 2015 NL Wild Card game.

That day would see the Cubs once again clash with the Pirates at PNC Park in the second game of a three-game series. In the 7-2 series opener, things between the two teams got heated, as lingering resentment over hit batters from the 2015 Wild Card game boiled over, resulting in multiple beanings.

The Pirates, who were expected to compete for the division title, sent Jon Niese to the mound. Coming into the game, the Pirates had lost six in a row, and found themselves four games behind the division-leading Cubs. Pittsburgh's odds of winning the NL Central stood at just 6.1 percent, while Chicago's were at 89.2 percent.

Arrieta, the reigning NL Cy Young Award winner who had eliminated the Pirates in the Wild Card game, would face them again at PNC Park on this night. The Cubs ace retired 15 Pirates in a row at one point, and went on to collect his sixth straight win in dominant fashion. He allowed only two singles and became the first Cubs starter since 1908—hey, that was a good year!—to win his first six starts of the season. He even helped out his own cause, smacking an RBI single in the second off Niese. The telling moment in the game would come even earlier.

Arrieta walked John Jaso and Andrew McCutchen to lead off the bottom of the first, bringing up David Freese. It was an early test for Arrieta, who had struggled with his command in his last couple starts—he had walked eight batters in his previous 14 innings pitched. Here though, Arrieta was able to retire Freese swinging, and then induced ground outs from Matt Joyce and Francisco Cervelli to snuff out the rally. The Pirates never truly threatened again.

In the second, Niese gave up two walks and hit two batters, as the Cubs touched him up for two runs. Two innings later, the Cubs got to him for four more runs and put the game out of reach. All told, the Cubs collected 11 hits, five walks, and seven runs, which was more support than Arrieta needed, as he threw seven strong innings of shutout baseball.

This win stands out as the first time in the 2016 season that the Cubs' chances of winning the division climbed over 90 percent. After this game, the Cubs' odds of winning the NL Central never fell below 91.7 percent. St. Louis and Pittsburgh occasionally made up ground on the Cubs, but never enough to truly threaten them for the division lead.

The Cubs also became the first team since the 2003 Yankees to start a season without consecutive losses through their first 25 games of the season. This particular game, highlighted by the dominant starting pitching and well-rounded offense, showcased the Cubs' greatest strengths—strengths that would serve them well on the quest for their first division crown since 2008.

The season was also emblematic of the Pirates' lost season. They started off well enough, but even before the bottom dropped out in June around the time of Gerrit Cole's elbow injury, there were warning signs. The aforementioned Niese was a below-replacement pitcher, as was Francisco Liriano. While the team's first-half hitting picked up the slack for the struggling Andrew McCutchen, the pitching definitely didn't. In the first half, the team's 112 FIP- was the fourth-worst in the majors, and second-worst in the NL. In the second half, the team's pitching improved, but the hitting dropped off sharply, as Gregory Polanco, Jordy Mercer and David Freese struggled, among others. Simply put, it just wasn't Pittsburgh's year.

July 15: Slipping Away

The St. Louis Cardinals entered the day seven games behind the division-leading Cubs. While the Cardinals' chances of overtaking the Cubs for the division lead didn't look promising, they were still realistically within striking distance, and they were also just a game behind the Miami Marlins and New York Mets for the second Wild Card. A victory over the Marlins on this day could position St. Louis not only to gain ground in the Wild Card race but the NL Central, too. The Cubs were hosting the Texas Rangers, who were leading the American League West by 5.5 games.

10 Things You Should Remember About the 2016 NL Central

1. 2015 NL Rookie of the Year Kris Bryant emerged in 2016 as an MVP candidate. The Cubs third baseman slashed .292/.365/.554, put up a .262 ISO, hit 39 homers and played fine defense.

2. Chicago's Anthony Rizzo popped 32 homers. Bryant shared with the media that Rizzo often told him "I'm your Prince," referring to Prince Fielder, who "protected" Miguel Cabrera in the Tigers' lineup during Cabrera's MVP seasons.

3. At -3.6 fWAR, the Reds' bullpen was the sixth-worst bullpen in baseball history, and their 103 homers allowed was 15 more than any team ever.

4. The Brewers acquired a trio of speedsters in Jonathan Villar (62 stolen bases), Hernan Perez (34) and Keon Broxton (23) for practically nothing.

5. Aledmys Diaz had a strong rookie campaign for the Cardinals. The Cuban-born shortstop hit 17 homers, and was an All-Star, and hit one of the

The Cardinals sent left-hander Jaime Garcia to the mound against the Marlins' disappointing free agent signing, Wei-Yin Chen. Chen was coming off a strong start against the New York Mets, having worked seven innings of three-hit, one-run baseball, but even with that start included, his 2016 ERA to that point was an inept 4.83, and his 4.51 FIP wasn't much better. Garcia, for his part, had pitched shakily in his previous outing against the Pittsburgh Pirates, allowing four runs in only five innings.

The two teams traded scoreless innings until the fourth, when the Marlins took a 1-0 lead on a Chris Johnson double that scored Marcell Ozuna. The Cardinals answered in the bottom half of the inning, putting up four runs on Chen with a solo shot from Stephen Piscotty and a three-run blast from Tommy Pham.

Miami tied the game in the seventh before St. Louis pulled ahead in the bottom of the inning with a pair of solo homers from Pham and Randal Grichuk. Pham's second homer was a bit of a statistical oddity, as it gave him three multi-homer games in his young career. He became one of just 28 hitters in major league history to have three multi-homer games in his first 80 career games, but what made it even more odd is that those games represented six of his 10 career homers. It was an unlikely but necessary boost for the Cardinals.

Another unlikely boost came from Aledyms Diaz, who reached base three times on this day and in general helped stabilize the infield after the team lost Jhonny Peralta for the season's first two months with a thumb injury, a thumb injury that would cost him more time as the season progressed.

Despite the feats from Pham, Grichuk, Piscotty and Diaz, Miami answered, tying the game in the eighth. The ageless Ichiro Suzuki pinch hit in the eighth inning as well, collecting major league hit No. 2,991; Ichiro would go on to notch his 3,000th career hit a few weeks later.

This furious flurry of action in the eighth would set up a dramatic showdown in the ninth between Seung Hwan Oh, the Cardinals' best reliever, and the fearsome combo of Giancarlo Stanton and Marcell Ozuna. Oh caught Stanton looking, but Ozuna doubled and came around to score on an RBI single from infielder Miguel Rojas to give the Marlins a 7-6 lead they would not relinquish.

Though the division race was the Cubs' to lose—and it didn't look like they were planning to give it up anytime soon—the Cardinals were set up to potentially gain some ground, and they let the game slip away. The Cardinals' play-by-play man, Dan McLaughlin, said, "You just get the feeling this is an important game to set the tone" for the three-game series, which the Cardinals ended up dropping to Miami. McLaughlin also went on to point out that the game summed up the Cardinals'

---

more memorable home runs of the season—his first career grand slam after taking a leave of absence to visit the family of José Fernández following the pitcher's death.

6. 2013 MVP Andrew McCutchen had a disappointing season. He belted 24 homers, one off his career high, but after hitting .292/.401/.488 in 2015 he hit just .256/.336/.430 in 2016, and put up the worst defensive numbers of his career (-28 DRS).

7. Cubs starter Kyle Hendricks had a breakout season. He put up 5.0 bWAR and 4.5 fWAR, and his 2.13 ERA was the best in the majors.

8. Joey Votto kept right on chugging, and was joined by Adam Duvall, whose 33 homers were a ray of light in an otherwise dismal Reds season.

9. Junior Guerra (2.81 ERA, 3.71 FIP, 2.5 fWAR in 121.2 IP) was another low-cost Brewers success.

10. Pirates prospect Josh Bell's first major league homer was a pinch-hit grand slam. He hit a respectable .273/.368/.406 line over 128 at-bats at age 23.

first half: poor defense late, the team's inability to add on runs, the struggles of the bullpen, and poor play at home. In fact, the Cardinals would finish with a below-.500 record at home for the first time since Busch Stadium III opened in 2006. They would finish 38-43 at home, a year after finishing 55-26 there. From 2006-2015, the Cardinals average home record was 49.1-31.8. So 2016 was a big break from the established norms for Cardinals baseball.

Meanwhile, the All-Star-studded Chicago Cubs manhandled the Texas Rangers behind six scoreless innings from Kyle Hendricks. The Cubs jumped on Texas lefty Martín Perez early to secure a 1-0 lead, and then tacked on five more in the sixth to give Hendricks and the bullpen ample breathing room.

After Hendricks came out of the game, the Cubs got lights-out relief work from their bullpen, as Carl Edwards Jr., Travis Wood, Pedro Strop and Justin Grimm combined for three scoreless innings. The Rangers managed just two hits off the Cubs' quartet of relievers, both against Wood. Said quartet was very important to the Cubs all year, as they combined for a 3.38 ERA in 235 relief outings, and they struck out 224 batters in 197 innings, which equaled a fantastic 27.9 percent strikeout rate.

The victory over Texas was Chicago's 54th of the season, and the team found itself sitting at 54-35 at the end of the day. With St. Louis' tough loss to Miami, the Cubs increased their division odds to 94.6 percent, and St. Louis' fell to 4.3 percent. The Cardinals would see their division odds stand at six percent or greater for only four more days throughout the 2016 season.

Still, the Cubs wouldn't take their foot off the gas. In the weeks leading up to the trade deadline, they traded for relievers Mike Montgomery, Aroldis Chapman and Joe Smith to further solidify their bullpen for a playoff run. They left nothing to chance, and as a result cruised, finishing with 103 wins and reaching 100 percent in the division odds as early as August 12.

The 2016 Chicago Cubs would go on to claim the World Series as wire-to-wire winners, joining the 1927 New York Yankees, 1955 Brooklyn Dodgers, 1984 Detroit Tigers, 1990 Cincinnati Reds and 2005 Chicago White Sox as the only teams to accomplish that feat.

The National League West View

by Stacie Wheeler

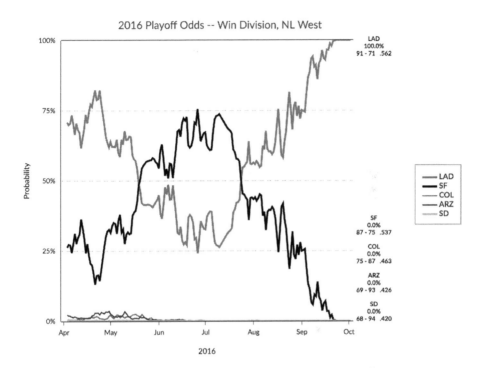

Fewer writers picked the Los Angeles Dodgers to win the National League West division before the 2016 season started than at 2015's outset. But while the San Francisco Giants and Arizona Diamondbacks were projected to be contenders, statistically the Dodgers' odds of winning their division were 70.5 percent before Opening Day, according to FanGraphs. They were tested all season, but they were tested as much by their own injuries—they would place a major league record 28 players on the disabled list in 2016—as they were by other teams. The most devastating injury landed Clayton Kershaw on the disabled list with a herniated disc in his back, a setback many thought would doom the Dodgers' season.

It was around the time of Kershaw's injury that many Dodgers observers were lamenting the loss of Zack Greinke, who signed with the Diamondbacks in the offseason. With his signing, Arizona thought itself ready to challenge the Dodgers and the Giants, but the Diamondbacks languished at the bottom of the division for most of the season. Neither Greinke nor their other new starting pitching acquisition, Shelby Miller, made a positive difference.

The Giants on the other hand, did get good returns from their new starting pitchers, Johnny Cueto and Jeff Samardzija. Adding them to an already strong team helped the Giants surge to a 57-33 record in the first half, the best record in baseball. San Francisco, with its history of winning titles in even-numbered years, held an eight-game lead in the NL West when Kershaw landed on the disabled list. The division, however, was in for a severe course correction.

Let's take a step back, to one week before his injury.

June 20: Kershaw Beats Nationals, Giants Waste A Bumgarner Gem

San Francisco had won 27 of its last 35 games, and eight in a row entering its series opener at PNC Park in Pittsburgh. The Giants were securely entrenched in first place, 6.5 games ahead of the Dodgers in the NL West, and their division odds stood at 72 percent. But after this day, on which the Dodgers defeated the Nationals and the Giants were outdueled by Jeff Locke and Clint Hurdle's bullpen, the momentum began to shift in favor of the Dodgers. Los Angeles increased their NL West division odds from 27.8 percent to 36.9 percent in just one day.

Kershaw was his usual dominant self and held the Dodgers' future NLDS opponents, the Washington Nationals, to one run over seven innings. There was absolutely no indication that he would go down with injury the following week. After the start, Kershaw had 141 strikeouts to just seven walks, for an unbelievable K/BB ratio of 20.1 while lowering his ERA to 1.57.

The Dodgers' offense wasn't great, but they did enough to earn the win, 4-1. Joc Pederson and Justin Turner both hit solo homers off of Yusmeiro Petit, who made an admirable start in place of an injured Stephen Strasburg. (Strasburg, whose late scratch with an upper back strain spoiled the highly anticipated matchup between the two aces, was off to a great start to the year going 10-0 with a 2.90 ERA before he was injured.) Turner's bat was as hot as the triple-digit temperature in Los Angeles during the series, and his 418-foot home run in the first inning extended his hitting streak to eight games. In that span he hit .467 with five home runs, putting his early season struggles (he was hitting only .247/.330/.325 at the end of April) behind him once and for all.

Kershaw struck out eight and walked none but was clearly tiring in the seventh inning due to the heat. The Nats plated their only run of the game in his final inning. Joe Blanton, who had all but cemented his role as the setup man, pitched a scoreless eighth inning and lowered his ERA to 2.15. Kenley Jansen entered in the ninth and picked up his 20th save. It was the 162nd of his career, and with it he surpassed Eric Gagne as the Dodgers' all-time leader.

Meanwhile, in Pittsburgh, the Giants squandered an excellent Madison Bumgarner start, which dropped their division odds to 62.7 percent. The 1-0 Pirates win ended their five-game losing streak and snapped the Giants eight-game winning streak.

Locke gave the Bucs a solid 6.2 innings of work, giving up just five hits without allowing a walk, a rare good start for a Pittsburgh starter in 2016. (Pirates starters finished the season with an average Game Score of 48, tied for next-to-worst in the NL.) Bumgarner, who had not lost a start since April 20, also only allowed five hits over his eight innings. The lone run came off the bat of an unlikely hero, catcher Erik Kratz, who hit his first home run of the year in the fifth inning. At first, it looked as though Angel Pagan had robbed Kratz of the homer to left field, but he slammed down his glove after being unable to hold on to the ball as he reached over the fence.

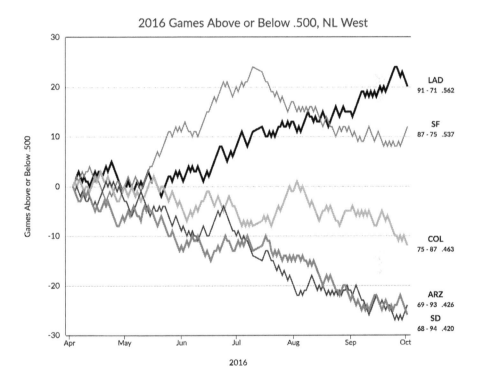

Hurdle went to setup man Neftali Feliz with two outs in the seventh and the tying run on second base with Bumgarner at the plate, an example of bullpen role redefinition that has evolved as managers and teams look to diminish the artificial importance of the save statistic. The shift in managerial bullpen decisions was subsequently and prominently successful in the postseason, most notably in the usage of Andrew Miller and Kenley Jansen. In this case, it worked in the regular season. Feliz retired

Bumgarner. Tony Watson and Mark Melancon followed with scoreless innings in the eighth and ninth to give the Pirates the team win.

After the Dodgers notched their sixth victory in their last seven games, and the Giants dropped the 1-0 contest against the Pirates, there was a 18.3 percentage point swing in division odds between the Dodgers and Giants, the largest one-day swing of the season.

June 24-27: A Lost Ace

After the Giants left Pittsburgh, it was the Dodgers' turn to travel there. They'd also had recent difficulty playing at PNC Park, but they came into the series having won six straight, three of which came via walk-off. Nevertheless, their division odds fell to a season-low 24.1 percent after they dropped the first three games of the series.

The final tally in the opener was 8-6, after a battle between the bullpens. The Dodgers had to turn to a virtually unknown starting pitcher, Nick Tepesch, after injuries to many of their starters—including Hyun-Jin Ryu, Brandon McCarthy, Alex Wood, Brandon McCarthy, and Frankie Montas. In this, Tepesch's lone start, he yielded five runs on seven hits in four innings. A couple of days later, he would be claimed on waivers by the A's, and then a couple weeks after that he would be claimed by the Royals. He didn't pitch again in the majors in 2016.

> ### 10 Things You Should Remember About the 2016 NL West
>
> 1. The Padres hit the reboot button. They lost 94 games, and traded away Andrew Cashner, Matt Kemp, Drew Pomeranz, Fernando Rodney, James Shields, and Melvin Upton Jr.
>
> 2. Padres general manager A.J. Preller was suspended 30 days without pay for deceptive practices during trades and withholding medical information.
>
> 3. 22-year-old rookie Corey Seager led the NL West with 7.5 WAR, second-best in the National League. He hit .308/.365/.512, and led all shortstops in baseball with a 137 wRC+.
>
> 4. Nolan Arenado featured in the MVP debate, as his 41 homers tied for first in the NL, and by Defensive Runs Saved (DRS) he was the best third baseman in baseball.
>
> 5. Giants shortstop Brandon Crawford excelled defensively, as his 21.3 Ultimate Zone Rating (UZR) ranked first among shortstops in the majors.

With the rotation in disarray, it was up to the Dodgers' offense. The bats did heat up, but four hits by Corey Seager were not enough to stave off the series-opening loss. Defensive miscues from Yasiel Puig in right field (overthrow) and Seager (dropped ball) helped Pittsburgh's cause and set the tone for the series.

Andrew McCutchen, who had not looked like himself at the plate for most of the year, appeared in vintage form in the second game. McCutchen homered twice, and his second shot—a three-run blast in the sixth—chased Kenta Maeda. On the other side, Pittsburgh starter Locke wasn't dominant, but he kept the Dodgers off the basepaths. The Dodgers scored their only run on back-to-back doubles from Scott Van Slyke and A.J. Ellis in the sixth, going 2-for-10 with runners in scoring position.

The Dodgers were dealt their biggest blow of the season in game three. Not only did the Pirates secure the series win with a 4-3 victory, but this would be the game in which they lost Kershaw, who was bested by Chad Kuhl, a rookie in his major league debut. Turner drove in all three runs for the Dodgers, but it wasn't enough, and Kershaw picked up his second loss of the season. He would not pitch again until Sept. 9.

While it was a losing affair for the Dodgers, it was also a turning point, as they would avoid a four-game sweep in Pittsburgh (something that hasn't happened since 1944). Scott Kazmir settled down after a four-run first inning, and the Dodgers scraped together five runs on seven hits and seven walks (three from leadoff hitter Kiké Hernández) en route to a 5-4 win. The victory was a microcosm of the season: The Dodgers rallied from an early deficit and relied on their stalwart bullpen.

With the win, the Dodgers' division odds rebounded to 29.3 percent, and they would win six of their next seven to boost themselves back up to 39.1 percent following a July 4th victory over the Orioles.

6. San Francisco's bullpen blew a major league-leading 30 saves, including nine in September, and their 21.1 percent strikeout rate ranked just 23rd.

7. LA's bullpen was much better, as its strikeout rate (26.1 percent) was fourth-best, and it held up even through 590.2 innings pitched, most in the majors.

8. Colorado's Jon Gray had six 10-strikeout games in his rookie season, tied for fifth most in the NL with Madison Bumgarner.

9. Jean Segura had a big comeback year with the Diamondbacks, who acquired him in a trade prior to the season. He led the team with 5.0 WAR, hit a career-high 20 homers, and stole 33 bases. He and teammate Paul Goldschmidt were just two of four players in the majors to have 20 HR-30 SB seasons.

10. The Rockies' middle infield duo of DJ Lemahieu and Trevor Story had great seasons. Second baseman Lemehieu led the majors in batting average (.348), while rookie shortstop Story led NL shortstops in homers, despite only playing 97 games.

While they would backslide a little heading into and out of the All-Star break, the team had proven it could sustain the loss of a key player.

Aug. 23-28: Gaining Ground

Los Angeles had built its division odds back up slowly following the All-Star break, but had been hovering in the 60 percent range for the previous two weeks, heading into an important three-game home series in late August. The Dodgers were a scant one game ahead of the Giants in the standings. This series, and the one that followed it, represented the Giants' best chance to get back into the NL West race.

The Dodgers came in with a two-game win streak, and won the first game of the highly anticipated showdown, 9-5. Seager, who would go on to shatter LA Dodgers records as a rookie shortstop, went 3-for-4. Gonzalez drove in four runs, and rookies Rob Segedin and Andrew Toles homered. The Giants' Bumgarner allowed five earned runs in five innings, a season high. Maeda's command wasn't as sharp as usual, and he had some communication problems early on with catcher Yasmani Grandal. However, Maeda did enough, and the offense and bullpen picked up the slack.

The second game of the series was closer. Rich Hill, a key trade deadline acquisition for the Dodgers, outdueled Cueto in the 1-0 Dodgers victory. He had been sidelined with persistent blisters, but demonstrated he was healthy and put his pitch arsenal on display over six innings of scoreless ball. The lone run of the game came on Turner's fourth-inning solo home run. The series win gave the Dodgers a season-high three-game lead in the NL West and improved their odds of winning the division to 81.5 percent.

The Giants shut out the Dodgers in the series finale, avoiding the three-game sweep and keeping hope alive. Acquired at the trade deadline, Matt Moore seemed to be the Giants' answer to the Dodgers' biggest weakness, left-handed pitching. Moore nearly no-hit Los Angeles for his first win with San Francisco, broken up by a Seager blooper to right field with two outs in the ninth. Moore was removed following the Seager base hit; he had thrown a career-high 133 pitches. Santiago Casilla needed only one pitch to retire Turner on a foul pop-up to close out the game and series.

The win decreased the Giants' deficit to two games in the NL West and lowered the Dodgers' odds of winning the division to 75.7 percent. Following this game, the Giants would fly home to meet with the toothless Atlanta Braves, while the Dodgers would host an NLCS preview series with the Chicago Cubs. Advantage, one would presume, Giants.

An extra-innings loss for the Dodgers coupled with a dominating shutout for the Giants on Friday seemed to confirm this turning point. The Dodgers' division odds dropped to 68.2 percent following the loss, with the Giants' climbing to 31.8 percent. That would be both the low and high point for each team for the remainder of the season.

The next afternoon, rookie Julio Urias struck eight over six innings of one-run ball, Seager would homer, and the Dodgers won, 3-2. Meanwhile, by the Bay, the Giants were forced to turn to their own, far less heralded rookie, Albert Suarez. Despite boasting a top-heavy rotation with Bumgarner, Cueto, Moore and Jeff Samardzija, the Giants didn't have a ton of starting pitching depth, and when Matt Cain landed on the disabled list for the third time on Aug. 18, the Giants briefly went to a four-man rotation before calling on Suarez. And while Suarez didn't allow more than three runs in any single start, he didn't pitch more than five innings in any of them, further taxing a weary bullpen.

Further impeding the Giants was manager Bruce Bochy playing a Sunday lineup on a Saturday—Brandon Belt, Buster Posey and Hunter Pence were on the bench. Braves starter Mike Foltynewicz held the remains of the Giants to one run over seven innings, and the Braves hung on to win, 3-1. The loss dropped the Giants' division odds to 23.4 percent. They would spend only another seven days with division odds in the 20 percent range, and by mid-September, they were firmly in the single digits, a division title that once seemed assured coldly slipping through their fingers.

Davis' Dinger, Cubs' Team Effort Shine Brightest

by Brad Johnson

Long live the 2016 Chicago Cubs. In 2014, the Royals reached postseason play and came up short. In their second attempt, they clinched the World Series. The Cubs cut their teeth in 2015 before going the distance this year. Unlike the Royals, it's hard to shake a feeling that Chicago will be back. Frequently.

Overall, this was a World Series to remember. Considering the stakes, Game Seven was one of the most thrilling games ever. The finale more than made up for the rest of the series, which occasionally lacked for tension and dramatic moments.

We like to do things differently around here. Rather than evaluate the postseason using common measures, let's spend the next few minutes looking through the lens of our pet statistic—Championships Added (ChampAdded). The stat has two components.

We begin with standard Win Probability Added (WPA). The outcome of a game is decided by each individual play. WPA measures the value of those plays by accounting for score, inning, base state (i.e. runner on first), and number of outs.

The second ingredient is a leverage index for each game—the Championship Value. As a team moves deeper in a series, its chance to win (or lose) the series increases. Obviously, games take on greater significance in a close series. Let's turn to the numbers.

Game Seven of the World Series is worth one full championship since it's a winner-takes-all contest. ChampAdded assigns a value of 1.000 to the game since the winner will receive the Commissioner's Trophy. All other games are worth a fraction of a championship. For example, had we seen a Game Seven of the LCS round this year, it would have been worth 50 percent of a World Series. Below is a chart that notes the total ChampAdded for each game.

Championship Value of Playoff Games										
	0-0	1-0	1-1	2-0	2-1	2-2	3-0	3-1	3-2	3-3
Wild Card Game	0.125	X	X	X	X	X	X	X	X	X
Division Series	0.094	0.094	0.125	0.063	0.125	0.250	X	X	X	X
Championship Series	0.156	0.156	0.188	0.125	0.188	0.250	0.063	0.125	0.250	0.500
World Series	0.313	0.313	0.375	0.250	0.375	0.500	0.125	0.250	0.500	1.000

Once we know WPA and Championship Value, we multiply them together to derive ChampAdded. The stat is expressed as a decimal like batting average and many other familiar stats. For example, a player with .500 ChampAdded will have singlehandedly produced 50 percent of a championship.

Starting with the Division Series round, every team had a 12.5 percent chance of winning the World Series. Teams that fail to win October glory are docked -.125 ChampAdded. In other words, they cede their 12.5 percent chance to another club. The World Champion Cubs contributed a total of .875 ChampAdded (1.000 minus .125 equals .875).

It is our tradition to use ChampAdded to identify a series MVP and a series goat, as well as the biggest play of the series. The MVP is the player with the most valuable series. The goat is the player who hurt his team the most. The play with the highest ChampAdded is considered the biggest play of the series.

AL Wild Card: Baltimore Orioles vs. Toronto Blue Jays

The American League East was a true battleground this season, so it was fitting that the AL Wild Card Game featured a pair of divisional foes. Both teams finished the regular season with an 89-73 record. They succeeded despite sharing similar flaws. Both offenses were inconsistent and volatile. Toronto received surprisingly good starting pitching to offset a thin bullpen. Baltimore's exceptional relievers bolstered a shaky rotation.

Fittingly, three of the four-run scoring plays in this game were home runs. José Bautista kicked off the action with a second-inning solo home run. Mark Trumbo responded in the fourth with a two-run blast. An unlikely hero, Ezequiel Carrera, singled home a critical run in the fifth. The game was tied, 2-2. It stayed that way until Edwin Encarnación hammered a three-run walk-off home run in the 11th inning.

In many ways, the end of this contest may have kicked off a (small) revolution. Orioles manager Buck Showalter opted to use enigmatic starter Ubaldo Jimenez in the 11th inning. Starters are used in relief all the time in the postseason, especially in extra innings. However, Cy Young Award candidate Zach Britton and his 0.54 ERA were waiting in the bullpen. While Britton watched, Jimenez allowed three straight hits, culminating in the Encarnación home run.

Game MVP: The Blue Jays won the game, but Orioles reliever Darren O'Day was the MVP. He entered with two on and one out in the bottom of the ninth. O'Day promptly induced an inning-ending double play from Russell Martin. He stayed on to toss a one-two-three 10th inning. The effort was worth .043 ChampAdded, or 4.3 percent of a championship.

Game Goat: No surprise here, Jimenez is the goat. He entered the game with one out in 11th inning and failed to record an out. Devon Travis singled, Josh Donaldson advanced Travis to third with another single, and then Encarnación removed all doubt with his home run. Jimenez was "rewarded" with -.053 ChampAdded.

Big Play: You'd think a walk-off home run is automatically the biggest play. And it was if you consider all of the events leading up to it. However, Travis and Donaldson did a lot of the dirty work. The trio of hits was worth .053 ChampAdded, but Encarnación's role was credited with just .022 ChampAdded. It was not the biggest play. In the fourth inning, Trumbo furnished the Orioles with their only lead via a two-run home run. His homer was worth .029 ChampAdded.

NL Wild Card: San Francisco Giants vs. New York Mets

Baseball purists were spoiled by the National League Wild Card game. The Giants and Mets both relied heavily on starting pitching to get them to the postseason. As such, a Madison Bumgarner versus Noah Syndergaard matchup seemed fitting, and had the makings of a duel for the ages. The last time Bumgarner pitched in the post-season, he contributed .869 ChampAdded. Syndergaard was no slouch last October either.

The pair of aces lived up to the hype. Syndergaard allowed two hits and three walks over seven innings. He tallied 10 strikeouts and looked untouchable for most of the evening. By comparison, Bumgarner managed only six strikeouts. However, he also authored a complete-game shutout. The postseason legend continues.

After eight innings, the score remained locked at 0-0, and Mets closer Jeurys Familia was called upon for the top of the ninth. Brandon Crawford led off the inning with a double, followed by a strikeout and a Joe Panik walk. The Giants' eighth hitter, Conor Gillaspie, then blasted a surprise three-run home run. With the newfound cushion, Bumgarner stayed in to close out his gem.

Game MVP: Complete-game shutouts are hugely valuable, especially when the game remains scoreless until the ninth inning. Now is a good time to note that pitcher hitting matters too. While Bumgarner is known for his adequate bat, he failed to record a hit in this game. He ended with .060 ChampAdded. It would have been .067 ChampAdded if we counted only the pitching component.

Game Goat: The theme of the Wild Card round: when you allow three runs in the last inning of the game, you are the goat. Familia ruined Syndergaard's gem, and his disastrous ninth inning cost him -.059 ChampAdded. It's the second consecutive postseason Familia played the role of goat.

Big Play: Gillaspie was credited with .049 ChampAdded for his game-winning home run. He also had a hit earlier in the game, giving him a total of .055 ChampAdded.

ALDS: Cleveland Baseball Club vs. Boston Red Sox

Cleveland limped into the postseason. Injuries to starters Carlos Carrasco and Danny Salazar left the pitching staff in a shambles. Josh Tomlin was the fifth starter for much of the season, and he was terrible in the second half. Cleveland needed him to fill the role of third starter behind Corey Kluber and Trevor Bauer.

By contrast, the Red Sox were healthy and loaded with recognizable talent. The offensive-minded club was led by soon-to-retire superstar David Ortiz. They were the clear favorites. As we were taught multiple times this fall, favorites can suffer stunning losses.

Game One featured Rick Porcello against Bauer. Porcello won 22 games during the regular season, but it was all Cleveland in this one. Jason Kipnis, Francisco Lindor and Roberto Perez all homered against Porcello, producing five runs in the process. Cleveland held on for a 5-4 victory.

This October, managers were careful to learn from Showalter's mistake in the AL Wild Card game. Cleveland manager Terry Francona called upon relief ace Andrew Miller to protect a 4-3 lead with two outs in the bottom of the fifth. The adventure started on a shaky note—Brock Holt doubled and then Mookie Betts walked before Miller struck out Ortiz to end the threat. He then dispatched the next five batters he faced as part of a two-inning, four-strikeout appearance. The outing foreshadowed the rest of his postseason.

While the first game was close, the second was a blowout. Kluber tossed seven scoreless innings, and Dan Otero and Bryan Shaw preserved the shutout. Meanwhile, David Price's postseason blues continued unabated. He allowed five runs in 3.1 innings as part of the 6-0 defeat.

Although the Cleveland never trailed in Game Three, it was a well-fought battle. With one on and one out in the eighth inning, Francona called upon Cody Allen to record the final five outs. The score was 4-2. Allen walked Ortiz. Hanley Ramirez knocked an RBI single. Allen was fortunate to escape the inning when Xander Bogaerts hit a sharp lineout to second base.

The ninth inning was equally stressful. Chris Young and Sandy Leon made quick outs, but Jackie Bradley Jr. and Dustin Pedroia reached base via a single and a walk. Travis Shaw worked a full count, but failed to deliver, and the brooms were out.

Series MVP: Cody Allen's two saves earn him MVP honors. He tossed three innings and tallied five strikeouts in his two appearances, good for .031 ChampAdded. By this measure, Allen is held accountable for the run that scored in Game Three, even though the actual earned run was charged to Bryan Shaw.

Series Goat: The Red Sox received quality starting pitching all season, but it failed them in the postseason. After allowing five runs on three home runs in an abbreviated start, Porcello was the chief goat. His flop was worth -.029 ChampAdded. Price deserves notice too. He isn't the top goat only because the Red Sox offense failed to do any damage against Kluber. Price's bad start was worth -.025 ChampAdded.

Big Play: Although Game Two was a lopsided affair, it also had the single biggest play of the series. Brandon Guyer opened the scoring with an RBI single in the second inning. Chisenhall immediately followed with a nail in the coffin—a three-run home run, good for .0.15 ChampAdded.

It's worth reiterating that a swept series affects game values. If the series had gone five games instead of only three, Travis Shaw's flyout would have been the biggest in the series. Since the Red Sox had such an uphill battle to advance, the series ending out was only -.011 ChampAdded.

AL Divison Series: Toronto Blue Jays vs. Texas Rangers

This was the rematch of the 2015 ALDS, also known as the "Bat Flip Series." There was certainly no love lost between these two clubs. Perhaps you recall a certain fight somewhere in the vicinity of second base.

Toronto cruised to a 9-1 victory in Game One. Marco Estrada delivered a superb 8.1 inning performance. Cole Hamels was battered for six runs in 4.1 innings. The Blue Jays were also in the driver's seat for Game Two. They scored five runs, all via four home runs against Rangers starter Yu Darvish. Texas threatened in the eighth inning, narrowing the score to 5-3. And that's where it finished.

Game Three featured a little bit of everything. Both teams scored early and often. Toronto led 5-4 heading into the sixth inning, when Mitch Moreland delivered a two-run double to put Texas in front. In the bottom of the sixth, Keone Kela inherited a bases loaded jam with one out. Darwin Barney fouled out to third base, and Kela had a chance to escape damage. Unfortunately, he uncorked a run-scoring passed ball. He later retired Carreram but the score was now tied, 6-6.

Without the passed ball, the Rangers might have won in regulation. Instead, the game went to extra innings. Rangers manager Jeff Banister tried to coax a third inning of relief out of Matt Bush, but the plan backfired. Bush allowed a leadoff double to Donaldson and intentionally walked Encarnación. Bautista went down swinging for the first out. Martin followed with a potential double play ball, but a throwing error gave Donaldson just enough space to scamper home to clinch the series.

Series MVP: Troy Tulowitzki raked in the Division Series. He slashed .462/.462/.846, with two runs and five RBI in 13 plate appearances. In addition to his bat, a quarter of his value was produced on the bases. He scored the tying run in Game 3. Most players would have scored on that passed ball. Tulowitzki was simply in the right place at the right time. With the running play included, he recorded .045 ChampAdded.

If we deduct credit for the theft of home, Roberto Osuna's .044 ChampAdded would have led the series. Osuna allowed one hit and struck out four batters over 3.2 high-leverage innings.

Series Goat: The Rangers got nothing out of their starting pitchers. Hamels and Darvish quickly handed the first two games to the Blue Jays. Colby Lewis continued the trend in Game 3. He lasted just two innings and allowed all five earned runs. The meltdown was worth -.034 ChampAdded.

Big Play: Moreland gave the Rangers their best chance to win Game Three. His go-ahead double was only worth .020 ChampAdded, and it was the single biggest play of a lopsided series.

NL Division Series: San Francisco Giants vs. Chicago Cubs

While the American League delivered one-sided series, the National League featured a pair of closely contested affairs. Chicago's World Series run kicked off with a duel between Jon Lester and Johnny Cueto. Both starters went eight innings. Javier Baez bopped a solo home run with one out in the eighth, prompting Cubs manager Joe Maddon to call upon Aroldis Chapman to finish the game.

The Cubs coasted to victory in Game Two. Starting pitcher Kyle Hendricks delivered the game-winning hit in the second inning—a two-run single to center. Reliever Travis Wood popped a solo home run later in the game.

Chicago's pitchers continued the onslaught in Game Three. Jake Arrieta opened the scoring against Bumgarner with a three-run home run in the second inning. This time, the Giants clawed back. Chapman blew a save in the eighth inning. Gillaspie delivered a go-ahead two-run triple, and Brandon Crawford promptly singled Gillaspie home.

With a 5-3 lead in the ninth, Giants reliever Sergio Romo walked Dexter Fowler and allowed a game-tying home run to Kris Bryant. Finally, in the bottom of the 13th inning, Crawford and Joe Panik both doubled to provide the death blow.

That was high tide for the Giants' even year magic. San Francisco led for most of Game Four, but a comfy three-run lead in the top of the ninth wasn't comfy enough. Derek Law opened the frame by allowing a single to Bryant. Javier López came in and walked Anthony Rizzo. Next up was Romo. He allowed an RBI double to Ben Zobrist. Will Smith served as the fourth pitcher in four batters. Willson Contreras drove in a pair to tie the game. Jason Heyward botched a bunt, but wound up on second anyway after an error. Bruce Bochy called for his fifth pitcher of the inning, Hunter Strickland. He allowed a go-ahead single to Baez.

Chapman struck out the side to complete a 6-5 victory and a 3-1 series win.

Series MVP: Baez delivered the killing blows in the first and final games of the series. Those two hits account for 85 percent of his .077 ChampAdded. Overall, he had a superb series at the plate, hitting .275/.412/.563, with four runs scored and two huge RBI.

Series Goat: The Giants bullpen was in freefall for most of the stretch run. Sergio Romo was part of the problem, and he definitely botched his role in this series. He did his best to lose Game Three, and his one shot at saving Game Four failed too. He was slammed for -.040 ChampAdded.

Big Play: Baez was big in Game One, and he was even bigger in Game Four. His ninth-inning, series-clinching single was worth .037 ChampAdded.

Before we permanently turn our backs on the 2016 Giants, let's applaud Gillaspie for another clutch performance. After teaming up with Bumgarner to carry San Francisco to the NLDS, Gillaspie played big roles at the plate in final two games. Without him, it's a much less interesting series. His Game Three triple was worth .035 ChampAdded and eventually led to the Giants' only win. Let's not forget, Gillaspie did his damage against Familia and Chapman. They say you can't predict baseball…

NL Division Series: Los Angeles Dodgers vs. Washington Nationals

Like the NL Wild Card Game, Game One of both NLDS series featured a prominent pair of starting pitchers—in this one, it was Clayton Kershaw and Max Scherzer. But two of the best starters in the NL looked decidedly mortal on this day. Scherzer allowed four runs through the first three innings before eventually settling down. Kershaw only lasted five frames, but he held the Nationals to three runs. The bullpens locked down the scoring, and Kenley Jansen contributed a two-inning save.

Game Two opened as Game One had, with a first-inning Corey Seager homer. But the Dodgers managed only two runs in this one. Daniel Murphy and catcher Jose Lobaton sparked the Nationals, with the latter hitting an unlikely three-run homer.

The Nationals clung to a 4-3 lead as Game Three entered the ninth inning. Dodgers manager Dave Roberts called upon Jansen again to keep the contest close. Instead, he allowed four runs.

With the Dodgers' backs against the wall, Kershaw took the hill on short rest for Game Four. It was a gritty effort. He entered the seventh inning nursing a 5-2 lead, but the lead evaporated, with Murphy tying the game with a two-run single. Finally, Joe Blanton staunched the bleeding by retiring Anthony Rendon on strikes.

Washington was just a run away from the NLCS. Blake Treinen started the eighth inning on a high note—a strikeout followed by a ground out. Then Treinen hit Andrew Toles, Andre Either tapped a pinch-hit single to the opposite field, and Chase Utley followed with an RBI single. Jansen slammed the door.

Game Five was epic in the sense that it was very long. Scherzer faced off against Rich Hill. Los Angeles trailed 1-0 until the seventh inning. Joc Pederson led off with a solo home run to tie the game, ending Scherzer's night. Nationals manager Dusty Baker called upon Marc Rzepczynski for one batter, Treinen for two, Sammy Solis for two more, Shawn Kelley for one, and finally Oliver Perez to record the final out of the inning. When the smoke cleared, the Dodgers had scored four runs. The half inning lasted eight batters and took over an hour to complete. The score was 4-1.

Leaving nothing to chance, Jansen was summoned after Grant Dayton allowed a two-run home run to Chris Heisey in the bottom of the seventh. With no outs and a runner on first, Jansen navigated his way through a bases-loaded jam, pitched the eighth without incident, and started the ninth.

Jansen was visibly tired. He started the inning with a strikeout, then walked Bryce Harper and Jayson Werth. Time for relief! In came Kershaw upon a golden steed, pitching on one day of rest. The Dodgers' ace beat Murphy and Wilmer Difo to conclude the series.

Series MVP: When Kershaw is on, he's completely unbeatable. It's safe to say he wasn't in top form for this series, but he did just enough to qualify as the MVP. Kershaw narrowly outpitched Scherzer in Game One, had his bullpen blow a solid Game Four outing, and recorded the final two outs of Game Five. All told, he earned .090 ChampAdded. Joc Pederson finished second with .082 ChampAdded.

Series Goat: Dayton appeared in four of the five games. He was tagged for five hits, two walks, three runs and a home run in 1.2 innings. Dayton was particularly bad in the pivotal Game Five. His -.079 ChampAdded was a hair worse than Rendon's -.077 ChampAdded. Rendon hit .150/.190/.300 and made several painful outs with two outs and runners on base.

Big Play: Justin Turner delivered the biggest blow of that pivotal Game Five seventh inning. His two-run triple tallied .051 ChampAdded. Pederson's game-tying home run to lead off the inning rounded up to the same .051 ChampAdded, while Ruiz's single chipped in an additional .045 ChampAdded.

AL Championship Series: Toronto Blue Jays vs. Cleveland Baseball Club

The defining feature of the 2016 Blue Jays was their collection of impressive sluggers. However, Cleveland held them to a mere eight runs over five games. Five of those runs were scored in Game Four—Toronto's only win of the series. Kluber and Ryan Merritt oversaw shutout victories in the first and final games.

Cleveland didn't beat up on Toronto either—it did just enough to win. Francisco Lindor's two-run home run against Estrada accounted for all of the action in Game One. Game Two went to Cleveland, 2-1. Lindor once again provided the game-winning hit, an RBI single to center in the third inning.

Game Three had early action as well. The two clubs traded blows through the first five innings. The score was 2-2. Jason Kipnis and Jose Ramirez contributed runs in the sixth via solo home run and an RBI single. The bullpens clamped down. Game Five was more of the same. Cleveland plated three runs through three innings. The bullpen did the rest.

Relievers played a critical role in the series. Cleveland's four wins featured zero runs scored by either team after the completion of the sixth inning. Francona leaned heavily on Miller and Allen for the late outs. Osuna and Jason Grilli featured prominently for the Blue Jays.

Series MVP: Miller ruined Toronto's fall. He tossed 7.2 high-leverage, shutout innings. He recorded 14 strikeouts and allowed just three hits. The Blue Jays barely challenged him. He accrued .083 ChampAdded.

Series Goat: Toronto's bats shared the role of goat. Martin took the worst of it due to a couple critical outs. He hit .118/.167/.118, with -.048 ChampAdded. Tulowitzki

(.111/.200/.111) and Encarnación (.211/.250/.263) weren't much better. Respectively, they contributed .046 ChampAdded and .041 ChampAdded.

Big Play: The opening blow was also the biggest play of the series. Lindor's two-run home run in the sixth inning of Game One broke the 0-0 deadlock and put Cleveland in the win column.

NL Championship Series: Los Angeles Dodgers vs. Chicago Cubs

As was the case throughout the postseason, National League teams fought hard for their conquests. The NLCS went six games deep, although the final four were one-sided. Chapman blew the save in the eighth inning of Game One, but Miguel Montero bailed him out with a grand slam. The Cubs cruised from there.

Game Two was another closely contested battle. Adrian Gonzalez led off the second inning with a solo home run off Hendricks. Kershaw and Jansen successfully protected the 1-0 shutout.

The rest of the series lacked for late-inning drama. Game Three went to the Dodgers by a 6-0 margin. The shutout streak ended during Game Four. The Cubs exploded for 10 runs. The barrage continued during Game Five, leading to an 8-4 Chicago victory.

In Game Six, Kershaw and Hendricks met for a rematch. The Cubs pushed five runs across against Kershaw. Meanwhile, the Dodgers were blanked by Hendricks and friends, and the Cubs had advanced to their first World Seres since 1945.

Series MVP: The Cubs have three ace-quality pitchers. In this series, Lester was the top dog. He tossed six innings of one-run ball in Game One, then repeated the performance with a seven-inning, one-run masterpiece in Game Five. His pitching alone was worth 10 percent of a championship. Once you deduct the squalid hitting, he totaled .081 ChampAdded.

Hendricks did his best to keep pace, but he fell on the wrong side of Kershaw in Game Two. Still, Hendricks provided .066 ChampAdded. Rizzo led the hitters with .061 ChampAdded.

Series Goat: Joe Blanton had a good season and a solid NLDS, but he was burned for five runs in Game One and allowed two more in Game Five. Both times, he was defending a tied ballgame. Anytime you allow three home runs in a short series, you're probably a goat.

Big Play: Speaking of Blanton, two of those home runs were the biggest plays of the series. The cake topper was Addison Russell's two-run home run in the sixth inning of Game Five. It accounted for .064 ChampAdded. Montero's grand slam contributed .055 ChampAdded.

World Series: Chicago Cubs vs. Cleveland Baseball Club

If only every series went the full seven games. It was generally agreed that the Cubs had superior talent. Cleveland had Francona the savant—he was undefeated in two previous World Series appearances.

Chicago received a surprise reinforcement in the person of Kyle Schwarber. He missed nearly the entire season with a serious knee injury. There was no way he could contribute. Right?

Game One went Cleveland's way, as the team recorded its fourth shutout win of the postseason, tying a major league record. Kluber did his part as the staff ace. Roberto Perez provided the fireworks by blasting a pair of home runs. As it turned out, they were unnecessary. The opposite happened in Game Two. Cleveland's only run scored on a wild pitch. Arrieta and the Cubs had a firm grasp on this one almost from the first pitch. Schwarber singled in the eventual game-winning run in the top of the third inning, en route to a 5-1 finish.

Here comes the shutout machine again. Cleveland broke the record with its fifth October shutout. This time, Tomlin battled Hendricks in a Game Three duel. Tomlin lasted 4.2 scoreless while Hendricks completed five frames. Cleveland summoned its relief ace, Miller, to finish off the fourth, fifth, and sixth innings. Shaw bridged the gap to Allen for another 1-0 win.

Kluber returned on short rest for Game Four, and he picked up where he left off in Game One. He threw six innings of one-run ball. Already up 4-1, Cleveland's offense thanked Kluber by adding a trio of insurance runs in the top of the seventh. The final score was 7-2.

As we know, the Cubs weren't interested in rolling over. Down three games to one, they pulled out a gutsy 3-2 win in Game Five. Francona's itchy trigger wasn't quite quick enough in this one. Bauer made it through three shutout innings, but the Cubs managed to plate three in the fourth. That was all they needed.

Tomlin pitched Game Six on short rest, and it showed. Tomlin, a command and control pitcher, was frequently ahead in the count. But rather than bury his 0-2 curve balls in the dirt, he left several hanging over the middle of the plate. Bryant opened the scoring in the first with a solo home run. Russell doubled home two more in the first. After the Cubs chased Tomlin in the third, Russell squared up Otero for a grand slam. The Cubs won comfortably.

Chicago sprinted to an early lead in the postseason finale. Kluber worked on short rest—again. This time, he struggled. His stuff was visibly diminished, especially his potent two-seam fastball. Dexter Fowler led off the game with a solo home run. All told, Chicago scored four runs against Kluber. The Cubs even managed to string together a couple hits versus Miller.

The Cleveland counterattack began in the fifth inning. With two out and Carlos Santana on first, Lester was called to relieve Hendricks. Kipnis tapped a swinging bunt and catcher David Ross botched the throw to first. Kipnis and Santana advanced to second and third. Next, Lester unleashed a wild pitch for the ages. The bounce knocked Ross off balance. Santana scored easily and Kipnis also scampered home all the way from second. Cleveland trailed, 5-3.

The fifth was a bad inning for Ross. The sixth offered an opportunity for redemption. With one out, Ross launched an important solo home run against Miller. This proved to be a critical run.

Fast forward to the eighth inning. The score was still 6-3 in favor of the Cubs. Chapman entered the game with two outs and a man on first. Guyer slugged a double, to make it 6-4. Up walks Rajai Davis. To this point, he had had a miserable series. This time, things were different. Chapman tossed a low-and-in fastball and Davis drilled it out over the left-field wall. New game: 6-6. The score remained tied through the end of the ninth.

With Shaw now pitching for Cleveland, there was a short rain delay between the ninth and 10th innings. Perhaps it messed with his rhythm. When play resumed, Schwarber opened the frame with a single. Pinch runner Albert Almora tagged up and reached second on a fly out to deep center, which prompted an intentional walk of Rizzo. Zobrist then delivered a go-ahead double. Another intentional walk and a soft single by Montero put Chicago up, 8-6.

Cleveland mounted one last attempt. As with the eighth-inning rally, Guyer and Davis were instrumental. Guyer walked, advanced to second and scored on a single by Davis. Earlier in the game, journeyman defensive specialist Michael Martínez—one of the worst hitters of all time—had replaced Coco Crisp. Nobody was left on the bench. Martínez predictably grounded out to cap the game and the 2016 season.

Series MVP: Even though Cleveland lost, Davis' Game Seven heroics make him the clear MVP. Remember the multiplier for Game Seven of the World Series. Whoever wins is the champion. Therefore, the top performer of that game is very likely to be the series MVP, according to ChampAdded. Davis earned 34.9 percent of a championship. He slashed a mere .227/.292/.409, but he showed up when he was most needed.

Rizzo led the Cubs with .262 ChampAdded. He clearly outhit Davis by batting .360/.484/.600. Which do you prefer? Timeliness or consistency?

Series Goat: Who had Baez as the series goat? After thriving in the first two rounds of the postseason, Baez completely disappeared. He hit .167/.167/.267, with 13 strikeouts in 30 plate appearances. One of those strikeouts was a weird two-strike safety squeeze play in Game Seven that almost came back to haunt the Cubs.

Big Play: Lo and behold. The top play of the entire postseason was Davis' home run against Chapman. That one swing alone was worth 40.5 percent of a championship. Erstwhile THT manager Dave Studeman said it was the third-biggest hit of all-time, behind Hal Smith and Tony Womack.

Zobrist delivered a big blow of his own in the 10th inning. His go-ahead double added 32.2 percent of a championship. The actual game-winning run off the bat of Montero was only .053 ChampAdded. Davis' 10th inning single was another .049 ChampAdded.

Playoff MVP: When we think about postseason heroes, we usually picture a dominating performance. For example, David Ortiz hit everything during the 2013 postseason. The following October was the Autumn of Bumgarner in which he nearly singlehandedly won a World Series.

Sometimes, a hero just happens to be in the right place at the right time. That's what happened with Davis. His final two plate appearances included three RBI and .454 ChampAdded. Unless he had mashed a second home run, there was nothing more he could have done toward ensuring a Cleveland victory. Overall, he led the postseason with .349 ChampAdded.

You see it, right? Where was Davis before those last two plate appearances? He was in the goat pen, with -.104 ChampAdded. Prior to the late-innings of Game Seven, he had cost Cleveland about one-tenth of a championship. A pair of big hits completely flipped the story.

Of course, Cleveland didn't actually win the World Series, despite producing the Playoff MVP. As is usually the case, the top 10 postseason heroes are composed primarily of the World Series champions. It was a team effort for Chicago, with Rizzo leading the charge. And how about a round of applause for Schwarber? His .091 ChampAdded, compiled in just one series instead of three, narrowly missed the top 10 list. Schwarber ranked 13th overall.

2016 Postseason Heroes	
Player	ChampAdded
Rajai Davis	0.336
Anthony Rizzo	0.312
Cody Allen	0.240
Ben Zobrist	0.230
Kyle Hendricks	0.210
David Ross	0.136
Michael Montgomery	0.120
Kenley Jansen	0.119
Brandon Guyer	0.113
Jon Lester	0.110

Playoff Goat: Shaw was the anti-Davis. Blowing the tie in the 10th inning of Game Seven dinged him for -.320 ChampAdded. Prior to that outing, he was on pace to be the 21st-best player, with .066 ChampAdded.

Baez's inclusion here is…complicated. He was our NLDS MVP, the popularly acclaimed NLCS MVP (he was credited with just .019 ChampAdded in that series), and his quick tags preempted multiple potential World Series rallies.

In the ninth inning of Game Seven, Baez "struck out swinging" according to the play log. Perhaps you remember the play. This is when Baez was asked to lay down a baffling two-strike safety squeeze. That play alone was -.189 ChampAdded. His aforementioned, ugly .167/.167/.267 line with 13 strikeouts in 30 World Series PAs fueled the rest of the negative rating. Despite earning the title of Vice Goat, Baez had a largely positive postseason from a player development perspective.

The Theo Epstein-led Cubs acquired Chapman at the seemingly high price of prospect Gleyber Torres and others. When they ponied up for the relief ace, I'm sure Cubs management didn't expect him to be the fourth-worst player of the postseason.

Obviously, that's a reductionist view to take. An overworked Chapman earned the vulture win in Game Seven after allowing the game-tying home run to Davis. All told, he matched Shaw's -.320 ChampAdded for the final game of 2016. Do the math and Chapman was at .160 ChampAdded prior to Game Seven. That would have landed him sixth on the MVP list. I guess the trade worked after all.

2016 Postseason Goats	
Player	**ChampAdded**
Bryan Shaw	-0.255
Javier Baez	-0.231
Mike Napoli	-0.196
Aroldis Chapman	-0.160
Francisco Lindor	-0.123
Jose Ramirez	-0.103
Dexter Fowler	-0.089
Anthony Rendon	-0.078
Michael Martínez	-0.077
Corey Seager	-0.072

References & Resources

For more on WPA:

- Dave Studeman, The Hardball Times, "The One About Win Probability," *hardballtimes.com/main/article/the-one-about-win-probability*

Commentary

The Year in Frivolity

by John Paschal

The year in baseball began with a slew of new rules, a lot of new netting and the same old new school/old school debate. First, Major League Baseball announced the advent of a 30-second clock to time coaching visits to the mound, meaning managers and pitching coaches would need to alter their offseason training regimens to include more jogging toward their golf carts. Second, MLB mandated a 20-second reduction in breaks between innings, a policy almost certain to accelerate the pace at which America's youth would ignore the National Pastime. Third, baseball also implemented new rules governing slides into second base, meaning, more or less, that baserunners would no longer imitate NFL linebackers and/or taekwondo masters but would instead glide tenderly into the bag, as if on a commercial for a Sleep Number bed, just prior to inviting the middle infielder to afternoon tea and perhaps a relaxing couples massage.

Ever watchful, MLB also recommended that major league ballparks extend their protective netting, a move designed to render the toothless demographic "more of a Monday-night bingo thing." Despite its paternal stance, baseball could do little to quell the cultural battle between its old-school and new-school fans, a battle that had bat flips as its cause and clickbait as its effect. With regard to an equally bloodless belligerence, U.S. baseball officials sought to thaw the Cold War frost by staging a game between the Tampa Bay Rays and the Cuban national team in Havana. Following Tampa's 4-1 victory, pundits predicted the Rays would win the American League East, provided, of course, the division expel the Blue Jays, Orioles, Red Sox and Yankees while inviting the Cuban national team and perhaps the 1969 Seattle Pilots.

Finally, in the run-up to Opening Day, MLB officials prepared for David Ortiz's final season with a candid proclamation to baseball's next generation of players: "Let Mr. Ortiz be a guiding light to all of you, that if you want a retirement tour complete with personalized surfboards and customized cowboy boots, you had better play for the Red Sox or Yankees."

What follows, fellow baseball fans, is a frivolous look at the irregular season.

April

In New York, the Yankees' season opener against Houston is postponed due to ice on the field and temperatures in the 30s. Later, in efforts to melt the ice in time for the rescheduled opener on April 5, club officials utilize the heat generated by a small collection of 1980s Astros jerseys.

On April 4, managers of four National League teams decide to slot their pitchers into the eighth spot in the lineup. Using similar lineup construction for a game against Texas, Seattle's Scott Servais slots catcher Chris Iannetta, who in 2015 batted .188 for the Angels, into the 10th spot.

On April 6, two days after handing the Padres the worst Opening Day shutout loss in major league history, the Dodgers blank them again, 7-0, making San Diego the first big league team to open a season with three shutouts. Afterward, Padres general manager A.J. Preller agrees to a trade sending three top prospects to the powerful Blue Jays in exchange for a run to be named later.

In the season's opening week, the Astros begin wearing football helmets during postgame interviews following each victory. During one interview, ace Dallas Keuchel is penalized for roughing the platitude, while during another, right fielder Colby Rasmus is flagged for intentional droning.

On April 10, writer Stephen King publishes a column in the *Boston Globe* decrying the protective netting that has gone up in Fenway Park, writing, "When do safety precautions steal away the pure joy of being there?" Sources later reveal that King plans to attend a game not to cheer on the Red Sox but to research his next horror novel, *Mouth Full of Lumber, Gums Without Teeth.*

Prior to Boston's opener at Fenway Park, the Red Sox honor designated hitter David Ortiz by showing a Big Papi video montage set to John Lennon's classic song "Imagine." Questioned about the song choice, officials note that while the ex-Beatle's ode to world peace might have seemed an odd fit, they couldn't find a song in the Lennon catalog titled "I Want My RBI and I Want It Now."

In mid-April, the Rays reveal that their training regimen includes virtual-reality technology. As part of his explanation, third baseman Evan Longoria claims that the high-tech goggles produce scenes so realistic he can "actually *hear* the isolated coughs from among our 8,000 fans."

While throwing batting practice during his rehab from Tommy John surgery, Texas starter Yu Darvish offers a pair of minor leaguers $1,000 each if either can hit a home run. Asked later if he might make the same offer during games, Padres starter James Shields admits that even with his $21 million salary, he "simply can't afford it."

In the 10th inning of a game in Philadelphia, Nationals outfielder Bryce Harper breaks a 1-1 tie by hitting a Jeanmar Gomez off-speed pitch over the wall and directly into the Phillies' bullpen restroom. Questioned later about the feat, Harper claims he would have just hit the ball behind a tree or a bush if catcher Carlos Ruiz had put down one finger instead of two.

Unhappy with the Turner Field playing surface amid their 4-11 start (1-7 at home), the Braves consider contacting the players union to pressure the club to improve the field. Days later, after losing their next two games to move to 1-9 at home, the Braves also consider contacting the union to complain that the stadium noise is "too boo-ish."

In late April, first-place Washington begins selling "Make Baseball Fun Again" merchandise at its store at Nationals Park. Meanwhile, in Atlanta, the last-place Braves begin selling merchandise that reads, "Make Baseball Fun For Once: Go Watch The Nationals."

May

Following a game in which the Cubs put Washington's Bryce Harper on base seven times, with six walks and a hit by pitch, Chicago first baseman Anthony Rizzo tells the press that "we ran out of things to talk about." Asked to clarify, Rizzo explains that he and Harper discussed astronomy, metallurgy, vermiculture and French literature but stopped when they got to politics and religion.

In LA, the Dodgers' Kiké Hernández and Yasiel Puig attempt to end their slumps by retreating to the training room and placing their bats in electric stimulation machines, which are typically used to treat injuries. Upon hearing of their efforts, slumping Phillies first baseman Ryan Howard takes a more direct approach by placing his bat on the floor and frantically attempting CPR.

In mid-May, ESPN reports that major league baseball games this season are longer—by an average of seven minutes—compared to games in 2015. Later, a team of MIT mathematicians determines the increase owes itself solely to the 10 home run trots executed by David Ortiz.

On May 19, reports out of Atlanta are that Braves shortstop Erick Aybar has gone to a hospital to have a chicken bone removed from his throat. Reports out of Toronto, meanwhile, are that DH Edwin Encarnación has gone to a hospital to have a chicken wing removed from his shoulder.

Days after Detroit manager Brad Ausmus punctuated his May 16 on-field tantrum by covering home plate with his hoodie, MLB posts the same hoodie for public auction, with proceeds going to charity. In related news, MLB also puts up for auction the sunglasses that flew off José Bautista's face when Rougned Odor punched him, with proceeds going to José Bautista's face.

On May 20, officials announce the City of Arlington will join the Rangers in constructing a new baseball stadium with a retractable roof. The lateral mobility of the roof, they add, will derive from a design modeled after the movements of José Bautista's jaw.

During the quarterly owners' meeting in New York, MLB's competition committee agrees to drastic rules changes that include eliminating the necessity for a pitcher to actually deliver pitches to register an intentional walk. In addition, the committee also agrees to eliminate the need for a pitcher to actually deliver pitches to register a strikeout of Chris Carter.

On May 20, outfielder Shin-Soo Choo returns to the Rangers lineup after six weeks on the disabled list and immediately strains his hamstring in his first game back, an injury that sends the veteran promptly back to the DL. The following day, in recognition of his feat, the International Society of Mayfly Enthusiasts presents Choo with its Lifetime Achievement Award.

On May 24, Boston outfielder Jackie Bradley Jr. hits a double off Rockies starter Jorge De La Rosa to extend his hitting streak to 28 games, halfway to Joe DiMaggio's record. In recognition, pundits suggest Bradley marry 50 percent of a sex symbol while calling himself Mr. Half-Caf.

Revealed in a *St. Louis Post-Dispatch* interview on May 25 is that Cardinals starter Adam Wainwright considers the proposed rule to shrink the strike zone next season "a horrible, horrible idea." Also considered a "horrible, horrible idea," per an interview in the *Obvious Observation Dispatch-Post*, is asking a pitcher how he feels about a rule that would shrink the strike zone.

During a game in Pittsburgh, D-backs chief baseball officer Tony LaRussa enters the Root Sports booth to confront Pirates broadcasters Greg Brown and Steve Blass about their comments regarding his history of hit-by-pitch controversies. Later, reasoning that they "really shouldn't have to," the broadcasters decline a reciprocal gesture of entering LaRussa's office to say the only reason he is in the Hall of Fame is that Nelson Cruz missed a routine fly ball.

Having opted against his usual batting gloves in efforts break out of a slump, Bryce Harper returns to the Nationals dugout after homering into the upper deck against St. Louis and promptly destroys the gloves with scissors. To further demonstrate his new gloves-free approach, Harper later descends the dugout steps and strangles Jonathan Papelbon with his bare hands.

During a pregame ceremony at Fenway Park honoring the 1986 pennant-winning Red Sox, observers note that former Red Sox third baseman Wade Boggs is wearing the World Series ring he won with the 1996 Yankees. During the ceremony, observers also note that former Red Sox first baseman Bill Buckner is not wearing the World Series ring he won for the 1986 Mets.

In late May, commissioner Rob Manfred uses the iconic *Field of Dreams* baseball diamond in Iowa to announce the multiyear Baseball Hall of Fame Tour will begin in July. The following day, Manfred uses the iconic *Bull Durham* alley, where Crash Davis punched Nuke LaLoosh in the jaw, to announce there's a lot of stuff the Hall of Fame Tour won't show you.

During a contentious series at Citi Field, the Dodgers ask the Mets to allow them to make marks in the outfield for defensive positioning. Upon consideration, the Mets agree to the request on the condition that the Dodgers let them leave a chalk outline of Chase Utley's body near home plate.

In late May, former Met Darryl Strawberry suggests that to become a better team, the current Mets should get into more bar fights. Meanwhile, experts suggest that to maintain their status as a small-market team, the A's should continue to argue over who ordered the salad at Applebee's.

June

After Pirates ace Gerrit Cole reaches first base on a single during a game in Pittsburgh, Angels first baseman Albert Pujols delivers what one reporter later calls "a stern lecture." Asked afterward about the lecture, Pujols replies, "I recited a condensed version of the famous Feynman Lectures on Physics, with emphasis on Maxwell's equations in free space as well as Lorentz transformations of the fields, but then I also told him to stop being an insufferable punk."

In early June, the airline JetBlue releases a commercial that features Red Sox DH David Ortiz attending a children's party, grabbing a baseball bat and taking a hard swing at a pinata to send its candy flying. Afterward, critics register their surprise that Ortiz has thus far issued zero complaints about being denied statistical credit for a ground-rule Dubble Bubble.

Following Houston's seventh straight loss to the rival Rangers—this one on a walk-off—Astros reliever Ken Giles surprises observers by claiming, "We have more talent than [the Rangers] team does." Afterward, the Astros validate his claim when Luke Gregerson blows a bubble with his nose and Luis Valbuena balances a spoon on his chin.

In Philadelphia for a final time before his planned retirement following the 2016 season, Cubs catcher David Ross takes time on June 8 to check the final item off his Philadelphia bucket list by running up the steps, a la Rocky Balboa, in front of the Philadelphia Museum of Art. Days later, with the Cubs in town for a series against the Braves, Ross takes time to check the final item off his Atlanta bucket list by repeatedly missing his exit, a la Pascual Perez, on Loop I-285.

On June 9, MLB hands a four-game suspension to Manny Machado after reviewing the Baltimore third baseman's soft punch to the head of Royals pitcher Yordano Ventura. Upon comparing the suspension to the eight games given to Rougned Odor, social media explodes with suspicion that MLB is biased not only on behalf of East Coast teams but also on behalf of terrible boxers.

In the eighth inning of a game against the Angels, New York's Chris Parmelee pulls a hamstring to become the fourth Yankees first baseman to hit the DL this season. The following day, after calling up a replacement from the minors, the team learns he, too, will be unavailable, owing to the fact that he lost consciousness inside the bubble-wrapped box.

On June 17, a newspaper story reveals that the Nationals keep a French press coffee maker in their dugout. Days later, another story reveals that in honor of manager Jeff Banister's lone appearance as a major league player, the Rangers keep in their dugout a Keurig Single-Cup.

During an on-field ceremony in Cincinnati, the Reds honor franchise icon Pete Rose by inducting him into the Reds Hall of Fame and retiring his number. After the unveiling, officials acknowledge that while they considered retiring Rose's jersey number, 14, they ultimately decided to retire a number more in line with his personal history, 11.5-110.

Following a start in which ace Clayton Kershaw allowed four earned runs in 5.2 innings, the Dodgers reveal that Kershaw has been suffering from a strained back, making him the eighth Dodgers pitcher to sustain an injury this season. Asked if the Dodgers staff is cursed or merely unfortunate, starter Scott Kazmir falls down and fractures his midsection.

In the aftermath of a Rangers-Yankees game that featured a controversial three-hour rain delay, pundits suggest MLB appoint a "weather czar" to rule on similar situations. Upon consideration, the commissioner complies with the suggestion by appointing an official weather czar whose first forecast is that "it will be a long, cold winter for the D-backs."

On June 28, the Rockies-Blue Jays game is delayed two hours due to an intense storm that drops large amounts of hail on the playing surface. Afterward, observers note they "haven't seen *that* much ice hit the field since David Ortiz last stumbled necklace-first into second base."

July

During the Nationals' Fourth of July game against the Brewers, outfielder Bryce Harper honors the U.S. armed forces by wearing cleats bearing the logos of the five military branches. In other games throughout the day, several players honor the U.S. Secret Service by wearing sunglasses.

Owing to extra-inning games and blowouts, a total of seven position players make pitching appearances during the Fourth of July weekend. Afterward, observers note that in efforts to pay further homage to America's independence from Great Britain, none of the players has requested emancipation from win-expectancy calculations, known otherwise as a "wexit."

In the aftermath of July 4, reports indicate MLB prevented Nationals star Bryce Harper from using a patriotic bat featuring a likeness of the Statue of Liberty. Per additional reports, MLB did allow Phillies outfielder Ben Revere to use a bat featuring the Venus de Milo "because, basically, he's got no arm."

After singling in the first inning of a game against the Nationals, Milwaukee's Ryan Braun is called out for having batted out of order. Speaking to the press after the game, Braun expresses embarrassment, saying, "The only thing more foolish than batting out of order would be apologizing to teammates, fans and the entire Brewers organization *before* getting caught."

According to a report in *The New York Times*, several major league ballparks have added designated spaces where disgruntled players can vent anger during a game by hitting a punching bag or otherwise throwing a tantrum. In response, social media users launch a debate as to whether the space should be called the Earl Weaver Suite or the Lou Piniella Room.

In an interview with baseball writer Buster Olney, Braves outfielder Jeff Francoeur claims 90 percent of major leaguers would prefer harsher penalties for players caught using performance-enhancing drugs. Later in the interview, Francoeur adds that the other 10 percent would prefer lighter penalties for players "who don't *knowingly* put PEDs in their bodies."

After hitting a 460-foot home run that bounced off the new Progressive Field scoreboard, Cleveland slugger Mike Napoli is greeted with a message on the same apparatus: "Mike Napoli, Please Don't Break Our New Scoreboard." Upon reading the news, longtime observers are reminded of a similar sign directed at pitcher and notorious playboy Bo Belinsky in stadiums throughout the 1960s: "Bo Belinsky, Please Don't Score In Our New Breakroom."

At the season's midway point, MLBShop.com reveals David Ortiz's No. 34 is its top-selling jersey. During a press conference to announce the results, the Red Sox DH is seen barreling into the room to make sure he is credited with a second-hand jersey sale at a Scituate thrift shop.

According to reports at the All-Star break, MLB and the players union have discussed the possibility of a Home Run Derby for pitchers as early as the 2017 All-Star week. Also discussed, per the same reports, are a Fielding Derby for designated hitters and a Massive Ego Derby for utility infielders.

As part of the ceremonies at the All-Star Game, Commissioner Rob Manfred announces that MLB's batting championships have been renamed in honor of two of history's greatest hitters: the Rod Carew American League batting title and the Tony Gwynn National League batting title. Manfred goes on to announce that after careful consideration, MLB has renamed one of the sport's most important designations the Chris Iannetta Mendoza Line.

Per reports on July 14, the 2016 All-Star Game drew a record-low TV rating of 5.4. In response, panicked Fox executives immediately scrap plans for new shows, *Downton Altuve* and *Better Call Odubel*.

Just prior to the start of the season's second half, Bovada oddsmakers publish their projected odds for major season-end awards, giving the Cubs' Kris Bryant an 11/4 chance of winning NL MVP and the Angels' Mike Trout a 7/2 shot at the AL MVP. In addition, Bovada installs Boston's Dustin Pedroia as a 100/99 favorite to be called "a gamer," and teammate David Ortiz a 1/1 favorite to become the subject of sentimental video montages set to treacly piano scores.

To kick off the second half, the Braves on July 15 host a Zombie Night complete with a zombie-themed bobblehead of catcher A.J. Pierzynski. Taking heed, the Diamondbacks later contact the Braves for advice about how to reanimate the corpse of pitcher Shelby Miller.

While promoting the ESPN documentary *Doc and Darryl*, former Mets star Darryl Strawberry tells reporters that on several occasions he had sex in the clubhouse between innings of games. Pressed for details, Strawberry adds, "Contrary to what sabermetricians have claimed in recent years, protection is important not only in the lineup but out of it, as well."

As the second half gets underway, reports emerge that MLB and the players union have discussed the possibility of returning to a 154-game schedule. Per additional reports, union leaders claim the main obstacle is ownership's insistence that players not only accept the late-1950s average annual salary of roughly $16,000 but also that they work as office-supply salesmen during the offseason, smoke Chesterfields and enjoy the zany antics of Lucille Ball.

On July 18, a day after teammates used Jobu from the movie *Major League* to perform a slump-busting ceremony on his behalf, Cleveland catcher Yan Gomes is carted off the field with an injury to his right shoulder and placed on the disabled list. Inspired, the Astros later endeavor a similar movie-based tactic by trying to make Carlos Gomez vanish in a field of corn.

On July 19, *The New York Times* reports that Roger Clemens, Roy Oswalt, Carl Everett and other retired players will join a team called the Kansas Stars to compete in the National Baseball Congress World Series. The newspaper also reports that to fund their endeavor, the old-timers will use the seventh-inning stretch to perform live reenactments of Cialis commercials.

In Houston, U.S. District Court Judge Lynn Hughes sentences former Cardinals scouting director Chris Correa to 46 months in prison for hacking into the Astros' player personnel database in 2014. After sentencing, the judge tells reporters he considered giving Correa a harsher sentence but later relented upon realizing that six months with the Reds bullpen would represent a violation of the Eighth Amendment's prohibition of cruel and unusual punishment.

In Chicago, starter Chris Sale is sent home and subsequently suspended by the White Sox after he uses a pair of scissors to destroy the throwback jerseys the team was supposed to have worn in a game versus Detroit. Meanwhile, in Tampa, third baseman Evan Longoria attempts to destroy the Rays' "throwforward" jerseys in a similar manner but is forced to abort the attempt when the scissors get stuck on the aluminum-alloy lettering that reads, "Montreal."

After designating 37-year-old pitcher Kyle Lohse (12.54 ERA in two starts) for assignment on July 26, the Rangers recall power-hitting prospect Joey Gallo and arrange a police escort to help him get to Arlington in time for the game. Afterward, Gallo tells the press that the only time the police escort failed to expedite the drive was when it arrived at the funeral procession for Lohse's career.

On July 31—the day before the trade deadline—Brewers catcher Jonathan Lucroy exercises the no-trade clause in his contract by vetoing a trade to Cleveland. According to sources, Lucroy nixed the trade not only because he remained skeptical of Cleveland's playoff chances but also because he had "never played quarterback" and "considered it far too late to learn the playbook."

August

Following his trade from the Padres to the Braves, outfielder Matt Kemp tells an interviewer he is "excited" to play for his new team because Atlanta is "a baseball town." Reminded that the team will move to a new stadium in Cobb County next season, Kemp amends his statement by saying he is "slightly less excited" because "Cumberland, apparently, is a baseball suburb."

In the first week of August, Cleveland's Mike Napoli begins using custom bats engraved with his popular new catchphrase, "Party At Napoli's." Meanwhile, with a league-worst ERA of nearly 6.00, Oakland's Sonny Gray begins taking the mound with an arm tattoo that reads, "Buffet At Gray's."

Following a Red Sox loss to the Mariners, Boston first baseman Hanley Ramirez injures his left wrist when he tumbles down the steps from the dugout to the club-house. Afterward, Statcast reveals Ramirez reached a top speed of 1.2 mph and had a route efficiency of 10.6 percent.

On Aug. 6, in recognition of the number-retirement ceremony for franchise icon Ken Griffey Jr., a flag that bears his No. 24 is hoisted above Seattle's Space Needle. Meanwhile, in recognition of Chone Figgins' performance following his lucrative free agent signing in 2009, a flag bearing his No. 9 is hoisted above the King County Wastewater Treatment Plant on South Jackson Street.

In a hastily arranged news conference on Aug. 5, New York's Mark Teixeira announces he will retire from baseball at the conclusion of the season. In response, the opponents remaining on the Yankees' schedule declare that given the timing of Teixeira's announcement, he will be accorded a "farewell mini-tour" in which he gets a 20-second shopping spree in the team store.

After rallying for a come-from-behind victory against the Blue Jays on Aug. 7, the Royals cite the influence of a praying mantis that entered their dugout and later adopt the insect as their Rally Mantis. Meanwhile, after losing eight of 10 games and scoring just 15 runs in their past eight contests, the Astros pin the blame on what they call the Regression Swarm Of Locusts.

From Boston comes the news, on Aug. 9, that the Red Sox will not honor the Yankees' Alex Rodriguez's retirement when the AL East rivals begin a three-game series at Fenway Park. Also announced is that Tom Brady and the Patriots will not host a Roger Goodell Appreciation Day, and that the corpses of 18th-century Boston protesters are still opposed to the Tea Act of 1773.

Days after sending Yasiel Puig to Triple-A Des Moines, Dodgers President Andrew Friedman says he is "disappointed" that the outfielder posted Snapchat images of himself partying with his new teammates. Reached for further comment, Friedman says he'd rather Puig behave like "the players in the old days, who used handwritten postcards to describe their nights of debauchery."

On Aug. 11, the Astros announce that as part of a 2017 renovation to Minute Maid Park, they will remove Tal's Hill in center field. The Astros also announce that, having studied the *Big League Guide to Ballpark Quirks*, they will replace Tal's Hill with Coogan's Bluff featuring Pesky's Pole.

In a mid-August interview, Commissioner Rob Manfred says he wants to implement a 20-second pitching clock to accelerate the pace of games. Later, Manfred adds that he hopes to implement a two-minute egg-timer whenever Oakland DH Billy Butler tries to stretch a single into a double.

On Aug. 21, reports emerge that Oakland's Billy Butler sustained an injury during a recent altercation with teammate Danny Valencia. According to sources, the altercation began after Butler and Valencia bickered about whose turn it was to unclog the clubhouse toilets.

During a road trip to Cincinnati, Dodgers outfielder Josh Reddick is forced to miss a game against the Reds after slamming a finger in his hotel-room door while receiving room service. In the time that follows, reports indicate that Reddick also sustained a Grade-1 glute strain while using the phone beside the toilet to request another mint on his pillow.

In late August, Reds slugger Adam Duvall says in an interview that if he could change one thing about baseball, he'd do away with the designated hitter. Days later, research reveals that Nostradamus predicted "the young fielder will become the older fielder, on the field of play in a single decade; he will slow his legs through graying hair, then he changes his mind."

As the month comes to a close, reporters disclose that a farmer in Canada has commemorated José Bautista's infamous ALDS bat flip by rendering the image in a corn maze. Meanwhile, in Texas, farmers across the state decline to render Rougned Odor's famous face punch in their own crops, reasoning that the image of Bautista's concussed left cheek will outlast the harvest.

September

In early September, the Boston Public School System begins offering students a pre-recorded wake-up call featuring Boston's David Ortiz. Per officials, students can choose from two options: the Gentle Wake-Up, with Ortiz saying, "Get out of bed and get ready for school," or the Urgent Wake-Up, with a series of *bleeeeeeeeeeps* and the sound of Big Papi smashing a dugout phone.

In the first inning of the Sept. 4 game against the Nationals, Mets infielder Wilmer Flores debuts his latest walk-up song: the theme from 1990s sitcom *Friends*. In the second inning, having slashed .198/.270./.327 since joining the Mets at the trade deadline, outfielder Jay Bruce debuts his own latest walk-up song: the theme from 1970s sitcom *What's Happening!!*

In early September, reports out of Hollywood reveal that Dodgers utilityman Kiké Hernández will make a guest appearance on the CBS soap *The Bold and The*

Beautiful. On Sept. 12, fans settle in to watch Hernández play catch with Quinn, which causes Eric to go into a jealous rage, which causes Steffy to console Eric, which causes Wyatt to suspect Steffy of cheating, which causes Eric to ask Bill to ask Brooke to have a talk with Wyatt, which causes Steffy to wonder if something is going on between Brooke and Wyatt, which causes Hernández to return to major league baseball where he can watch Madison Bumgarner pitch to Yasiel Puig.

On Sept. 14, the Yankees sign DH Billy Butler days after the A's released him following his fight with a teammate. To make Butler feel at home, the Yankees first take turns punching him in the jaw and then engage in group flatulence in efforts to recreate the smell of the A's locker room.

Following an investigation in mid-September, MLB issues a 30-day suspension to Padres GM A.J. Preller for his role in withholding medical information on players involved in midseason trades. In efforts to further teach Preller a lesson, officials withhold information on how he can loosen the straps from which he is suspended, and ways by which he can reach food and water.

When Cincinnati reliever Blake Wood surrenders a two-run homer to Pittsburgh's Jung Ho Kang in the seventh inning of a game at Great American Ball Park, the Reds bullpen establishes a big league record by having yielded its 93rd home run of the year. Asked if the record might damage the bullpen's collective psyche, manager Bryan Price replies, "No, but given the way our relievers continue to whip around to watch the flight of the ball, it might damage their collective spine."

A day after the Cubs clinch the NL Central, team President Theo Epstein dons a disguise—a fake mustache and soul patch—to sit among joyous fans in the Wrigley Field bleachers during Chicago's 10-inning defeat of the Brewers. Later, in a separate ruse, at least one Chicagoan dons a Theo Epstein disguise to sit among joyous fans at a succession of Wrigleyville bars.

Just prior to the Cardinals-Rockies game on Sept. 19, the Rockies are compelled to close the Helton Burger Shack after St. Louis outfielder Matt Holliday's batting practice home run breaks a pane of glass at the popular concession stand. Seizing the entrepreneurial opportunity, Holliday immediately creates the Matt Holliday Weight-Loss Plan, wherein a 240-pound baseball player arrives at the burger joint or taco stand of choice and immediately destroys its food-prep area.

Days after the Mets sign former football player Tim Tebow to a minor league contract, sources reveal Tebow's No. 15 is the best-selling Mets jersey at a prominent online retailer. Taking advantage, the Mets immediately announce the debut of the Failed NFL Quarterbacks Collection, featuring JaMarcus Russell Jockstraps and Ryan Leaf Sliding Pants.

In the sixth inning of the Giants-Dodgers game on Sept. 19, benches clear after San Francisco starter Madison Bumgarner shouts, "Don't look at me!" at Yasiel Puig following the LA outfielder's ground ball back to the mound. Shortly afterward, Bumgarner consents to an agreement that allows Puig to look at him through a third party, e.g., Buster Posey or Hunter Pence, while also consenting to seek outpatient treatment for Puig Derangement Syndrome.

In late September, MLB.com releases a new Statcast metric called "Barrels," which pairs launch angle and exit velocity to determine the best-struck balls and the players who most often deliver them. Later the same week, in efforts to also recognize players such as Jonathan Papelbon, Yordano Ventura and Madison Bumgarner by pairing on-field behavior with prevailing attitude, the site also comes up with a metric called "Knobs."

On Sept. 23, the Mariners suspend Steve Clevenger for the remainder of the season after the six-year veteran tweets disparaging comments about the Black Lives Matter movement. Later, consensus around baseball is that black lives do matter but backup catchers don't.

Upon singling in the sixth inning of Atlanta's Sept. 28 game against the Phillies, first baseman Freddie Freeman extends his hitting streak to 30 games. Questioned later, Freeman says, "Due to the fact that, unlike Jackie Bradley Jr., I lacked the foresight to get myself drafted by a media-favorite team, even *I* wasn't aware of the streak."

On Sept. 29, a sixth-inning thunderstorm in Pittsburgh forces the finale of a four-game Cubs-Pirates series to end in a score of 1-1. Asked afterward about his run-scoring sacrifice fly in the third inning, Pittsburgh phenom Josh Bell replies, "I'm just here to help this team tie."

On Sept. 30, just prior to Boston's season-ending series against the Blue Jays, groundskeepers at Fenway Park mow into the outfield grass the iconic image of David Ortiz pointing his fingers to the sky. Meanwhile, a local gardener creates a series of topiaries that depict Big Papi renting a pair of 18-wheelers to transport his farewell gifts to his suburban estate.

Pitch Framing Was Doomed From the Start

by Jeff Sullivan

Here's a little exercise for you. Which teams would you consider to have forward-thinking, stat-friendly front offices? Go ahead, list them off. I'll even play along.

I don't know where you start. The Dodgers, obviously. And the Cubs, of course. You have to make sure to fold in the Rays and the A's. The Yankees have a massive analytics department. The Mariners took a step forward with Jerry Dipoto. The Phillies have changed under Matt Klentak. The Twins are looking to get more analytical under their new management. Cleveland has to count, and so do the Astros, and the Cardinals, and...

It goes on. *Every* front office has some sort of analytics department. Even the Royals! Especially the Royals. Major league baseball, overall, has gotten smarter. It's no longer enough to just hire some smart guy in a suit. Smart guys in suits are everywhere. Any hiring has to be considered in context.

In a sense, analytics doomed analytics. At first, they seemed powerful. You could find market inefficiencies everywhere. And so early adopters were able to benefit. But then came the later adopters, and then came the last adopters. Numbers are no less powerful than they used to be, but there's less relative power to be wielded when everyone's trying. A given front office now would have a massive advantage over an organization run by a bunch of stubborn throwbacks, but such organizations are so near to extinct they're almost hypothetical. So the comparison doesn't have any meaning.

That's the larger trend. That might be *the* trend, as major league baseball goes. The sabermetric movement has been fully embraced. But I mostly want to talk to you about a similar trend on a much smaller scale. It's not the easiest thing to prove, but it's plenty easy to discuss, and I feel it works as a legitimate theory. As analytics arguably doomed analytics, pitch framing seems likely to doom pitch framing.

Pitch-framing analysis has been moved to the back burner. It's a product of the PITCHf/x system, and it was deeply exciting, but many have moved on from PITCHf/x to Statcast, because it's the shiny new thing, and it's impossibly informative. "Exit velocity" and "launch angle" have turned into commonplace terms overnight. We've already learned so much about hitters. We've already learned so much about pitchers. And, importantly, we're beginning to learn about defenders. Statcast is going to get us places.

But pitch framing didn't go away when the attention did. And, if I can give you some background: Pitch-framing statistics represented a major breakthrough. They were made possible by PITCHf/x around 2008 and 2009, and the greatest public efforts were made by Mike Fast, Max Marchi, Matthew Carruth and Dan Turkenkopf. Maybe you've been reading baseball analysis for a few years. Maybe longer. But, maybe not so long. It was groundbreaking stuff. What the numbers indicated was that pitch framing, or pitch receiving, could be worth dozens of runs in a season, by preserving or stealing strikes. More, the different methods mostly agreed with one another, and they tended to show year-to-year sustainability. There was signal, which meant there was talent.

The closest José Molina ever came to being a superstar was on the internet. On the internet, he was the face of pitch-framing statistics. According to numbers from Baseball Prospectus, the way Molina caught was worth 36 extra runs in 2008. The next year, it was worth another 19, and then that went up to 24 in 2010. Pitch framing was specifically cited as a reason why Molina wound up with the Rays. Molina always had a talent, but, at last, its real value could be quantified.

Not that Molina was the only catcher who stood out. The numbers have also celebrated guys like Russell Martin, David Ross, Jonathan Lucroy and Francisco Cervelli. On the other side, when there are players who are good at something, there have to be players who are less good. The opposite of Jose Molina was Ryan Doumit. Unlike Molina, Doumit could hit. But, as it turns out, Doumit couldn't catch. His framing in 2008 cost his team an unfathomable 63 runs. The next year, in less time, he cost his team 29 runs. Then 24. Doumit was a defensive negative. The impact was worse than one would've imagined.

All right, let's pause. Think about what was happening when the ball started to roll. It was being demonstrated, for the first time, that there were real differences in value among catchers, just based on how they caught. That actually flew in the face of prevailing sabermetric consensus at the time. Evidence mounted as the teams continued to shift toward being more number-savvy. Just in theory, what do you think would happen?

You'd think smarter teams would start to seek out good receivers. You'd think, additionally, that smarter teams would attempt to *develop* good receivers. That's not as easy as just flipping a switch—that requires a lot of video work, to see what catching techniques help and what catching techniques hurt. But, just in general, you'd think pitch framing would be more heavily prioritized. What happens when something gets prioritized by an increasing number of teams?

At first, there were inefficiencies to be taken advantage of. The Rays, for example, got Molina for cheap. Some teams were skeptical of the framing data. Yet, over time, most teams have been turned into believers. Any executive or coach you talk to would agree that catchers have some degree of influence over the strike zone. Now we have well-established numbers for that ability. It's not anything to be ignored. And when every team wants to get better at something, something that was only recently discovered, you look for the laggards to catch up to the leaders.

Every team wants a good-receiving catcher. Every *pitching staff* wants a good-receiving catcher. Every organization wants to develop good-receiving catchers. And it even feels like something a player can just learn. If a hitter is going to adjust to hit for more power, odds are, that same hitter is also going to strike out more often. There should be no such drawback with attempting to improve how a catcher catches. It's just learning appropriate technique. Bad-receiving catchers might be helped. Then you'd have a catcher who just made himself better. No downside.

Stories have gotten out to the public. There were articles written about the Astros trying to improve the way Jason Castro caught. There were similar articles written about the Angels and Chris Iannetta and Hank Conger, and there were articles written about the Padres and Nick Hundley. There have been more such stories, and there have been countless additional stories that just weren't or haven't yet been written. Teams continue to work on this. The A's have had a system implemented in earnest for about the last 18 months. No team wants to settle for a Doumit-type catcher anymore.

We might as well get to some actual evidence. To this point, it's all been theory. The theory is that, over time, gaps between teams and catchers should narrow. Bad-receiving catchers should start to disappear, raising the baseline. The best catchers, after all, can't improve much, but the worst ones sure can.

The most advanced numbers out there come from Baseball Prospectus, so that's what I've used here. Using its data, I calculated for each catcher framing runs above or below average per 7,000 opportunities, going back to 2008—7,000 being roughly the number of opportunities a starting catcher will have in any given season. In that way, it's like UZR/150. I narrowed to only catcher-seasons with at least 2,000 framing opportunities, and in the plot below, you can see each season's standard deviations within the catcher pool.

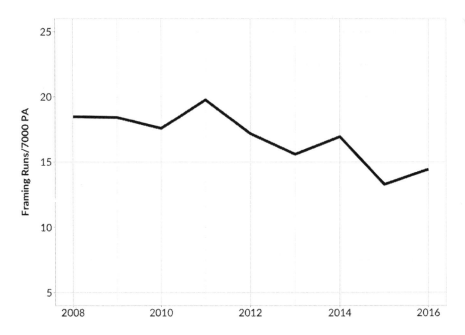

Team Framing Runs/7000 PA Standard Deviation

There remains, of course, an existing gap between the best and the worst catchers. This is all still very new, as a statistical measurement. But it's worth noting that the two smallest standard deviations have come in the last two seasons. A smaller standard deviation means a lesser spread. It supports the idea that the gap is gradually getting smaller.

As an alternative plot, here's the year-to-year average of the top 10 framing catchers, in terms of runs above average per 7,000 chances.

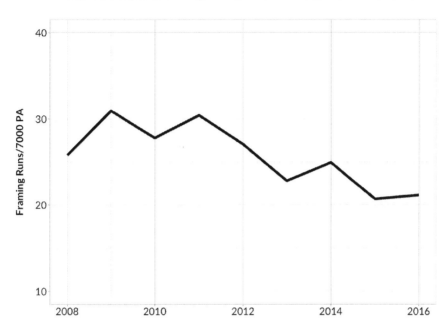

Top 10 Player Framing Runs/7000 PA Standard Deviation

Similarly, you see a drop, with the two lowest averages coming in the last two years. In 2011, the top 10 catchers were, on average, 30 runs better than the mean. In each of the last two years, the average has been a hair above 20. It doesn't make too much sense that the best-receiving catchers would be getting worse. The other explanation would have to be that the average catcher is just improving. Just for fun, here's the top and bottom 10 for the 2016 season:

Top 10 & Bottom 10 Catchers by Runs/7000, 2016			
Catcher	Runs/7000	Catcher	Runs/7000
Miguel Montero	28.4	Alex Avila	-14.8
Yasmani Grandal	27.7	Carlos Ruiz	-14.8
Buster Posey	25.3	Ryan Hanigan	-15.3
Jeff Mathis	23.4	Jarrod Saltalamacchia	-15.4
Tony Wolters	18.1	Nick Hundley	-15.9
Jason Castro	18.0	Chris Iannetta	-18.3
Kevin Plawecki	17.9	Robinson Chirinos	-18.6
Roberto Perez	17.7	Bryan Holaday	-19.3
Tyler Flowers	17.5	Juan Centeno	-22.4
Caleb Joseph	17.4	Dioner Navarro	-24.3
Rene Rivera	17.4	Ramon Cabrera	-39.5

To mix it up, here's something on the team scale, now using information from FanGraphs. It's pretty easy to calculate, for a team's season, the difference between the number of strikes and the expected number of strikes. Obviously, there would be a relationship between this measure and pitch-framing ability. The more extra strikes a team gets, the better the receivers, and vice versa. I ran the numbers for every team's season since 2008, and here are the year-to-year standard deviations.

Strikes - Expected Strikes Difference Standard Deviation

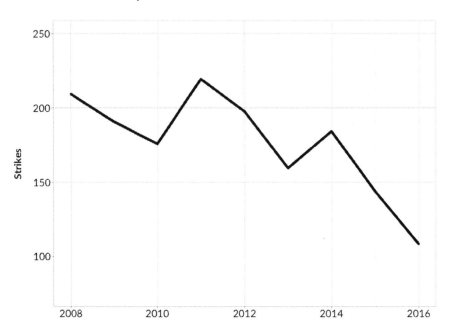

This is fairly striking. The standard deviation in 2011 was 219 strikes. By 2016, that number dropped to 122, or 56 percent of what it had been. The two lowest standard deviations have come in the last two years. Going back to 2011, the difference between the best team and the worst team was 964 strikes. Last year, the difference was 437 strikes.

That's still a difference. That's still a pretty substantial and significant difference. But the differences have gotten smaller, which is what we would expect. Should the trend continue, the differences will get smaller still. Perhaps not smoothly, perhaps not year after year after year, but in the big picture the gap should get smaller. Evidence suggests more teams are on board with pitch-framing ability, and as that happens, the best framers have less of a relative edge.

Over the course of the nine seasons we have this data for, things have changed quite a bit. We can see just how much they've changed in this table of year-to-year differences for each team:

Adjusted Expected Strike Difference, 2008-2016										
Team	2008	2009	2010	2011	2012	2013	2014	2015	2016	Total
Brewers	72	89	377	482	452	445	406	243	151	2,716
Braves	376	501	333	440	343	57	-189	-250	-102	1,510
Cardinals	330	276	265	176	175	116	-131	15	25	1,245
Diamondbacks	102	267	80	224	199	79	306	-24	-35	1,197
Yankees	306	68	-221	210	243	278	220	22	69	1,194
Reds	434	247	278	138	208	-4	-34	-108	-64	1,096
Giants	-109	84	17	252	130	-38	159	101	145	741
Astros	-13	-126	168	87	32	-1	123	133	178	580
Nationals	-25	-16	200	298	138	25	-12	-79	-137	391
Phillies	162	200	75	-34	117	28	-42	-107	-68	330
Orioles	22	192	81	28	-61	-77	99	-20	46	310
Angels	42	-5	51	149	29	-11	80	-53	4	286
Blue Jays	182	-68	28	-19	-29	85	-181	-12	155	140
Padres	-68	-143	-4	-232	40	146	310	118	-36	132
Cubs	-93	-82	97	-7	-19	-129	-115	180	203	35
Red Sox	-16	-122	-219	26	75	81	90	-40	41	-84
Dodgers	244	68	-55	-202	-213	-43	-103	62	111	-130
Rays	-232	-6	-134	-205	179	163	89	53	-47	-139
White Sox	-107	-31	-64	-51	-122	-28	-45	267	-199	-380
Mets	-89	-125	-159	-147	111	-140	-2	36	79	-437
Royals	99	57	-46	-170	-142	-99	-101	-97	-67	-565
Pirates	-463	-353	2	-202	-319	187	135	303	101	-607
Athletics	22	-132	-99	-168	-117	41	-66	-169	-131	-819
Rangers	-269	45	-154	-138	-135	-131	-150	75	6	-851
Twins	5	56	10	85	-220	-346	-361	-94	-124	-990
Rockies	-131	-13	-60	-146	-188	-148	-220	-219	64	-1,060
Mariners	-234	-318	-315	-157	-312	-132	233	86	-97	-1,248
Tigers	-180	-346	-123	42	-105	29	-160	-276	-137	-1,256
Cleveland	-54	-205	-284	-482	-298	-135	-62	-86	-56	-1,662
Marlins	-316	-61	-124	-277	-189	-298	-276	-60	-77	-1,677

Quality pitch framing isn't going to be rendered irrelevant, certainly not as long as there are humans responsible for calling balls and strikes. But remember the example of a hypothetical old-school, backward front office. That front office might get savaged in the market today, but that front office also doesn't really exist. Likewise, a truly bad pitch framer would score horribly now. The average only gets better and better. But there just won't be many truly bad pitch framers. When everyone is a good receiver, no one is a good receiver.

As long as there are umpires, and not robots, there will be a gap. We will never see a day when every single catcher in baseball is identically good at catching pitches. It is a skill, and only so much can be taught. Yes, anyone can improve his forearm strength. Yes, anyone can improve his wrist strength, and the way that he positions himself behind the plate. These are fundamentals. But there's an instinct component. There's anticipating where pitches are going to go. Taller catchers will be better up in the zone; smaller catchers will be better down in the zone. It's not realistic to believe the average draft pick can be coached into becoming another José Molina. Some of that ability was innate.

But some of it wasn't. Some of that ability *can* be coached. Maybe even much of that ability. And now that that ability can be recognized, it could end up selected for, in drafts and internationally. Teams are running out of excuses for having lousy receivers, and eventually, it stands to reason any advantages are going to be slight. Maybe the gap between the best and worst catchers gets trimmed to 20 runs. Maybe it gets trimmed to 10. It's nothing that will happen overnight, but it looks like the process is already underway.

Pitch-framing numbers answered questions we didn't know we had. A new statistical category emerged out of nowhere, and before long, the research proved its own worth. That was the birth of the revolution. Every team now wants good-receiving catchers. Every team, additionally, wants to develop more good-receiving catchers. The market is going to end up flooded with good-receiving catchers. By then we'll no longer recognize them as good-receiving catchers. Pitch-framing is sufficiently important that baseball teams will prioritize it right into insignificance.

References & Resources

- FanGraphs & Baseball Prospectus
- Ben Lindbergh, Grantland, "Sabermetrics Gets Soft," *grantland.com/the-triangle/2014-saber-seminar-mlb-sabermetrics-gets-soft*
- Alden Gonzalez, MLB.com, "Iannetta focused on improving pitch framing," *m.mlb.com/news/article/113148786/los-angeles-angels-catcher-chris-iannetta-focused-on-improving-pitch-framing*
- Eno Sarris, FanGraphs, "Jason Casto on Pitch Framing," *fangraphs.com/blogs/jason-castro-on-catcher-framing*
- Corey Brock, MLB.com, "Hundley, Padres catchers working on framing," *m.mlb.com/news/article/69454498/nick-hundley-padres-catchers-working-on-framing-pitches*

Baseball Cards and the Value of Value

by Patrick Dubuque

When I was nine, my parents and I visited a co-worker of my father's for dinner. I don't remember it, don't remember the meal, or the house. My memory's not too good. I think his name was Ray. Ray collected baseball cards. I don't remember the cards, either; neither he nor I wanted me to touch them, I'm sure. I can only mark the date because Ray, at the end of the night, gave me a beat-up copy of the December 1987 *Beckett Baseball Card Monthly*, with Kirby Puckett staring wearily past the camera. I only remember that because I still have it. It's even more beat up now; I have to be careful opening it for fear of tearing the cover off the staples.

The cover of the Dec. 1987 issue of *Beckett Baseball Card Monthly*

I took the magazine and launched into the box of baseball cards that had accumulated in my room, payment in exchange for waiting as my mom shopped at drug stores. I didn't know who any of the players were, unless they were the hometown Mariners, and rarely then. Few of the games made it onto television in the '80s, and it wasn't a franchise that made it onto SportsCenter. So, slowly, I took each card and looked it up in the magazine, hoping to find the name that indicated this card was "worth something."

Most of them weren't. The cards were generally worthless, a string of Iorgs and Garbers and Boddickers. Except for one: an ugly brown-and-green bordered card, its blurry figure running away from the camera, face hidden, hunched awkwardly. It looked like the most worthless thing in the world, objectively. At the bottom, three lines:

> TONY GWYNN
> OUTFIELD
> PADRES

The card was worth $15. Or, adjusted to kid rates, $15,000.

My mother, an instinctive scrapbooker, bought a plastic page to put it and the other valuable cards together to keep them safe. I wanted to put the Gwynn in the top-left slot, keep them in order of value, but I was afraid it might fall out. So I put it in the center, along with the other cards worth more than a dollar: the Danny Tartabull rookie, a Ryne Sandberg Sportflics card. I forget the others.

I took them to church that Sunday to show my friends after the service. I don't remember if they were impressed; I hope so. Then I put them down, and we pretended we were knights and athletes in the sunlit basement of the reception hall with its Boy Scout toys and equipment. I went home. Later that afternoon, I realized the page, all the cards, were gone.

"You must have left them at church," my mother said, and we went back there, had someone unlock the doors, patrolled all the places they might have been left and then the places they might have been moved. They were, of course, gone. Except my memory's not very good, and I didn't remember taking them home, but I also didn't remember not taking them home. So when we got back I tore the house up, looking for those cards. I did it again the next day, and the next week. Even months later I'd go into the laundry room, with its high shelves filled with craft supplies and empty shoeboxes, looking in places they couldn't be. I couldn't believe those cards could be gone.

———————————————

It was a blow, but it didn't keep my myopic nine-year-old self from collecting baseball cards. There was something in that price guide that fascinated me, even more than the televised games or the plastic Wiffle ball bat in my yard. I was a math kid; I loved numbers, loved the puzzles they could offer. In some ways the price guide was like a dictionary, translating unrecognizable names into comfortable integers. But despite knowing their prices, I never considered selling them. What fascinated me was the concept of value.

Long before the modern measurement of man—the wins above replacement—long even before Bill James' ragged and thought-provoking Win Shares, Dr. James Beckett provided the first true measure of baseball players. Living in a remote corner of the American League, baseball cards were often the sole means for seeing their faces. Their histories were rarely more than their statistics. And the invisible hand, as recorded by those lines of numbers next to lines of names, dictated which players were worth plastic sleeves and pages.

The question: how closely does this monetary value align with more modern statistical evaluations, like Wins Above Replacement?

In this study, I selected an assortment of rookie cards between the eras of 1954 and 1980 and tracked them from the first *Beckett* magazine in November of 1984 to today. This selection was based on my own capricious nature, as well as several factors: Hall of Famers, players famous for a single moment or season, and players whose legacy may have shifted for some reason over time. The goal: to measure exactly how well the forces of capitalism align with our modern sabermetric assessment of ballplayers, and to see which names are actually the biggest bargains.

The reason for 1954 as a starting point: 1952, the first mainstream issue of the Topps Chewing Gum Co., suffered from low print runs, the iconic Mickey Mantle, and heavy inflation thanks to romantic collectors. The 1953 set is seen as the 1952 for collectors who can't afford 1952 cards and sees a lesser but noticeable inflation, as well. From 1954 forward, set values follow a fairly predictable trendline downward, meaning we can isolate a player's value more easily from the rarity of the set in which he can be found.

And 1980 is an equally logical stopping point. In 1981, Topps lost its monopoly over trading cards, allowing rivals Donruss and Fleer to enter the market. This created potential for confusion over rookie cards, when one company would include a player in a set one year but not another. It also marked the dawn of the "Traded" or "Update" set, a small (generally 60-100 card) subset sold directly at card shops to collectors instead of at grocery stores. These rarer supplementary sets often offered first cards of exciting players, but collectors were unsure of whether these were true "rookie" cards. Regardless, their existence muddies up the value of players and is better avoided.

Two variables remain to be tackled. The first: Until 1973, Topps didn't issue its sets all at once, but instead rolled them out in multiple series. However, the company often front-loaded its recognizable stars early in the set to make them available early, while leaving the lesser-known, younger players for the later versions when kids might already be tuning out from a lost season or the promise of football. For that reason, high-numbered cards are significantly more valuable than their low-numbered counterparts. This can be solved by normalizing the card values within a set by dividing them by the value of common cards—the forgettable players that round out every roster and pack.

The second is that in the early days of baseball cards, the priorities of collectors—at that point, namely, children—were different than those of today. The current model is one in which, excepting other factors like scarcity, a player's rookie card is his most valuable issue, with future years falling along a more-or-less logarithmic curve. But in the old days, kids didn't care so much about rookie cards; they wanted the star players that year, and didn't think about investing so much as flipping. So the rookies, especially the September call-ups, were often crammed two to four to a card, little smiling heads squared off like Brady Bunch characters. Separating out these values is tricky, but we can approximate it by looking at a player's second-, third-, and fourth-year cards, and extrapolating the rookie value along the same logarithmic curve as other stars with solo rookies. For players who are truly inextricable, like the 1978 Topps Alan Trammell/Paul Molitor rookie, the only choice is excluding them.

The most valuable rookie cards of the post-1953 era are Roberto Clemente ($2,200), Hank Aaron ($1,800), and Ernie Banks ($1,500), all from the 1954 set. The other four-digit members are Sandy Koufax ($1,200) and Pete Rose ($1,000). No surprises here, as these are some of the greatest players in the game's history. But let's strip away the aforementioned variables and adjust each card against the base value of the commons surrounding it, with the following formula:

$$Value = fWAR / (card\ price\ /\ common\ price)$$

A card with a value of one, then, would be one in which their career WAR is equal to its relative price. If a card is worth $100, but it's so rare and old that the Don Blasingame next to it is worth $20, we could say this card has the same value as a five-dollar card surrounded by one-dollar commons. It's not a perfect system, as we'll see, but it produces some interesting results. First, here is a ranking of the most overpriced Hall of Famers:

Most Overpriced Hall of Famer Rookie Cards					
Year	Player	fWAR	Card Price	Common	Value
1968	Nolan Ryan	107.2	$500	$2.00	0.43
1955	Sandy Koufax	54.5	$1,200	$12.00	0.55
1969	Reggie Jackson	72.7	$300	$2.50	0.61
1954	Ernie Banks	63.3	$1,500	$15.00	0.63
1978	Eddie Murray	72.0	$80	$1.00	0.90
1973	Rich Gossage	31.3	$30	$1.00	1.04

The most overpriced baseball card, adjusted to era, is one of the most iconic: the 1968 Nolan Ryan. Amazingly, this holds true after Ryan's cards dropped more than 500 percent in price since its peak in the late stages of his career in 1994 ($2,672, in 2016 dollars). Koufax's inclusion is unsurprising, given his lack of twilight, as is perhaps Mr. Cub, whose extended decline phase is overshadowed by his role as face of the franchise. (The 1954 and 1955 common prices, compared to issues before and after, feel a little undervalued, hurting their cause.) Gossage is narrowly more overrated than fellow closer Bruce Sutter, but strong feelings about this position are probably more closely tied to the calculation of WAR than to Gossage's $30 rookie card.

This leaves two rather surprising, and almost opposite, famous sluggers, in Reggie Jackson and Eddie Murray. Jackson's reputation was based almost as much on his style and his timing as his pure offensive output, while Murray accumulated his greatness fairly quietly. You would think Reggie-mania, with the New York presence and the October heroics and the chocolate bars, would have faded and made Jackson, if anything, underrated. Meanwhile, Murray's rookie card just seems to be priced too high. Contemporaries with similar values (Rickey Henderson, George Brett) had better careers, while those with similar careers (Gary Carter at $20, Robin Yount at $50) come far more cheaply.

On the other end, the most underpriced Hall of Famers:

Most Underpriced Hall of Famer Rookie Cards					
Year	Player	fWAR	Card Price	Common	Value
1964	Phil Niekro	78.5	$80	$15.00	14.72
1957	Jim Bunning	66.9	$150	$20.00	8.92
1963	Willie Stargell	62.9	$120	$15.00	7.86
1971	Bert Blyleven	103.3	$20	$1.50	7.75
1962	Gaylord Perry	100.5	$80	$5.00	6.28
1965	Tony Perez	58.9	$80	$8.00	5.89
1966	Don Sutton	85.9	$60	$3.00	4.30

Phil Niekro is easily the most underappreciated member of the Hall by these standards. His $80 price tag isn't unreasonable, but it fails to take into account how rare the card actually is. The only explanation is that Niekro just never looked the part: the snow-white hair pouring out from under the '70s Braves cap, the achingly slow delivery, the slower knuckleball. Perhaps this explains Stargell's presence as well; the slow, hulking home run hitters of yesteryear possess numbers that pale in comparison to the modern standard, but we're talking about a first-ballot Hall of Famer.

Blyleven and Perry get here in part because people simply don't realize that after Ryan, they're the two most valuable pitchers of the post-deadball, pre-steroid era. Sutton and Bunning were also seen as compilers. But the presence of anti-sabermetric pick Tony Perez is surprising. There is one thread that ties them together: All these players were late-ballot inductees, and it seems that as a general rule, players who sit on the waiting list for a decade may get just as nice a plaque, but their reputations seem to suffer to a degree with collectors.

As a curiosity, I also selected a smattering of non-Hall players, either with interesting careers, legitimate Hall cases ignored, or other sources of fame. These were the players who were overrated:

Selection of Most Overpriced Non-Hall of Famer Rookie Cards					
Year	Player	fWAR	Card Price	Common	Value
1965	Masanori Murakami	1.2	$40	$2.50	0.08
1970	Thurman Munson	40.9	$100	$1.00	0.41
1958	Roger Maris	36.9	$500	$12.00	0.89
1957	Bobby Richardson	6.3	$125	$20.00	1.01
1964	Lou Piniella	12.3	$30	$3.00	1.23
1971	Steve Garvey	37.8	$30	$1.50	1.89

Murakami's value to the sport obviously exceeds his on-field production, being the first Japanese player to play in the majors, and the appreciation for his accomplishment altered dramatically. In 1990 his rookie card was worth two dollars; by 1997, after the arrival of Nomomania, it had risen to its current $40. Maris' legacy rests on a single season, and nostalgic investors are willing to pay more for it than they would the entire careers of Brooks or Frank Robinson. Being a Yankee, when it comes to baseball cards, also never hurts.

This theme continues with the surprising ranking of Thurman Munson, an excellent catcher whose tragic death could be thought of either as adding to his legacy or cutting it short. Munson's name is one rarely brought up these days outside New York; an all-around ballplayer, he holds no records to be threatened, and his achievements predate the modern video age. And yet. Meanwhile, among also-Yankees, Lou Piniella's presence, as half-manager, is easy to understand. (Joe Torre, it should be noted, falls right around the median of the scale.) Richardson's greatness is even more easily isolated than Maris', so the only surprise is that he's only fourth.

Garvey's inclusion will satisfy statheads, although his price is only a third of what it once was. In his defense, the 1971 set, a beautiful black-bordered triumph of '70s aesthetics and engineering, is incredibly difficult to find in near mint condition. The corners in particular scuffed easily, scaring Topps away from the color black for thirty years. So Garvey probably is a little overpriced for at least one reason beyond his control.

Finally, a table of the most underpriced players of the Topps era.

Selection of Most Underpriced Non-Hall of Famer Rookie Cards					
Year	Player	fWAR	Card Price	Common	Value
1956	Larry Jackson	53.9	$12	$12.00	53.90
1970	Jerry Reuss	52.1	$1	$1.00	52.10
1974	Steve Rogers	50.2	$1	$1.00	50.20
1955	Camilo Pascual	52.0	$15	$12.00	41.60
1961	Willie Davis	53.7	$15	$8.00	28.64
1973	Rick Reuschel	68.5	$3	$1.25	28.54
1964	Jimmy Wynn	52.8	$6	$3.00	26.40
1971	Bobby Grich	69.2	$4	$1.50	25.95

It won't take long to find a pattern here. The underrated list is a veritable Who's Who of Hall snubs and elite-level members of the Hall of Very Good. Larry Jackson, who was essentially the ace of the Cardinals for the better part of a decade, has never been more than a common in any price guide from 1984 to 2016. His career has been completely forgotten outside a few passages in Jim Brosnan's The Long Season. Collectors show obvious disdain for the career No. 2 starter and the above-average hitting center fielder.

(Perhaps the most underrated rookie of all time, ironically, is also the most over-rated: Jerry Koosman, who takes second billing on his own card to Nolan Ryan. The poor 62-win pitcher can't even stock up on his own rookie cards without paying a fortune.)

It's clear the sabermetric revolution has not caused older collectors to revisit their judgments on men like Bobby Grich and Reggie Smith (who just missed the cut). In that sense, collecting is a little like baseball itself: People only care about winners. Make the Hall, and your rookie card will be worth something, eventually; fall short, and well, you better have set a single-season record or donned a bunch of pinstripes. Otherwise, there's just another man to take your position and number.

The thing about collecting baseball cards, however, is that unlike actual baseball, there's no way to win. People can collect and celebrate however they want. But if an enterprising collector were interested in maximizing his or her talent for the dollar, the 50-win player is by far the way to go. Besides, there are plenty of pictures of Babe Ruth and Hank Aaron all over the place. It's the Camilo Pascuals of the baseball world who deserve cards to commemorate them. After all, as fans, our memory isn't too good.

I never got another Tony Gwynn rookie card. Sometimes I'd see it under the glass shelves at baseball card shops, back when there were still baseball card shops. But even if I'd been able to save up the cash to buy one, I never considered buying back something I already owned and putting a finite price on my own stupidity. As I grew older, Gwynn's legacy grew as well, and the card went up in value: $30, then $70. At some point the baseball card bubble burst, and my earning power outpaced its value. But at that same point, I also had to start paying rent. I wasn't Ray. couldn't afford to be an adult and still be that much of a kid.

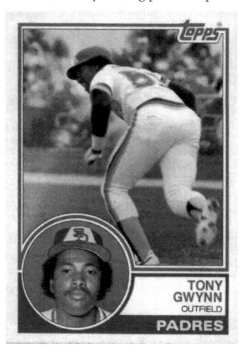

The other day I gave in and checked on eBay. It was $2.70, shipping included. The nice thing about card collecting these days is that if you don't care about condition, cards are pretty cheap. So I decided to be a kid for a day and bought it. When it arrived, it was just like I didn't remember. The green and the brown popped off the white cardboard. It was gorgeous.

It was too gorgeous. It was also coun-terfeit. The images were reproduced exactly, no mark of a reprint and no distinctive fuzz of a printer. But the card stock was white, not the brown card-board of 1983. It almost does the job. It looks like my childhood, but isn't, quite. Perhaps the counterfeit card is a better encapsulation of recapturing youth than a real card would be - a perfect memory of an imperfect thing.

References & Resources

- Dr. James Beckett, *Beckett Baseball Card Monthly*, Dec. 1987
- Dr. James Beckett, *Beckett Baseball Card Monthly*, Dec. 1990
- Dr. James Beckett, *Beckett Baseball Card Monthly*, Feb. 1994
- Dr. James Beckett, *Beckett Baseball Card Monthly*, Dec. 1997
- Dr. James Beckett, *Beckett Baseball Card Monthly*, Dec. 2001
- Dr. James Beckett, *Beckett Baseball Card Monthly*, Dec. 2006
- Dr. James Beckett, *Beckett Baseball Card Monthly*, Dec. 2011
- Dr. James Beckett, *Beckett Baseball Card Monthly*, July 2016

The Complicated Relationship between Sports Writing and Fandom

by August Fagerstrom

All sportswriters have their moment. That moment when their inner kid wants to come out. That moment when, even if just for a split second, they involuntarily begin to lose sight of their professionalism and revert back to their days as a die-hard fan, before the journalism classes and the deadlines and the re-written game stories silenced that irrationally over-exuberant part of their personality that gave every sports fan his or her identity growing up.

It never actually gets there. The inner kid never makes it all the way out. The professionalism always emerges the victor. Barring extenuating circumstances, most reporters who have advanced far enough in their careers to live out the sort of experiences that might tug at that retired part of their personality are far enough removed from fandom to successfully stifle the urge. But they'd be lying if they said, from time to time, it never came close.

It's the childhood heroes that do it. For Sportsnet's Shi Davidi, it was former Toronto Blue Jays second baseman and Hall of Famer Roberto Alomar passing him in the press box and casually telling him he made some good points on his television segment earlier that day.

For MLB.com's Jordan Bastian, it was being in the champagne-soaked clubhouse of his hometown Chicago Cubs after they won the 2015 National League Wild Card game while striking up a conversation with noted Cubs fan Eddie Vedder, the lead singer and guitarist of Bastian's favorite band, Pearl Jam.

For the *Los Angeles Times'* Pedro Moura, it was arriving to the press box at Dodger Stadium on crutches to find Vin Scully, the voice of Moura's earliest baseball memories, sitting in his seat, and then Scully getting up, pulling the chair back, and guiding the hobbled Moura in.

For Cleveland.com's Zack Meisel, it was spending an inning apiece in a suite at Progressive Field with Kenny Lofton and Jim Thome while conducting interviews for a story on the 20-year reunion of the 1995 American League champion Cleveland team, whom Meisel grew up watching.

For me, it was standing on the field during batting practice at Progressive Field—the stadium once known as Jacobs Field, the stadium that made me fall in love with baseball—talking about Francisco Lindor's defense with Omar Vizquel, my favorite player growing up as a Cleveland fan, then serving as first base coach and fielding instructor for the Detroit Tigers.

Without those men and those teams, it's possible none of us sportswriters wind up choosing the career path we all chose. And then we get to meet those men and cover those teams while doing the job those very men and teams inspired and…we don't get to enjoy it. The experiences are cool, yeah, and they make for fun stories, but we don't get to enjoy it in the moment the way 13-year-old us would *want* us to enjoy it. We enjoy it through a muted spectrum of professionalism, an involuntary hardening of the childlike senses of wonder and awe that captured our minds and spirits at a young age, eroded naturally—and out of necessity—with enough time spent on the job.

And that's kind of sad. And it's one of the most interesting side effects of this job, something one might not consider when choosing their journalism major in their freshman year of college as a rabid sports fan with an interest in telling stories, someone who wants to spend the rest of his life in or around a game he loves, who might not realize the birth of his professional self might also incur the death of his fan self.

"Three years ago, the Indians opened in Toronto, and I was doing a story on Robbie and Sandy Alomar," Meisel said, "and to talk to Roberto Alomar, he sent a handler to pick me up from my press box seat and bring me to his private suite, and we sat there for a few innings and chatted. Tell that to 12-year-old Zack and he's going to collapse. But, I don't know, I guess you just have such a different perspective when you've done this for a little bit that it becomes a completely different feeling. And to a part of me, honestly, that kind of sucks. I wish there was a part of me that thinks about the experiences I've had—that we've all had—and just wants to drool over how cool it all is. But it's hard to do that because we're all used to it and you have to be in the moment and be professional."

It's something I've spent a lot of time thinking about, the relationship between fandom and writing, since I began covering my hometown Cleveland team in 2013, eventually moving across the street from Progressive Field, which has served as an extension of my home office now for several years. And it's something that's pertinent to me now more than ever, as that same hometown team is in their first World Series run since the 1997 team that was responsible for my first memories of baseball, the genesis of my interest-turned-obsession-turned-career.

Because this World Series run has only confirmed what I've already known since I was just a couple weeks into my first gig covering the team several years back, something I've almost had to come to terms with in recent years, as it's a shift that was completely out of my control when it occurred, and a shift that my younger self never could have imagined was possible: I am no longer a Cleveland baseball fan. I haven't been for some time, and I can't ever envision myself being a true, rooting "fan" of a baseball team ever again.

We all know the feeling: that uninhibited, visceral, emotional reaction to a big moment in a game played by our childhood, hometown team. It's a lot like love; we don't know where it comes from, and we may never quite understand it. It can't be forced, and it can't be stopped. I haven't felt that feeling in years with regards to Cleveland, nor has most any sports reporter you'll talk to about their hometown team, and it's a phenomena that's difficult to explain and almost impossible for others who knew the younger, fanatical version of ourselves to understand.

"The idea of ever cheering for, not just the Dodgers, but any sports team, is so boring to me at this point," Moura said. "My friends and people who have known me for a long time ask me this all the time, because if you knew me in high school and you know me now, you'd wonder, 'What the heck happened?' You'd be confused about how this kid who was so obsessed suddenly has no rooting interest whatsoever. What I always try to say, the simplest way to put it is, you root for your own self-interest in almost all things, as long as it doesn't harm someone else. And in this job, you're always rooting for the best story. In some cases, that means for the team to win, it some cases it means for the team to lose. It really depends on what happens on a nightly basis. But it can never be about the team."

It's a simple shift in priorities. It comes with the territory. It comes with getting to know the players themselves, them becoming more than just faces on a television screen or members of our fantasy teams or characters in a video game the way they were when we were kids. It comes with these people becoming just that: *people*. Humans. Humans at their job, and the irrationality that would be having one's *own* emotions invested in the successes or failures of the people with whom one covers on a daily basis.

Davidi, aside from covering his hometown Blue Jays, teaches post-graduate journalism classes at Centennial College in Toronto, and being able to set aside fandom in favor of objectivity is something not all of his students have been able to go through with.

"Some people get it right away, some people know it beforehand, and for some people it's a process," Davidi said. "We've had students who have been like, 'I can't be this dispassionate about things. I want to work on the PR side or the team side or whatever.' And some have."

Davidi tells a story to his students about covering the gold medal hockey game between Canada and the U.S. in the 2010 Winter Olympics, when Sidney Crosby scored the now-infamous game-winning goal in overtime for Team Canada, the nation's team for the nation's sport, the team that transcends any Canadian NHL organization. Davidi recounts the goal going into the net, the buzzer sounding, a country erupting, while he and his colleagues with the Canadian Press calmly looked up at the scoreboard to note the time of game for their stories.

"One of the students was like, 'You didn't stand up and cheer?'" Davidi said. "Of course not! You're not there to cheer. You can enjoy what you just saw, and I just saw one of the coolest moments ever in Canadian hockey, and I appreciate that, but I'm not there to be like, 'Yeah! That happened!' I'm there to relay the information.

"I ended up writing a story that day about how Sidney Crosby's goal ended up securing himself a place in Canadian hockey lore, kind of like the goals Paul Henderson and Mario Lemieux scored on the international stage, and that's where some of your inner fan comes out, because you can remember what those goals felt like, and what this goal is going to mean for generations. You can tell the story around that, and that's something people are going to connect with. But you can't be a fan in that moment, because you wouldn't be doing your job. You're going to miss opportunities and you're not going to see the things you need to see."

Davidi's experience at the Olympics perfectly encapsulates what happens to one's fandom when one gets into this business. It's not that the innate ability to derive pleasure from sporting events just disappears completely; that would make this job absolutely miserable, and it would do the same to one's output.

"I think it's really important that you should always be a fan of the sport, and that you should always root for it," Davidi said. "If you're just going through the motions and you're completely dispassionate and have no curiosity, it's going to be reflected in what you produce. So I think that's important. But if you're going to be a fan of the team, I don't think you're doing anybody a service, because you can't be emotional in a fan way when you're covering a team. You just can't be riding the rollercoaster. It's for fans to ride the roller coaster. Your job is to explain the hows and the whys."

What happens is, that fandom simply begins to manifest itself in different ways. Like, for instance, rather than fandom being something that occurs in the *present* to inform one's emotions, one's *past* fandom becomes a journalistic tool, something upon which to draw to inform one's work, the way Davidi was able to use his memories as a fan of the goal scored by Lemieux in 2002 to connect with his readers on an emotional level regarding Crosby's goal in 2014, or the way Meisel has leaned on his adolescent experiences as a Cleveland fan as a way to relate to his readers regarding the emotions they're likely feeling during the club's 2016 postseason run.

"This is cool for the city and the place I grew up in and all that," Meisel said. "But I think more than anything, it allows me to do my job better in covering what's happening right now."

"People ask me now, 'How excited are you that the Indians are in the World Series?!' And I'm like, 'Yeah, I'm excited because I get to cover a World Series and because people care about my work.' This isn't Kenny Lofton and Albert Belle making the World Series, so it's not that same attachment."

Fandom becomes a tool, rather than a response. And it shifts, rather than disappears. Every writer quoted in this story, as well as myself, experienced a similar transformation, in that we've all actually become much bigger fans of the *game* in the wake of losing our allegiance to a particular ballclub.

"The one thing I've always said about it is, I may no longer live and die with one team, but I'm a bigger baseball fan than I think I was when I was a kid," Bastian said. "I can now watch any game and get just as much out of it, and maybe even more out of it, than I did when I was younger. I'm not living and dying, I'm actually paying *more* attention to the game as a whole, rather than whether my team won or lost or missed that pitch or got screwed by the umps, because I'm more into trying to learn the analytical side of it, and I'm into good stories, and it allows me to flip on any game and think that game in its singular self is awesome. I think that's where the family member or friend wouldn't understand. I care about the game, not the name of the team on the uniforms."

It doesn't necessarily have to be the case that in order to write in sports, one has no choice but to abandon their inner, or even outer, fan. In our changing media landscape, fans have agency over where and how they consume their content, and with a wealth of well-written, well-reasoned and informative fan blogs existing for every team, readers are no longer forced to consume the more rational, operational perspective provided by reporters who don't take the same emotional journey as fans.

Take McCovey Chronicles, for instance, the San Francisco Giants community run full-time by Grant Brisbee as part of the SBNation blog network since 2005. Despite remaining an admittedly biased Giants fan throughout his writing career with a Twitter bio that includes the confession, "I do not break news," Brisbee has amassed a following of more than 30,000 on Twitter and has grown McCovey Chronicles into one of the internet's go-to locations for Giants news and analysis, while rarely stepping foot in the team's clubhouse.

"I think that's my niche," Brisbee explained, "to be the fan. I'm not going to compete with the beat writers, so to have someone who's on the couch yelling at the TV just like the reader is sort of what was available to me."

"I'm getting mad at the same things they're getting mad at. I'm complaining about the same things. We'll have disagreements, me and the readers, but at the same time, we're all coming from the same place. We're all just totally biased and we're all rooting for the same thing."

Brisbee's place within the baseball writing community is a unique one, as he is perhaps the most prominent voice, who, as he puts it, continues to "wear his biases on his sleeve." But even in a role that, by choice, has allowed him to maintain his fandom amidst a sea of objectivity, even he has not been immune to the unintended consequences that come with the job.

"Even when I'm watching Travis Ishikawa win the pennant in 2014, there's a part of me that's not in the moment so much, because I'm thinking, 'Oh shit, what am I going to write about? What am I going to say?' I'm trying to craft," Brisbee said. "So even for me, there is a level removed where the lows aren't necessarily as low, and the highs are maybe a little bit muted because I'm also on the job."

Brisbee does have clubhouse and press box access whenever he wants it, but he's found that his time spent rubbing shoulders with the team in the Giants' clubhouse only reinforces his desire to rest comfortably within the niche he's carved out for himself over the last decade, to not fly too close to the sun by embedding himself too deeply within the game.

He remembers feeling self-conscious about the fear of someone like Hunter Pence or Barry Zito—the butts of many of Brisbee's jokes that oftentimes serve as the backbone for his engaging, whimsical writing style—potentially recognizing him in the Giants' clubhouse. He remembers a game in which Brandon McCarthy, an athlete with whom he has become friendly over Twitter, pitched poorly against the Giants while playing for the rival Dodgers, leaving Brisbee in a difficult position. A position that, in a way, compromised his ability to work through the perspective of a writer that connects with his readership by means of their shared fandom.

"If it's a normal Dodgers pitcher, I'm on Twitter just having a blast," Brisbee said. "But I was very quiet that night, very very quiet. I like the guy, so I'm not just going to sit there and poke him in the eye, especially when he might see it. So that's sort of an example of what I don't want."

"[Giants reliever] Derek Law follows me on Twitter, and I get weird about it. I'm not going to block him, but I kind of prefer they don't know who I am at all."

For more traditional beat writers and reporters, it's the time spent around the game, our proximity to the players themselves, that play a role in naturally divorcing ourselves from our fandom. In Brisbee's case, it's the fandom itself, and his desire to maintain it, that pushes him away from the proximity to the game. Even on opposite ends of the spectrum, being involved in this industry in any way can radically alter the way we consume the game on a fundamental level, whether we like it or not.

This business is not for everyone, especially considering the realities one faces along the way that can lead one to becoming jaded and losing their allegiances, whether occurring behind the scenes or front and center.

Take Moura, for example, who, besides growing up a Dodgers fan in Los Angeles, was also once a fan of one of Los Angeles' NBA basketball teams, the Clippers, a team he covered while attending college at the University of Southern California.

"I saw that the players, on the nights that they lost, that they didn't really care that they lost," Moura said. "And that was really jarring to me at age 20 or so. I try to explain that to people. This is their job, and they're going to try as hard as they can for themselves and for their employers to succeed, but if they do not and they tried hard, they're going to be totally fine with that. In most cases, it's not going to really affect them beyond 20 minutes or so after the game. So why would it affect someone else?"

At the same time, Moura was covering the USC athletics program, which was in the middle of investigations by the NCAA regarding rules violations that resulted in former football star Reggie Bush having to give up his 2005 Heisman Trophy, while both the football and basketball teams were stripped of dozens of wins, including the 2004 football team's national championship, and forced to sit out postseason play in 2010, as well as 2011 in the football program's case.

Before ever completing his journalism degree, Moura had seen enough of the inner workings of the sports industry that by the time he landed a job out of college covering his childhood Dodgers for the *Orange County Register*, the idea of any emotional attachment rooted in fandom clouding his objectivity was a nonexistent concern.

"By that point, I had already become so jaded by USC and the idea that I was supposed to root for this school that I knew was doing a lot of bad things and things I didn't agree with," Moura said. "My job was to report on them, and I would get emails from alumni and things like that saying, 'Oh you're a traitor!' and things like that."

"Even when I was 17, 18, as I started to become more aware of everything else that was interesting in the world, I stopped caring so much about the games and who won. It was a gradual thing, I think, from like age 16 on, and then aided along for certain by my experiences in journalism in college."

And the emails Moura received in college from alumni calling him a traitor were child's play compared to the treatment Meisel received during his senior year as editor-in-chief of *The Lantern*, Ohio State's student newspaper, after he broke the news of head football coach Jim Tressell's attempts to cover up repeated NCAA violations, which led to the resignation of the beloved, championship-winning, hometown coach.

Meisel, 21 at the time, was suddenly thrust into the middle of a national scandal, and wound up on SportsCenter, on Deadspin; a feature story was written about him for ESPN.com. He received hundreds of emails and tweets from incensed Ohio State supporters, calling him a hack and a traitor, some going as far as to issue threats of physical violence and even death, with one message saying that Meisel and his co-editor, James Oldham, were the "most likely candidates to be found dead" in the nearby Olentangy River.

Even though Meisel's mother and grandmother were left rashly wondering whether he would be best served leaving the journalism industry entirely, perhaps to go into witness protection, Meisel himself actually felt better off for the experience, more prepared to enter the industry full time, if not jaded at a young age.

"It gave me a dose of what this job can be in the most hectic times, and it was good to get that out of the way," Meisel said. "There have been other times since where I've written something controversial and I was able to fall back on what I went through at Ohio State and was able to stay grounded and kind of be relaxed about it. I mean, I kind of went through the craziest experience of my journalistic life first, and so that kind of helped make everything easier from then on. It definitely numbed me in terms of fanbases and rooting for teams I once cared about."

When the Cleveland Cavaliers won the NBA title earlier this year, I went ballistic. I hadn't been emotionally attached to my hometown baseball team in years. Covering the Cleveland Browns for a single season in 2014 for the *Akron Beacon Journal* not only eradicated any shred of Browns fandom I had remaining, but turned me off from the NFL, and completely away from football as a whole. I haven't watched a football game since the end of that season. The Cavs were all I had left.

I watched LeBron James and that Cavaliers team break the city's 52-year championship drought at a Cleveland sports bar in downtown Manhattan with a group of friends and Cleveland sports fanatics from high school. When the clock hit 0:00 and Cleveland became a city of champions for the first time in my lifetime—for the first time in the majority of any Ohio native's lifetime—we quite literally danced on tables, swung from the ceilings, popped champagne and danced the night away. I immediately called my father, watching from back home in Ohio, and although we couldn't really hear one another amidst the hysteria, we cried on the phone together.

Since that Cavs championship, I've done a lot of thinking regarding the nature of fandom, what it means to me, and what its role is both inside of our industry and outside of it, and the motivation behind my writing of this article was meant to be as therapeutic and revealing for me as much as it was meant to be (hopefully) informative and entertaining for you.

The weird thing is, as much as I've tried to get excited about this upcoming Cavs season, as they bring back almost the same championship roster in an effort to repeat their title run, I just can't do it. No matter how hard I try, I find myself ambivalent. And I think I realized something: I am no longer a fan of the Cavs, either.

Most any sports writer will tell you that, in place of being a fan of an individual team, they're a fan of the story. And when I was cheering and dancing and laughing and crying with my friends in that Manhattan bar the night the Cavs brought a championship to Cleveland, I wasn't doing those things as a Cavs fan, even though I didn't realize that at the time. I was doing it as a fan of the *story*.

Above all else, I was doing it as a fan of my dad, who's been as die-hard a Cleveland sports fan as they come for his entire life, who's damn-near the entire reason I got myself into this crazy industry I love so much to begin with, who finally got to see the teams he's spent his entire life rooting for call themselves champions, something he'd no doubt questioned would ever come to fruition at countless times throughout his adult life. I did it as a fan of LeBron James, and *his* story, making good on his promise to bring joy to the area that made him who he was, the area that had so desperately been seeking that joy since long before it produced James. I did it as a fan of my friends, who grew up Cleveland sports fans alongside me, and I did it as a fan of my city, and the several hundred strangers from that city who danced the night away with me in that Manhattan bar 460 miles away from home.

I'm writing this the day before Cleveland and the Cubs kick off the 2016 World Series. By the time you've read this, one of those teams will have broken their far-too-long-lasting championship drought, bringing that same joyful hysteria the Cavs incited in a fanbase that's long overdue. I will be at every one of those World Series games, sitting in the press box, working, alongside one of my mentors and former co-workers, Jordan Bastian. And one of us will see our once-beloved childhood baseball team win a World Series in person, and neither of us can say exactly how we might react. How we might feel. *If* we might feel. Jordan has a guess.

"I think I'll feel like I need to get down to the clubhouse because I have a deadline," Bastian said. "That's one of those things where, and it almost sounds like a cliché like what the players would say, 'Oh, I haven't taken a lot of time to reflect back on it, I'm sure when the smoke clears, blah blah blah,' but I honestly think it's kind of the same thing. I'm sure it would be like, 'Oh, wow, they did it. That's really cool for my city, and for all my friends I grew up with and my family that are still Cubs fans, but I've got to get downstairs.' I think if there would be any kind of emotional reaction, it would be reflecting back on friends and family or things like that, or thinking about how long my grandpa was such a die-hard fan. It would no longer be about myself and instead would be about that sentimental side of it."

When one becomes a sports writer, one often loses the very part of oneself that planted the seed for their future career, and that can be a difficult and strange reality to come to terms with. And it's definitely not for everyone, and I would never fault someone who's not willing to make that trade. Part me of misses being a fan. Part of me misses it dearly, and is sometimes jealous of those who continue to experience the unbridled jubilation that comes with fandom, and even the crushing lows that make the highs that much sweeter. A part of me misses that life, even though a part of me can no longer fathom it. What I'm fairly certain of is that there's no right or wrong or best way to take part in all of this. What I'm absolutely certain of is that I wouldn't trade my perspective for the world.

References & Resources
* Special thanks to Jordan Bastian, Grant Brisbee, Shi Davidi, Zack Meisel and Pedro Moura for their time and insight.

Reckoning with Baseball's (and America's) Amphetamine History

by Jack Moore

Major League Baseball's history with drugs doesn't begin with the bottle of Andro discovered in Mark McGwire's locker. No, the history of performance enhancing drug use in baseball dates back at least to Pud Galvin's use of a serum derived from animal testes in 1891. The widespread use of more modern pharmaceuticals, though, dates back to the 1940s, when amphetamines became the first performance-enhancing drug to gain widespread use in professional baseball clubhouses.

The next quarter century represented a Wild West for drugs in the game. With no oversight, amphetamine use went unchecked for years. Unlike the story we typically are told regarding performance-enhancing drug use in baseball, which solely places blame on the players, classed as a group of dirty cheaters, baseball's amphetamine story shows the way drugs truly become institutionalized in a sport. It doesn't happen without the help of team owners and doctors, and even society at large.

German forces in the Blitzkrieg of 1939 were fueled by a drug called Pervitin, better known as methamphetamine. The Germans did not stick with their drug regimen for long—issues with addiction and recklessness swiftly discouraged the plan—but that did not stop Allied forces from looking into their own form of chemical troop enhancement. By 1943, benzedrine sulfate was a part of every Air Force pilot's emergency kit. "Go pills," despite their dangers, were used as a method of both fighting fatigue and boosting morale, and the American military continues to use them even now.

To trace the history of widespread performance enhancing drug use in major league baseball locker rooms, we have to start here, with the American military's use of benzedrine sulfate as a pepper-upper for fighter pilots. After the Allied victory in 1945, a number of those returning fighter pilots returned to their jobs as baseball players, Ted Williams most famous among them. They brought with them their knowledge of benzedrine sulfate's pick-me-up power—if it could help them on their flight runs, it certainly could help them get through the comparatively light grind of 154 baseball games over a six-month season.

An early advertisement for benzedrine sulfate tablets bragged, "For men in combat, when the going gets tough," the tablets saved lives by "sustaining their mental efficiency by overcoming the symptoms of fatigue." In reality, clinical studies as early as the 1930s suggested amphetamines lacked efficacy at producing anything but a feeling of euphoria. Military leaders noticed the downsides—recklessness and addiction chief among them—but decided to keep using them for their impact on soldiers' "fighting spirit."

The military has continued to use go pills to this day, the only exception being a four-year moratorium between 1992 and 1996. But when the Air Force began regular bombing runs over the Balkans in 1996, the go pills returned, necessary to fuel pilots over the hundreds or thousands of miles of flight required for the missions. In every conflict since World War II—most notably the Korean War and the Vietnam War, both of which included many baseball players - we have continued to feed our soldiers' fighting spirit in pill form.

Drug use in baseball existed before World War II, but the first widely used drug for performance-enhancement purposes was amphetamines. Anybody in a clubhouse who was skeptical just had to ask their former pilot teammates about the beneficial properties of the drugs. Throughout the 1950s and 1960s, amphetamine use was a regular part of clubhouse life that was totally unknown by the public. It took until players spoke up, most notably Jim Bouton in his revelation of the league's greenie habit in his seminal autobiographical work *Ball Four* in 1970, for the news to spread to the rest of the country.

While Bouton was the most prominent player to note the league's amphetamine habit, he was not the first or only one. Jim Brosman published a book called The Long Season in 1960, an autobiographical account of his tumultuous 1959 season, in which he started with the St. Louis Cardinals and was eventually traded to the Cincinnati Reds. Brosnan's work did not garner the national attention Bouton's work would receive a decade later, but it did include an account of the Cardinals' amphetamine use, provided by their team doctors. Here's one particularly illustrative exchange between Brosnan and a Cardinals doctor:

> *"Where's the Dexamyl (a combination barbiturate and amphetamine), Doc?" I yelled at the trainer rooting about in his leather valise..."There's nothing here but phenobarbital and that kind of stuff."*
> *"I don't have any more," said Doc Rohde. "Gave out the last one yesterday. Get more when we get home."*
> *"Been a rough road trip, huh, doc? How'm I goin' to get through the day then? Order some more, Doc. It looks like a long season."*
> *"Try one of these," he said.*
> *"Geez, that's got opium in it. Whaddya think I am, an addict or something?"*

In the wake of *Ball Four* and Bouton's claim that 40-50 percent of baseball players were regularly using amphetamines, the nation's attention turned to drug use in sports in earnest for the first time. In October of 1970, the California State Assembly's Health and Welfare Subcommittee on Drug Abuse and Alcoholism convened "to explore the extent to which drugs play a part in athletic competition." The committee was chaired by California State Assemblyman William Campbell and included fellow State Assemblymen Gordon Duffy, Kent Stacey, Larry Townsend, Henry Waxman and Pete Wilson. Among those interviewed were team doctors for the California Angels and San Francisco Giants, Dr. J.V. Rasinski and Dr. Eldor Siler, respectively. Both denied providing amphetamines to players, but their testimony still revealed much about baseball's drug policies—or lack thereof.

> Chairman Campbell: What would be the policy that you would follow then? Are the guidelines set down by the National American League [sic] as it related to drug use?
> Doctor Rasinski: We've never received any formal statement at all about this—formal or informal—from the American League.
> ...
> Assemblyman Townsend: Why don't they have any medical directives about....
> Doctor Rasinski: I'm not familiar with their governing boards or with their policy set-up. I can't speak for the organization. I'm employed by the California Angels.
> Assemblyman Townsend: It seems ridiculous since they have rules governing almost every other aspect of the profession, they must be concerned about drug usage amongst the players.

Drugs might as well not have existed as far as organized baseball was concerned. As Assemblyman Townsend points out, major league player contracts have had all sorts of behavioral restrictions—most notably against gambling—for decades. Thus, baseball's lack of any sort of policy can easily be seen as a tacit endorsement of the game's drug culture, particularly given Brosnan's description of how easy it was to get these drugs from team doctors. Cardinals doctor I.C. Middleman (seriously, that's his name) also told *Sports Illustrated* in 1969, "We occasionally use Dexamyl and Dexedrine [amphetamines]....We also use barbiturates, Seconal, Tuinal, Nembutal. ...We also use some anti-depressants, Triavil, Tofranil, Valium....But I don't think the use of drugs is as prevalent in the Midwest as it is on the East and West coasts."

We know now, and we actually knew fairly well then, that amphetamines are not terribly effective as performance enhancers. In *Ball Four*, Bouton recalled a story about a pitcher who was shocked to see his manager coming out from the dugout to pull him from the game. The pitcher began to protest, telling the manager he was feeling great, like the "king of the mountain." That was until the manager informed him his last three pitches had been blasted out of the park and that it was definitely time to hit the showers. Study after study dating back decades has suggested the same thing: The performance-enhancing qualities of amphetamines are almost entirely illusory.

But that belief matters far more, and the euphoric sensations provided by amphetamines made it very easy for players to feel like they were excelling when they were on the drugs, and for players to feel like they need the drugs to prepare for game day. The conflicts created by this situation became apparent as the California Assembly continue to question the doctors for the Angels and Giants.

> *Assemblyman Duffy: Okay. But now what if someone else is using—an athlete is using the drugs—a drug or stimulant, for example, not that you prescribed. I'm not impugning your motives at all, or your ethical background. But it was obtained somewhere else, either legally or illegally. What would you do then?*
>
> *Doctor Rasinski: I would first tell the coach, and of course tell the general manager also. We're employed by the general manager. And we have an understanding at the Angels that we will not use anything like this. If it comes to my knowledge that this is being used, then I'm supposed to tell him.*
>
> *Assemblyman Duffy: Now, if they did nothing, then what would you do?*
>
> *Doctor Rasinski: I don't know what else I could do.*

Giants doctor Eldor Siler offered similar sentiments.

> *Assemblyman Duffy: Well, let me ask you the same question. All right, now if you found that there was some athlete on your team who was using—you believed they were using amphetamines, for example, what would you do?*
>
> *Doctor Siler: Well, I guess, it's been answered by—what was said a minute ago. I would report it.*
>
> *Assemblyman Duffy: You would report him. Now, what if they did nothing? The athlete did nothing and the management of the team did nothing? What would you do then?*
>
> *Doctor Siler: Well, I don't really know where I'd go.*

The testimony from these doctors doesn't just reveal the depths of baseball's apathy regarding drugs until it started to become a public relations issue in the wake of Bouton's revelations. It also shows how wildly unprepared baseball was to deal with the potential health issues around amphetamines, which far outpace those of anabolic steroids.

"They are way, way more dangerous," Penn State professor Charles Yesalis, one of the foremost experts on sports doping, told the *Pittsburgh Post-Gazette* when baseball finally clamped down on amphetamines as part of the 2006 drug agreement. "They can stone-cold kill you on the spot." They are also highly addictive and can create dependencies quickly. Is a manager or general manager faced with a player with an amphetamine addiction going to help him get off the stuff, even if it means he can't play in the interim? Or are they going to do their damnedest to make sure he's on the field the next day?

Amphetamines remained a staple in major league locker rooms for more than three decades after the California State Assembly dragged the state's baseball doctors in front of a committee and after similar hearings took place on a national level three years later. When David Wells released a career autobiography in 2004 entitled *Perfect I'm Not*, 34 years after Bouton's *Ball Four*, he claimed amphetamine use in the game was "rampant." Players like Tony Gwynn made similar claims, although never until after their retirement.

Baseball went through multiple massive cocaine scandals and the steroid catastrophe in those decades, yet when amphetamines were included in the 2006 drug agreement, they were treated largely as an afterthought. Mark Kreidler, writing for ESPN about the amphetamine ban, said "amphetamines are so old school that many observers just assumed they'd never be addressed," with the fact that players like the venerated Willie Mays used them to get up for games somehow making them acceptable.

We are now over a decade into baseball's drug testing era, which began in earnest with the adoption of the Joint Drug Prevention and Treatment Program in spring 2006. For fans who have lived through the steroid era and the backlash that followed, the scene Brosnan described of players nakedly asking a team doctor to supply them with performance enhancers is surreal. But the world he describes isn't just one in which drug use is widespread and in which teams are turning a blind eye. Rather, it's a world in which drug use was accepted and even supported by the teams themselves.

Those in baseball have all sorts of logic for why amphetamines were okay—or at least not worthy of the same moral panic as steroids. Jerry Crasnick wrote in 2006 for ESPN as the new amphetamine ban approached, "the more commonly held view is that stimulants are performance 'enablers' rather than performance 'enhancers.'" He quoted one anonymous management official who said, "It's a get-you-out-there issue more than anything else."

There has always been an arbitrary line drawn in sports between "restorative" and "enhancing" drugs, where the former are deemed acceptable and the latter are deemed to be cheating. Nobody would suggest painkillers or treatments like cortisone shots, used to get over injuries and back on the field, are cheating. Steroids, meanwhile, are capable of producing obvious visual changes to the body. The contrasts between a Jason Giambi or Barry Bonds rookie card and the bodies they had when they were blasting home runs in the early 2000s are simply too apparent.

But this is a simplistic view of why players take steroids. It's not just to be bigger, to have more home run power or velocity on their fastballs. It is, for many, a search for the same kind of restorative effect as amphetamines were thought to provide for players in the mid-20th century. Players take steroids to build a body that can withstand the 162-game grind, and they take them so their bodies will heal from the inevitable bumps and bruises of the dog days of summer with a quickness. The line between these drugs is much blurrier than many baseball observers would have you believe.

Perhaps we are more likely to understand amphetamine use because of how relatable it is. Benzedrine sulfate was marketed to the general public in the 1930s through the post-war days for its "striking effect upon mood" and ability to provide "a sense of increased energy, mental alertness, and capacity for work." The Journal of the American Medical Association contained advertisements for benzedrine sulfate to treat "The Patient with Mild Depression," whose symptoms included:

1) apathy, discouragement, and undue pessimism; 2) subjective difficulty in thinking, in concentrating, and in initiating and accomplishing usual tasks; 3) subjective feelings of weakness and exhaustion; and 4) hypochondria (undue preoccupation with vague somatic complaints, such as palpitation or gastrointestinal disorders that may have no organic basis).

In other words, the human condition. It wasn't until the 1960s that the federal government began to place restrictions on the medical use of amphetamines and until 1971 for it to be classified as a Schedule-II controlled substance (having a high potential for abuse and dependence, but accepted medical uses). They still remain in heavy use among the general public, as amphetamine-based prescription drugs like Ritalin and Adderall have become common in workplaces and on college campuses to keep up productivity in these heavily competitive worlds.

It's important to consider this history when we look at the way drugs in baseball have been dealt with, both in terms of punishment and in terms of the stories we tell about them, in this new era. Baseball seems determined to solve the steroid problem through heavier and heavier punishments for players, and the union, spearheaded by sanctimonious comments from players who have already made their money, has gone right along with this strategy. It's an approach that suggests the evil of drug use comes only from the players, one that ignores how and why these drugs make their ways into the games in the first place.

The pressure of professional baseball, major league and minor league, force players into difficult situations in which they have to balance their morals and their health against the chance of earning their first major league paycheck or holding their tenuous grip on a roster spot. When steroids entered the game in the 1980s, right alongside the amphetamines that had already been around for years, they were entering a culture in which it was accepted that you would do whatever it took to stay on the field—play through whatever pain, and take whatever drug necessary to make it work. This approach was preached and accepted by team owners, managers, commentators, and fellow players—even fans. It was an ingrained part of baseball culture, and it went far deeper than some greedy players looking to play beyond their normal capacities.

If baseball actually wants to solve its drug problem—whether it's with amphetamines, steroids, human growth hormone or whatever the next big thing turns out to be—it will have to reckon with this history. It will have to acknowledge the problem goes far deeper than the greed of the players. It will have to acknowledge that the very structure of the league, in which a select few earn huge paydays while the bulk of the professional class toils for sub-minimum wages, encourages a dog-eat-dog mindset that demands players do whatever it takes to succeed, including drugs.

It will have to acknowledge that a program that treats players as adversaries only encourages those players to hide their use and avoid getting help. And it will have to acknowledge that, if baseball truly wants to be a drug-free sport, the responsibility for the mess we're in now resides with more than just the players. It also resides with the managers, executives, owners and doctors who helped create this culture. Although the 1970s and 1980s seem like the distant past, today's baseball leaders grew up surrounded by the drug culture of the time, and their approach to the problem remains informed by the outdated attitudes of that era. Until baseball's leadership can get past its obsession with policing players as a singular response to drugs, the game will remain stuck in the same cycle of scandal and punishment it has been in since the 1980s, ruining lives and careers until those in power decide to wake up and actually do something about the root of the problem.

References & Resources

- Robert Smith, NPR, "A Different Kind of Performance Enhancer," *npr.org/templates/story/story.php?storyId=5314753*

- Jon Bonné, NBC News, "'Go Pills': A war on drugs?," *nbcnews.com/id/3071789/ns/us_news-only/t/go-pills-war-drugs*

- Jim Salisbury and Todd Zolecki, *Philadelphia Enquirer*, "Baseball's problem with pills Amphetamines are widely used, the commissioner said. Selig hopeful on 'greenies' ban," *articles.philly.com/2006-03-08/news/25415047_1_amphetamines-clubhouses-bud-selig*

- Mark Kreidler, ESPN.com, "Baseball finally brings amphetamines into light of day," *espn.com/mlb/columns/story?id=2225013&columnist=kreidler_mark*

- Jesse Hicks, *Distillations*, "Fast Times: The Life, Death, and Rebirth of Amphetamine," *chemheritage.org/distillations/magazine/fast-times-the-life-death-and-rebirth-of-amphetamine*

- Jerry Crasnick, ESPN.com, "Kicking amphetamines," *espn.com/mlb/columns/story?id=2289509&columnist=crasnick_jerry*

- Jim Bouton, *Ball Four*, 1970

- Jim Brosnan, *The Long Season*, 1960

- Hathi Trust Digital Library, "Proper and improper use of drugs by athletes. : Hearings, Ninety-third Congress, first session, pursuant to S. Res. 56, section 12 ... / June 18 and July 12 and 13, 1973.," *babel.hathitrust.org/cgi/pt?id=pst.000015501806;view=1up;seq=510*

- Bil Gilbert, *Sports Illustrated*, "Problems in a Turned-On World," si.com/vault/issue/43044/70/2

- David Wells and Chris Kreski, *Perfect I'm Not: Boomer on Beer, Brawls, Backaches, and Baseball*, 2004

Mud Is Chaos

by Eno Sarris

We nerds hate chaos. I feel I can call you that because I don't think it's an insult, and also because you're reading this book. Anyway, to nerd out on a subject is to want to know a ton about a subject, and to know a ton is to really isolate the parts and understand them. Chaos is the thing that puts the things you know in a blender to produce the smoothie that is The Unknown.

In baseball, one of the key ingredients in that smoothie is mud. And, as with any of the mud food your toddler might make, it's leaving an upsetting taste wherever it goes.

The nominal idea is this: New balls, since 1938, have been rubbed up with mud bearing the Lena Blackburne seal of approval in order to "remove the gloss" as the rulebook addition that year phrased it. It all started with Ray Chapman being beaned and dying in 1920, and it took 18 years for Blackburn to transition from player to manager, where he first instituted regular rubbing up of the baseballs. So we've been mudding up the baseball for 80 years in order for pitchers to have a better grip on the ball.

The problem—other than the chaos that results from introducing a lightly regulated process concerning the main piece of league-provided equipment—is that nobody seems to love the idea any more. "Don't rub the balls up at all," said Dodgers starter Rich Hill. "I'd rather they just got rid of the mud," said Rockies reliever Adam Ottavino. "Look at some of these balls, and they're darker than dirt," said Twins second baseman Brian Dozier.

If you ask around, as I did, you'll quickly find how disparate the rubbing process can be. There's no guidance, is the first thing you'll notice. "I learned 36 years ago from George Mitterwald, a coach of the A's, when I was 12 years old," said Oakland's visiting clubhouse manager, Mike Thalblum, and that's the best-case scenario. He was taught by a coach, closer to the beginning of time. Others just learned from the last assistant, or worse, from the tub itself.

"Apply a small amount of mud to the palm of your hand," begin the meager instructions on the Lena Blackburne *Original* Baseball Rubbing Mud. And that's all some minor league parks have for the ballboys instructed to rub up the balls before the game. "We had a big problem last year because they were almost black," laughed Giants catcher Trevor Brown. "The kids that were coming in to rub them were bat boys, they didn't know. I'd get one and just hand it back to the umpire and then get one and hand it back to the umpire."

A jar of Lena Blackburne "Original Baseball Rubbing Mud" in the Oakland A's clubhouse

But even on the major league level, the way each clubhouse attendant goes about applying the mud can be very different. Two attendants modeled their method for me.

Thalblum's was more old-school. He'll take a dab, throw it on the ball, and then rub using his bare hands in a circular motion around the leather, avoiding the seams. "Some guys will put it on the ball, some guys will put it in their hand, some guys will use gloves, some guys use a sponge, but this is the original way, so this is the way I do it," he said as he finished a ball.

Over in Colorado, they're more new school. Allan Bossart, the director of clubhouse operations, used to be the ball-rubber. "I used to be the umpire's assistant, and I did it with gloves—they said you could get infections, but also, you get a more consistent motion," he felt. But really, it's just about who taught him: "I was shown 10 years ago with gloves, so I do it with gloves."

The players have even noticed a difference in color from park to park. Giants reliever Javier López said that "the balls we use here in SF are a little bit darker than most," and what if that had something to do with the power-suppressing park factors in the ballpark? Chaos. "It's the same mud, it's just how much you use it," he said. But still.

Not only is there a great deal of variance in how the balls are rubbed, there seems to be a difference in when the balls are rubbed up.

Players are sure the balls sit for a while after being rubbed up. "Balls in Arizona are very dry, very slippery," said Ottavino. "It feels like dust on the ball after they dry up, especially when they're all sitting in the bag together." San Francisco's López echoed the sentiment: "I only notice if it's been done in advance because the ball gets slick and flaky and dry." Even Bossart knew about it—"you have to watch out for that crumbly mumbly on the baseball"—but not from personal experience at his park, of course.

Oakland A's reliever Sean Doolittle was sure that some spots let them dry out over the course of a series: "Sometimes the balls sit for a while after they've been rubbed up and the mud dries out and it almost gets dusty and slick." Randy Marsh, the director of major league umpires and a 28-year veteran of umpiring, agreed that in the past, this might have happened, but now the process is more "secure."

"For years, the plate umpire rubbed the balls, he always did it himself," Marsh said. "That went on for years and years. Then the clubhouse attendants got involved in it, trying to make a few bucks and help us out, too." That process grew over the years, but then there was some trouble. "There have been a couple places where one team said the balls were not rubbed up enough, and another said they were rubbed up too much, because of the way their starting pitcher wanted it."

"It's all a secure process now," Marsh said. "They rub the ball up and they're inspected by the plate umpire that night, to make sure they are consistent and rubbed up correctly. Then a security guard comes and gets them and he holds them until the game starts." But there are still wrinkles.

In Oakland, they do it the night before. "They're still going to feel the same way tomorrow," Thalblum assured me. That was his opinion. Hill, who pitched in Oakland for four months, felt a bit differently. "If I rub the balls up, before the game, it dries up and it sucks up the wetness. It's slick," the lefty said. "If you take mud, what does it turn into? Dust."

But, if it's normally fine in Oakland, that's still Oakland. Wet, soggy, sea-level, cool Oakland. What about in dry, mile-high Colorado?

In Colorado, there's a camera on the balls most of the time. A security guard has to escort the balls any time they travel from or to the humidor. Scrutiny has created a monster. "We put them in for three weeks," says Bossart of the balls. "The umpire's assistant will come in about five hours before the game and rub them up and then put them back in. The rule of thumb is whatever time they've been out for, they go back in for. Then, about a half hour before the game starts, the resident security officer escorts the balls to the umpire room, where they can inspect the balls, and they go to the field with an escort."

And yet, despite their best efforts to keep the ball wet and tacky, home and visiting players all pointed to Colorado as a place where the ball is slick. "Some days, even in Colorado, they're perfect, said López, before adding "and some days..." before trailing off. "They're slick in Denver, mostly because it's hard to get moisture on the ball," said Ottavino, poking open another bag of worms.

That sort of thing begets the chaos we've been talking about—grip issues, and hitters not being able to see the seams—but there's another element of chance that's introduced with mud. "Flyball distances are very sensitive to the air drag on the ball, which in turn is sensitive to the surface roughness," said physics professor, baseball enthusiast and Hardball Times author Alan Nathan. "It is quite possible (even plausible) that there might be some variation in the drag on otherwise identical balls due to differences in the mudding." And park factors are already pretty tough.

Ottavino began talking about coping mechanisms he's begun using because of the mud factor. Prompted by my asking about the fact that the clubhouse attendants have to rub up balls to send to the minor leagues, he had a few interesting exclamations. "I won't even throw a minor league ball," he laughed. "I won't even play catch with one. Major league ball is a major league ball, you have to get used to that. Otherwise what's the point."

He takes that attitude even further. Ottavino so wants to mimic game situations that he'll throw out balls after throwing them a couple times in the bullpen. "You almost have to practice getting a new ball that sucks," he said. "When you're warming up, don't get comfortable with a ball and let it hit the ground and keep throwing with it. Immediately get a new one every time to make it realistic. If the ball even touches the ground, I get a new one. In the game, you get a new ball every other pitch."

There are other coping mechanisms, too. And here's where the chaos begins to spiral into a real problem. The mud is supposed to help the players get a grip on the ball. It might not be doing the best job. So players have resorted to other methods.

When I questioned Thalblum about the necessity of rubbing, he defended it. "The balls are too slippery without it," he said. "And if I had some lotion I'd show you what it feels like with lotion, It's really grippy. Lotion, sunscreen, or some guys obviously use pine tar."

We know all about this weird fact of baseball: Pitchers everywhere are using secondary substances to improve their grip. Like Eddie Harris said in *Major League* —"I have to put anything on it I can find,"—real-life major leaguers are passing on the Vagisil and using sunscreen lotion and pine tar to get a grip. Ninety-eight percent of the time we look the other way, but then in big moments, a plucky manager will call out the egregious offender, and suddenly we're all wringing our hands about pine tar on Michael Pineda's neck. And that's the way it has to be—"You wait for a complaint from a team before you go undressing someone out there," said Marsh. "They have to tell you exactly where they think it is. You're not going to go out there and start taking clothes."

Waiting for a complaint about something we look the other way on most of the time is unfair, and it seems to happens only when the manager really needs the win. "Especially when a guy is really good in game three of a series," laughed Phillies catcher A.J. Ellis.

Or in the World Series when a 42-year-old Kenny Rogers shut down the Cardinals with pine tar on his hand. Rogers was confronted during a dominant Game Two win that year, but umpire supervisor Steve Palermo said the crew determined that the substance on his hand was dirt and asked him to wash it off before the second inning. The Cardinals, who lost the game but won the series, called it "blatant" after the game (in hitting coach Hal McRae's words) and weren't satisfied with the ruling.

On some level, the random is fine. It separates a computer simulation from real life. It makes the game interesting, and it introduces chance. No projection system will ever perfectly capture and predict baseball, and we want it that way.

But when chaos and chance beget unfairness, then it becomes an issue. Especially when there might be a better way, a model, in the game of baseball.

In Japan, every ball arrives at the park in shrink wrapping. The balls are opened and handed to the catcher. Put in play right out of the bag. And it works. Because the balls are manufactured to be grippy. "They had a little tack on them," remembered López.

We'd eliminate a fair bit of chaos with this one move, and probably not the move Dozier wanted—"Use some sort of mud that's white, that'd be perfect. That would solve everything." That suggestion would make the balls more visible, but it wouldn't get at the underlying problems of inconsistency and complacency to foreign substances on the ball.

With a tacky ball that's white, the hitters and the pitchers would be happy. There would be no need to rub up the balls anywhere, there wouldn't be dry mud in some places and dark, wet balls in other places. We might even keep pitchers from having to resort to lotion and pine tar, and if that were the case, the game would follow the rule book more often and we wouldn't have another Rogers situation.

Of course, chaos is a squirrely thing. You shoo it out of one corner, and it up and resides in another corner. In a year that saw the second-most home runs of all time, there's been a lot of talk about the ball being juiced. That sort of talk cost Ryozo Koto his job as commissioner of the Japanese league, Nippon Professional Baseball. And Kenta Maeda just told us the ball moves more here in America, especially on change-ups and sinkers. Due to the relationship of the seams to the leather—which may have something to do with creating a tacky ball—those pitches don't get as much movement in Japan.

If we move to a tacky ball, we may invite a whole host of other problems.

We started with one problem—the rubbing up of balls is "unregulated" as Ellis put it, and "everyone's dimensions of rubbing the ball are different" as Bossart said—and that thread led us into more sinister territory. But any solution may be just as difficult and introduce just as much entropy into the game we know and love.

So maybe we should just embrace it. Learn to love the mud. Jump right in. It keeps us from being robots.

References & Resources

- Several interviews conducted over the course of the 2016 season
- Doug Miller, MLB.com, "The Mudville Line," *m.mlb.com/news/article/40289696*
- ESPN.com, "Questions linger over substance on Rogers' left hand," *espn.com/mlb/playoffs2006/news/story?id=2635538*
- Bryan Hoch, MLB.com, "Pineda ejected for having pine tar on neck," *m.mlb.com/news/article/73145346/yankees-right-hander-michael-pineda-ejected-for-having-pine-tar-on-neck*
- Eno Sarris, FanGraphs, "Kenta Maeda, Then and Now," *fangraphs.com/blogs/kenta-maeda-then-and-now*

On Baseball, Writing and Finding Your People

by Sara Nović

When I was a kid, baseball fandom was confined to the limits of my immediate family, or more often than not, a solitary activity. I've loved the game for as long as I can remember, but as a Mets fan raised in Philadelphia I was, (outside our house at least) markedly alone in my devotion to the team. I saw my first Mets game at Veterans Stadium, and over the years I was twice a direct target of the Phanatic's antics, including once when he gave me a noogie on the Jumbotron. Being a girl with a passion for baseball, too, could be isolating. None of my school friends knew about the games or the players, so I talked shop mostly with my dad and grandma, and the one person with whom I could trade baseball cards was my little sister, who collected them only because I did.

This suited me well enough as an introvert, but it was an incomplete picture of what baseball could be. Then, in 2005, I moved to Boston to go to college. The Sox had just broken their curse in the previous season, and I found among people there an almost unanimous love of the game and the team—one that transcended age and gender and race, and pressed out beyond the city limits and across state lines: the Red Sox Nation.

Simultaneously, I was learning another thing that had made me strange back home—the notebooks filled with ideas and stories and bad poetry that I hid beneath my mattress—might also be the makings of membership in a kind of collective. Around the tables of literature seminars and writing workshops, I was slowly becoming part of the literary community.

I survived the shock of my first Boston winter and soon found myself in front of a television for the Sox home opener. The cameraman scanned the stands, packed and rowdy, and eventually settled on Stephen King and his son, both reading novels as the game began. One dorm mate commented that reading at the game was a waste of money; another said yeah, well, King had plenty of it, but I was transfixed, a different kind of revelation dawning. Reading a book on a sunny day at the ballpark seemed to me an ideal afternoon, and here on the screen was proof that not only could I be in community with other baseball fans and other writers, but perhaps there was also a communal tie between the two.

Many writers have professed their love of the game. King himself, along with Stewart O'Nan, compiled evidence of their devotion to the Sox in their book *Faithful*. Myriad novels have included baseball as a central subject or theme, including Robert Coover's *The Universal Baseball Association, Inc., J. Henry Waugh, Prop.*, Chad Harbach's

The Art of Fielding, Philip Roth's *The Great American Novel*, and Bernard Malamud's *The Natural*.

Other authors' attachment to the sport, though less overt in their work, has been noted by those closest to them. Stephen Crane, author of *The Red Badge of Courage*, played baseball while studying at Syracuse University with what teammates once called a "fiendish glee," and was accused by professors of working harder on the diamond than in his academic courses. My own team, the Mets, claim several famous writer fans, including comedians/writers Jerry Seinfeld and Chris Rock (with Kevin James, Ray Romano and Jon Stewart also regulars at Citi Field), and the late Pulitzer Prize-winning author of *To Kill a Mockingbird*, Harper Lee. Lee's friend Marja Mills once described her as a "rabid Mets fan" and her biographer, Charles Shields, noted that she often wore a Mets cap around town.

And then there is Roger Angell; author of numerous baseball-themed essay collections, former fiction editor of and frequent contributor to the *New Yorker*, he was once nicknamed, to his chagrin, "the poet laureate of baseball." But whether or not the moniker accurately represents the quality of Angell's prose is less interesting than the fact that such a phrase even seems a reasonable thing to say. There could be no poet laureate of football, for example, though Wimbledon did appoint the British writer Matt Harvey the official poet of the tournament in 2010. In any case, the number of writers fascinated by the game, and the notion of literature and baseball so intertwined at their cores, speak volumes about the special relationship between the two. Which of course raises the question—why?

The obvious answer lies in baseball's unique pacing, which allows for a certain kind of multitasking. Like King and his son, one can enjoy both a novel and baseball game simultaneously—the languid tempo of each are so similar that it's easy to move between them. Even non-writers probably have experienced the satisfaction of "background baseball," a game on the TV or radio making everyday tasks a bit more pleasurable.

When I lived in Sunnyside, Queens, a few years ago, I often took the 7 train out to Citi Field for a weeknight game. I'd climb up to section 504 and read a novel, or write a new scene for a story I was working on, then put it down and watch the game and the sunset. I was both bolstered by the feeling of being in community with other fans, happy to sit alone and let my mind wander. Time is perhaps the most valuable thing one can give a writer, and baseball is generous this way, providing viewers with the luxury of being able to sit for an hour or two with no expectations upon them. In an interview with Salon, Angell put it well: "You can watch the game and keep score and look around and take notes. Now and then you even have time to have an idea."

While other sports are tied to the clock and artificially adrenaline-pumped because of it, every move in baseball is both organic to that particular matchup, each play deliberate and its speed inviolable to outside pressures (except, perhaps, the weather).

This, I think, is what makes the sport both a safe haven for writers and a metaphor for the work we do.

When writing fiction, so often I fail to fit a story into the constraints of shape or length I, or someone else, had envisioned for it. And now at work on my second novel, I feel anxious about getting it all done. People, well-meaning, of course, constantly ask me how the new book is going and when it will be ready. Their inquiries coat my thoughts and I plod along all day, dismayed by the amount of time it takes to complete a single page, scene, or sentence. Then I think of baseball—a long game in a long season, a slow, methodical progression toward the win—and I feel better. Nothing good can come of rushing the pitcher or swinging for swinging's sake, and best of all, if I can keep step with the greats on and off the field, I am in good company. This book, like this game, will take just as long as it needs to, and it will be the better for it.

References & Resources

- Stephen King & Stewart O'Nan, *Faithful*, 2005
- Robert Coover, *The Universal Baseball Association, Inc., J. Henry Waugh, Prop.*, 1971
- Chad Harbach, *The Art of Fielding: A Novel*, 2012
- Philip Roth, *The Great American Novel*, 1995
- Bernard Malamud, *The Natural*, 2003
- Stephen Crane, *The Red Badge of Courage*, 1895
- Rick Burton, *Syracuse University Magazine*, "Syracuse and a Civil War Masterpiece"
- Harper Lee, *To Kill a Mockingbird*, 1960
- Marja Mills, *The Mockingbird Next Door: Life with Harper Lee*, 2014
- Charles J. Shields, *Mockingbird: A Portrait of Harper Lee*, 2006
- Steve Kettmann, Salon, "Roger Angell," *salon.com/2000/08/29/angell*
- Caroline Davies, *The Guardian*, "Quiet, please: Wimbledon appoints its first official poet," *theguardian.com/uk/2010/may/19/matt-harvey-appointed-wimbledon-poet*

The Dark Age of Cuban Baseball Has Begun

by Eric Longenhagen

On Aug. 31, 2016, Jet Blue flight 378 left Floridian soil for Cuba. It was the first commercial flight across the Florida Strait since 1961 and a watershed moment in the history of Cuba/U.S. relations. Just 106 miles separate Havana from Key West, but the ideological and legislative barrier between the two nations has kept them completely apart since the early 1960s.

The most prominent common cultural touchstone shared by the two nations for the last half century has been baseball. As political relations between the United States and Cuba begin to normalize in present day, the cultural and economic landscape of the island are poised to undergo rapid change. Baseball will not be exempt from these alterations, and indeed there is sizeable evidence and opinion within baseball that in anticipation of things to come, changes to the landscape of Cuban baseball already are well underway. And they may not be for the better.

To understand the current state of Cuban baseball and try to predict where it's heading, it's important to consider how 20th century Cuban politics are impacting the game today. Between 1953 (when the Cuban Revolution, led by Fidel Castro, began) and 1962, Cuba's government and its relationships with global powers underwent substantial, dramatic change. The Revolution reached a tipping point in 1958 when the U.S. government decided to cease weapon sales to incumbent Cuban President Fulgencio Batista despite dissent from prominent U.S. officials, including U.S. Ambassador to Cuba Earl T. Smith, who later told a Senate subcommittee he thought that, either through extreme stupidity or via misinformation propagated by Communist sympathizers within the State Department, the U.S. government was responsible for Castro's rise to power.

Batista's militaristic reign in Cuba was unsavory. His repressive, dictatorial ways (which included public executions) helped ignite the revolution that would ultimately usurp him, but the United States was willing to look the other way because of its own financial interests in the island at the time and because Batista was helping keep Communism, which the U.S. did not want on its doorstep, at bay.

When Fidel Castro rose to power and came to the U.S. to meet with then-Vice President Richard Nixon, it became abundantly clear to the U.S., despite reportedly charming presentations by Castro, that his intentions were not so financially favorable. The Eisenhower Administration imposed trade restrictions on Cuba (most prominently ceasing oil supplies, which Cuba began to receive from the Soviet Union among many other subsidies) that were expanded upon in 1962 after John F. Kennedy had taken office. Shortly after that, personal travel between the two countries became forbidden.

This ended the relatively narrow band of time, between when Jackie Robinson broke baseball's color barrier and the start of the Cold War, during which Cubans like Luis Tiant and Tony Perez found their way to the majors and had robust careers. Though political administrations in the United States would tweak aspects of the embargo several times in the coming decades, this initial iteration of what Cubans often call a "blockade" (despite no physical military blockade restricting trade) christened modern Cuba and, because the two are inextricably linked, modern Cuban baseball.

It was at this time, because of the embargo, that the structure of Cuban baseball changed. Focus shifted toward cultivating Earth's best national team as a way to show that Cuba was thriving, even though the island began relying more and more heavily on financial aid from the USSR. The travel restriction aspects of the embargo also meant players now needed to defect should they want to play in major league baseball which. Those factors combined with the harsh punishment of Cubans caught trying to defect, kept virtually all baseball talent on the island for the next 50 years.

Cuba's entire population is roughly equivalent to Ohio's, and yet for five decades Cuba dominated international baseball competition, winning 25 of the 28 International Baseball Federation tournaments in which it participated. Until the Beijing Olympics in 2008, Cuba either won or reached the championship game in 50 straight international events. Perhaps the athletic and political pinnacle of this run was an Olympics gold medal in 1996 for an undefeated Cuban team on American soil.

This run of excellence has come to an abrupt end as we stride into the 21st century.

It was also around '96 that a modest flow of talent began to make its way from Cuba to the majors. Cuba remained competitive (though no longer dominant) into the 2000s, but as more and more stars and prospects have left for the majors, the island has been unable to produce enough high-level talent to replace them.

Currently, many international scouts consider Cuba to have virtually no major league-ready talent and precious few prospects worth exceeding MLB's international amateur signing bonus rules to sign. Players of all ages have departed from Cuba to varying levels of success in the majors, and the deluge of talent in the States has left Cuba dry.

This decade has seen an explosion in Cuban imports. Fewer than 30 Cubans defected for professional baseball in North America during the entire 1990s; in 2015 alone, upwards of 75 athletes left the island. Players who would be the Cuban stars today (Yasiel Puig, Yoenis Céspedes, Jose Iglesias) are established big leaguers. The Cuban stars of tomorrow (such as 17-year old left-handed pitcher Adrian Morejon, who signed for $11 million in July and whose fastball was up to 96 mph during Fall Instructional league) are developing under MLB's resource-obsessed umbrella.

This exodus undoubtedly has been exacerbated by America's fascination with Cuba and its baseball. Modern technology in America has made domestic athletic accomplishments increasingly tangible and immediately visible. Sports fans can see highlight videos of high school basketball players on their phone in just a few seconds. In contrast, Cuba's isolation from much of the Western world kept its athletes shrouded in mystery and intrigue well into the 2000s.

It wasn't until Céspedes' 2011 workout video went viral that American baseball fans got more than a fleeting glimpse of Cuban talent. That video is a surreal 20 minutes of Céspedes performing various feats of strength and doing very little actual baseball activity before thanking former Green Bay Packers running back Ahman Green and spit roasting a pig. Céspedes began an era of Cuban defectors disdainfully known to older Cuban ballplayers as "The Reggaeton Generation." It began a run on Cubans with monster tools and a flashy style of play. Fans and executives became somewhat obsessed and have bled the island dry of its talent.

The Dark Ages of Cuban baseball are upon us, though some in baseball would argue their harbinger came in the 1980s when then-Soviet leader Mikhail Gorbachev instituted an era of reform in the USSR called *Perestroika*. As the sun set on the Cold War, *Perestroika's* policy reforms and the diplomatic tensions and economic instability they created are generally regarded as significant accelerants toward the dissolution of the Soviet Union in 1991.

It also led to the end of Soviet economic support to Cuba. The island was so dependent upon Soviet aid (according to a 2005 volume of *The Journal of Latin American Studies*, trade with the USSR comprised 70 percent of Cuba's economic dealings at the time of *Perestroika*) that *Perestroika* was effectively the death writ of the Cuban economy. This began the still extant period of economic hardship in Cuba known as "The Special Period" in which Cuba, forced to fend for its financial self without a powerful sponsor, began to slowly but steadily fall into a deepening, country-wide poverty.

This, along with the country's inescapable human rights issues, is what American baseball sources cite as the primary reason for the deluge of Cuban player defections in the 21st century. As the quality of life in Cuba has continued to erode since Perestroika, players have been more apt to undertake the risks associated with defection, a process that often is dangerous and unsavory for the athletes involved. It's not a coincidence that major league baseball saw the first real wave of Cuban defectors in the early 1990s, just after the official collapse of the Soviet Union in 1991. Talents like Rey Ordóñez and Liván and Orlando Hernández began to trickle in, providing American baseball scouts and executives with their first look at how the island's marquee talent measured up to major league competition.

The turn of the century brought the World Baseball Classic, which provided scouts with more looks at Cubans against elite competition and more confidence that many of them could contribute to big league teams. As the number of defections increased, so too did the number of zeroes on the checks Cuban players were cashing. Jose Contreras' $32 million deal with the Yankees in 2002 was a lucrative signal to talented Cubans who were toiling away in Series Nacional on the increasingly poor archipelago. Younger players like Kendrys Morales (age 21 at defection), Yunel Escobar (22) and Aroldis Chapman (21) began to leave the island.

As Cuban defections have reached their apex in the last few years, the demographics of the players in question have skewed younger, with some leaving Cuba at age 14 or 15 to establish residency in Haiti or other South American countries and begin working out for scouts in pursuit of a deal by the time they're 16. With nearly all the veteran players gone (Yulieski Gurriel's defection a symbolic end of the era) and prospects being poached pretty much as soon as they're identified, some are concerned Cuban baseball will die as major league baseball turns it into just another resource for amateur talent.

Like much of the rest of Cuba's culture, baseball was left to incubate on the island free of American influence during the decades of the Cold War. Impoverished and repressed though they may be, Cubanos have created a unique and beautiful culture around their hardship and, as economic relations with the United States begin to normalize, many have mixed feelings about a more prosperous but impure Cuba packed with vacationing frat boys. The island's government has made it clear to its citizens that tourism is going to be a priority, and makeshift restaurants and hotels already have begun popping up because, as one scout told me, "Cuba is becoming interested in capitalism but not democracy."

Some international curators are concerned American "overfishing" of baseball talent in Cuba will effectively destroy the country's enthusiasm for consuming and playing the sport and ultimately harm the quality of MLB's product as world youth turn to other sports. Others contend that, so long as major league teams are willing to pay players millions of dollars, kids will take an extra round of ground balls even if they'd rather be playing soccer.

Both parties, MLB and Cuba, have incentive to change the current system. Major league owners have paid a pretty penny for Cuban talent in recent years, and not all of it has been good. If and when Cuba is open for business, the owners will sit down at the bargaining table with Cuba to iron out a deal, and their priority will be to save money. Alternatively, Cuba's government likely will seek a situation that most financially benefits Cuba.

This intersection of incentives has many within baseball anticipating a posting system similar to the one MLB has in place with the Korea Baseball Organization (KBO). In that system, a player from a KBO team is posted, and major league teams can place sealed bids in an effort to win exclusive negotiating rights with the posted player. If the KBO team accepts the highest bid, the player can negotiate only with the major league club whose bid was accepted.

If this system were adopted in Cuba, it potentially would allow the Cuban government to offer its players to a robust open market of major league teams while the players get little leverage in negotiations. This also would allow major league owners to avoid the massive payouts Cuban defectors like Yasmany Tomás received when all 30 teams were allowed to negotiate.

Nippon Professional Baseball (NPB) in Japan once used this posting system, but the current Collective Bargaining Agreement capped NPB posting fees at $20 million, with all teams that bid $20 million able to engage in contract negotiations with the posted player. Pitcher Masahiro Tanaka was the first player posted under these rules. He garnered the maximum posting fee and a seven-year, $155 million deal. The last player posted under the previous NPB system (and current KBO system) was Yu Darvish, a prospect superior to Tanaka. Darvish's negotiating rights were won with a $51 million bid from the Texas Rangers. He signed a six-year, $60 million deal.

The current KBO model also would allow Cuba to retain players into their prime (as Cuba would be allowed to determine when a player was posted) and help restore respectability to the game on the island (which may become an economic asset under economic reform). At the same time, the system would illustrate resurgent baseball on the island as a representation of the success of New Cuba just as it once was touted as a triumph of Cuban socialism.

Several people in the baseball industry believe that anticipation of such a system is another reason talent has fled the island as players seek deals more representative of a full market than the one that might be waiting for them when the Cuban Thaw is complete. It's an ironic theory when you consider that any sort of organized pipeline between the two entities is almost universally touted by the American media as a way of ending the often harrowing nature of defections.

Ironically, as Cuban players have looked to take their skills to the United States more frequently, American interest in bringing major league baseball to Cuba as part of future expansion has increased. MLB commissioner Rob Manfred, when asked about the possibility of expansion into Cuba, responded, "a lot would have to happen in Cuba to get to a position where it could support a team economically."

Several barriers prevent short-term expansion of major league baseball into Cuba. The primary one is that most Cubans don't have any sort of income, let alone the kind of disposable incomes a major league team would need to siphon away from a city's populace to support a team. Even if Havana were to become an economically fertile city, it may not have enough people to support a team. Havana's estimated population is about 2.1 million people. The only metropolitan statistical area under two million currently with a major league team is Milwaukee (just shy of 1.6 million as of a 2014 Census Bureau estimate). Smaller American cities, like Memphis, have been able to support a major pro sports team when it's the only ticket in town and cities with comparable populations to Havana, like Kansas City and Cleveland, have supported more than one.

That Manfred has had responses for questions about Cuba holstered and ready for immediate use is a sign that MLB has discussed internally the possibility of eventually expanding there. But it would take decades of reform in Cuba and decades worth of evidence of the positive effects of those reforms for Cuba to have the infrastructure to support an major league team—and for MLB to feel good about planting its flag in the ground there.

In the meantime, scouts have identified about a half dozen prospects currently on the island who may be of big league interest. The best is 20-year-old outfielder Luis Robert, a well-built and projectable athlete with a shot to be a middle-of-the-order hitter with above-average bat-to-ball skills and plus raw power. Robert should at least be a valuable defender in an outfield corner, if not play a viable center field. That would take some of the pressure off his bat and allow him to profile as an everyday player even if his offensive tools mature to just around average.

Two other outfielders, Victor Mesa Jr. (known as Victor Victor in Cuba) and Julio Pablo Martinez also are intriguing to scouts. Some are convinced Mesa, who has deep familial ties in Cuban baseball and is essentially the heir to the Cuban baseball throne now that the Gurriel brothers have defected, will remain on the island, while others think too much money is involved to consider sentimentalities. The compact Mesa has less physical projection than Robert but is a better bet to stay in center field and has some pull power. Martinez is a free-swinging outfielder with above-average speed and has shown an ability to golf homers out to his pull side, but he may never make enough contact to be more than a platoon option or fourth outfielder.

Three other prospects of note are pitchers. Right-handed pitchers Hector Mendoza and Yunier Cano both flash mid-90s fastballs, but Mendoza has strike-throwing issues, and Cano's repertoire is shallow. Many scouts think both will end up in relief should they defect. Diminutive lefty changeup artist Livan Moinelo might one day have three average or better pitches, but few are convinced he has the physical make-up to handle a starter's workload in the States.

While all of these young men are solid, if flawed, prospects, they're a far cry from the freaky tooled-up athletes who have invaded North American diamonds over the past half-decade.

Despite recent dialogue between President Barack Obama and leaders in Cuba, many in baseball as well as governmental circles remain hesitant to predict the immediate future of Cuba/U.S. relations, as much of it depends on the outcome of the 2016 U.S. Presidential election. President-elect Donald Trump, just weeks before the election, publicly stated he would undo recent decisions made by President Obama that have reopened diplomatic dialogue with Cuba. Shortly thereafter, reports of Trump conducting illegal business in Cuba during the late 1990s began to surface.

How this might impact short-term relations with Cuba now that Trump is set to become president are difficult to predict.

It requires a good bit of mental gymnastics to envision a bright future for Cuban baseball. Either major league teams will continue their perpetual raid on the island's talent before it ripens on Cuban soil, or there will be a system that exploits the players while benefitting the government and suppressing overall costs for major league owners will be enacted. It's also possibile that economic reform in Cuba occurs in a way that renders baseball on the island relatively meaningless from a financial standpoint, which would give the government little incentive to funnel resources toward developing talent.

Regardless of what occurs, it appears as though the golden age of Cuban baseball, one of the most important and symbolic athletic eras in the history of sports worldwide, already has met an abrupt end.

References & Resources

- Hugh Thomas, *Cuba: The Pursuit of Freedom*, 1971
- Peter C. Bjarkman, *Cuba's Baseball Defectors: The Inside Story*, 2016
- MLB, Collective Bargaining Agreement, *mlb.mlb.com/pa/pdf/cba_english.pdf*
- J. Gordon Hylton, Marquette Law Faculty Blog, "Milwaukee: Still the Smallest Metropolitan Area with a Major League Baseball Team," *law.marquette.edu/facultyblog/2013/05/30/milwaukee-still-the-smallest-metropolitan-area-with-a-major-league-baseball-team*
- Marisa Guthrie, The Hollywood Reporter, "MLB Commissioner on Foreign Expansion to Cuba and Mexico, Instant Replay and Drone Cameras," *hollywoodreporter.com/news/mlb-commissioner-foreign-expansion-cuba-833160*
- Patrick Oppmann, CNN, "Report: Trump violated law by doing business in Cuba," *cnn.com/2016/09/29/politics/donald-trump-cuba-business*
- Gilbert A. Harrison, *New Republic*, "Setting Up the Scapegoat Who Will Be Blamed for Cuba?," *newrepublic.com/article/105062/setting-the-scapegoat-who-will-be-blamed-cuba*
- Jeffrey Cook and Serena Marshall, ABC News, "Historic Flight From US Touches Down in Cuba," *abcnews.go.com/International/jetblue-set-off-historic-flight-cuba/story?id=41717301*
- Rebecca Sanchez, Elissa Curtis and Rachelle Klapheke, MSNBC, "Remembering the Cuban Revolution," *msnbc.com/msnbc/remembering-fidel-castro-and-the-cuban-revolution*
- John Woolley and Gerhard Peters, The American Presidency Project, "Speech of Senator John F. Kennedy, Cincinnati, Ohio, Democratic Dinner," *presidency.ucsb.edu/ws/index.php?pid=25660*
- Danielle Renwick, Brianna Lee, and James McBride, Council on Foreign Relations, "U.S.-Cuba Relations," *cfr.org/cuba/us-cuba-relations/p11113*
- BBC News, "Timeline: US-Cuba relations," *bbc.com/news/world-latin-america-12159943*

The José Fernández Joy Award

by Joon Lee

The idea of potential, more than most things, holds a lot of weight in society. Through high school and college, I've heard many young people talk about what they want to do with their lives. They want to travel the world and experience culture. They want to become a doctor and save lives. They want to write about some athletes playing a kid's game. That time is on their side, that somebody could potentially do anything, keeps people going. If somebody makes a mistake, there's time to turn things around. There's time to make things right.

Potential elicits two drastically different emotions dependent on the tense. When considering the future, there's nothing more exciting. America is built on the idea of potential; it's one of the things that makes this country great. My parents came to the United States, carrying a two-month-old version of myself, because they felt as if living here, away from all of their family and friends, presented the best opportunity for our future. The potential to live the life they desired simply was higher in the U.S.

It's the reason why José Fernández attempted to defect from Cuba on three separate occasions. Beyond all the politics that come with living under a communist regime, the pursuit of playing major league baseball represented the American dream for him. It's how he kept his perspective on the field, never taking things too seriously, but seriously enough to be the best at this craft.

It's the reason why I loved watching Fernández, why lots of fans loved watching him on the mound. Through his bright, wide smile, Fernández looked like each one of us playing pick-up ball with our friends, except at a much higher level. Fernández's right arm threw pitches with more movement than I thought was humanly possible outside video games. On top of being a ball of joy on the field, his performance made him the rare baseball player who was just impossible to dislike. You admired his performance on the mound, and you admired how much he enjoyed playing the game.

For even the old guard of baseball, Fernández's love for the game was undeniable. In a piece reported for *Sports Illustrated* by S.L. Price, utility man Chris Johnson recalled meeting him upon joining the Marlins. When Johnson was an Atlanta Brave, he and Fernández got into an altercation after Fernández disrespected him and his team by admiring a home run. Johnson felt nervous about meeting the pitcher in wake of their previous animosity.

"I couldn't have been more wrong," Johnson told Price. Fernández welcomed Johnson immediately and Johnson realized he'd been wrong about his new teammate.

"He's not showing up any player up," Johnson said. "He's out there completely free, having as much fun as possible. And then him getting out of Cuba, we talked about how he got caught and went to jail and didn't see his mom, and didn't know how long he was going to be in jail because they don't tell you over there: stuff I never knew. I'm mad at myself for having that altercation."

But what Johnson told Price next defines Fernández's legacy, looking past his ability to manipulate a baseball like an air bender.

"He changed me," Johnson said. "I smile. Before, I was always intense and took the game as a job and had to make it, and had to stay in the big leagues, had to get the contract, had to be the guy. No. You didn't have to do anything. You made it, you got to the big leagues. You're in the United States of America, got a beautiful family. This game is fun. He played the game how I played the game in Little League. That's how everybody should be in the big leagues."

For all the talent Fernández possessed—and really, that talent was infinite—the most notable thing about his presence on a baseball field was not his ability to snap off breaking balls like nobody else in the sport or that he could make some of the greatest athletes in the world look as if they had never played baseball before. It was the pure joy he exuded on the field, the kind of joy you see in a toy store, the kind of joy you see in the Little League World Series.

In the wake of Fernández's passing, many folks began to brainstorm ways they could honor the pitching prodigy. The idea that resonated with me was creating an award honoring the player who best embodied the spirit of having fun while playing baseball, in memory of Fernández. Joy, of course, can be embodied in so many different ways, whether that's through the exuberance Fernández brought to the field over the day or through pure goofiness, like Adrián Beltré.

Among the awards that Major League Baseball presents on an annual basis, the Cy Young, Hank Aaron and the Relief Man (named after Mariano Rivera in the American League, Trevor Hoffman in the National League), and the batting titles (Rod Carew in the AL, Tony Gwynn in the NL) represent the accolades named after a player. The trend amongst these players is the legendary greatness each demonstrated at their particular skill set, unmatched by few in the game's history.

Fernández's youthful playing style will be forever youthful. His death at 24 years old will ensure that his memory will always be of child-like exuberance and enthusiasm for the game. For all of the magic Fernández brought to the mound, he somehow was even more of a lightning rod as someone passionate for the game of baseball. For all of the great enthusiastic spokesmen for the game through its history, Fernández stood out because of everything he could've brought to the game at a time when many claim baseball needs to do a better job of luring eyes away from the glow of our smartphones.

Of course, if this award were to become a real thing, Fernández deserves the inaugural honor. But there are other players who embody this spirit of the game. And as the world around baseball continues to speed up, with Snapchat, Instagram, Twitter and whatever else is invented in the coming years, these players will only continue to become more and more important to the sustainability of the sport.

Francisco Lindor

A lot of things make Francisco Lindor one of the most fun players to watch on a nightly basis. Over the course of 2016, Lindor was not only one of the most consistent hitters at the shortstop position, he routinely made plays in the field that left people in awe. The 22-year-old Cleveland star undoubtedly would be one of the most talked-about young stalwarts in baseball if he was playing in a major market.

Lindor finished the year with 6.3 fWAR, second among full-time shortstops, behind just Corey Seager. Much of this value comes from the glove. Lindor ranked second in baseball this year in FanGraphs' defense metric (Def), just barely behind Brandon Crawford, and well ahead of everyone else. That doesn't make Lindor a slouch with the bat, either; he finished sixth in wRC+ behind Seager, Carlos Correa, Asdrubal Cabrera, Jonathan Villar and Xander Bogaerts. Combined with some postseason heroics, he emerged this season as a player you can't take your eyes off.

On top of his performance, there's a lot to love about Lindor. He plays with extremely high energy and is not afraid of a little flair. Once the postseason hit, Lindor unveiled cleats reading "BelieveLand." He plays with confidence and exuberance and, like Fernández, always seems to have a smile on his face while he's out there on the field. Oh, and he changed his walk-up song to the *Space Jam* theme.

Lindor is among the most underappreciated players in this game. Throughout Cleveland's season, Lindor represented one of the major backbones of the team's success. He has a smile that takes up half of his face, practically a magnet for the television cameras. The combination of electric play on the field and Lindor's style makes him one of the game's brightest stars.

Adrián Beltré

My freshman year of college, the biggest (dumbest) argument I got into with one of my friends was over whether Adrián Beltré was a Hall of Famer. I remember turning very red, becoming dumbly frustrated and just generally being stubborn about anyone not thinking Beltré was undeserving of being in enshrined in Cooperstown. Almost four years later, it's undeniable that he ranks among the all-time greats at third base.

Except in his 48-homer 2004 season, Beltré's entire career has been relatively under the radar. But he's consistently, year after year, put up fine numbers. In his age-37 season, Beltré finished with a .300/.358/.521 line with 32 homers while continuing to play some of the best defense at the position.

But what's most notable about Beltré is how he plays the game. He always has a smile on his face, he still messes around with Elvis Andrus, and he still runs away whenever opposing players try to touch his head. Beltré dances around on the baseball field and still mashes dingers on one knee. For as much fun as Beltré has on the field, he performs just as well, the essence of his lovability as a star.

This desire to have fun developed later in his career. In an ESPN profile, Beltré explained that early on, he was so focused on making money for his family that he forgot why he loved playing the game. Then his wife gave him a talk.

"My wife helped me understand everything's not about baseball." It's what you like to do and you get paid for it, but once you're off the field, you have a life. Once I had a baby, I understood that I'm a husband and a father and that's going to come first."

"Then I started enjoying the game," he continued. "I could just go out there and do my job—work hard at it—and let my talent take over."

It's this perspective on the game that makes Beltré a pleasure to watch.

Mookie Betts

The main joy of watching Mookie Betts play baseball is his ability to makes things look effortless. Betts is visually memorable, listed at 5-foot-9, but actually shorter, a scowl on his face, his bat swinging back and forth. He's a striking combination of physically unimposing and incredibly intimidating. When Betts uses that whip-like bat speed and strikes a line drive that zips through the infield in the blink of an eye, it's somehow surprisingly expected.

His numbers at the end of the 2015 season suggested an incoming power surge in 2016, but when he ended 2106 with 31 homers and finished the season hitting clean-up, people were surprised nonetheless. It's the charm of Betts; you're fully aware this guy is one of the best athletes in the sport today—his bowling and basketball accomplishments are well documented—but when he excels at something new—playing the outfield, hitting for home run power—it still raises an eyebrow.

Watching Betts marvel on the field was accented this year when the Red Sox outfield crew began to dance after every win. First, it was a simple "Hit Dem Folks" rendition that slowly grew more complex, integrating a player of the game photo opp that eventually evolved into a dance spotlight. This is when Betts really showed his versatility, breaking out "The Macarena," the "Jump On It," and "The Carlton."

As a Red Sox fan, it's especially fun to think about the ceiling for Betts, or the lack thereof. In just two full seasons, he not only has proven to have an impact bat, but his conversion to the outfield has been an overwhelming success. While adjusting to a new position, Betts led the league in defensive runs saved with 32, a full 10 runs ahead of the second-place finisher, Adam Eaton. That same 10-run gap separates Eaton and ninth-place finisher Brett Gardner.

Mike Trout is head and shoulders above every other player in baseball right now, but Betts leads the pack of that next tier, where he stands with few peers.

Munenori Kawasaki

"Thank you very much. My name is Munenori Kawasaki, I come from Japan, I am Japaneeeeese. My teammates gave me an opportunity, so I wanted to do something about it."

And with one spontaneous, high-energy postgame interview, Munenori Kawasaki entered the consciousness of baseball fans.

To put it bluntly, Kawasaki is by far the least accomplished major leaguer on this list. He's a fringe major leaguer who has hit .237/.320/.289 and has posted 1.3 fWAR and wasn't on the roster as the Cubs went into postseason play. That shouldn't diminish his ability to have fun while playing the game. My editor reminded me before I started writing this article that I wouldn't be able to use any GIFs or embed any videos for this ink-and-paper Annual. Too bad. There's no player whose joy is more unjustly captured by mere words.

Kawasaki became a viral sensation with his endearing enthusiasm for learning the English language and his willingness not to use a translator for interviews. Given he's still learning the language, it shows Kawasaki's self confidence that he's comfortable his humor and sensibilities will shine through despite the language barriers. It's this confidence that led to Kawasaki telling SportsNet Canada, "I'm drunk. We don't need bananas, we need champagne," during the flurry of playoff celebration post-game interviews.

[Insert Munenori Kawasaki dancing montage YouTube video here] Wait, that's not how books work? Ahh, go on YouTube and look it up. It's worth the watch.

Trea Turner

Turner has one of the most exciting skillsets in baseball, combining electric speed with an excellent approach at the plate. For the entire first half of the season, many clamored for the Nationals to bring up the 23-year-old dynamo from the minors to have man center field or second base. And when he finally came up, boy did he make an impact.

While playing 73 games for the Nationals, Turner posted a 162-game pace of .342/.370/.567 with 29 homers, 89 RBI, and 73 stolen bases, with 31 doubles and 18 triples. There has never been a player in baseball history who has put up a comparable season. Of course, it's a moot exercise to compare those extrapolated numbers to players who played full seasons, but it does give a sense for the type of ridiculous impact Turner made after earning a full-time job in the big leagues. Among Turner's peers in fWAR were Bryce Harper (3.5), although Harper needed almost exactly double the games.

Combined with the fact that he looks like a 13-year-old boy in the outfield next to his bearded fellow outfielders in Harper and Jayson Werth, Turner is truly one of the most eye-catching talents in all of baseball. His rare combination of speed with, well, just about everything else makes him someone whose potential career makes your mind wander, thinking about all of the possibilities.

Adam Jones

This summer while interning at *The Washington Post*, I went down to Camden Yards to report on the cultural transition of Hyun Soo Kim. Orioles public relations staff told me to wait in a certain part of the clubhouse for Kim when Adam Jones, sitting slouched in a chair, yelled over.

"Hey, what's up," Jones said.

"Hey, how's it going," I said as I turned back around.

"Dude, I'm your elder. Doesn't Korean culture say you're supposed to bow and greet me?" Jones said with a chuckle and a big smile. He then told me to come over to his locker, eager to talk about how much he enjoyed learning about South Korea from Kim.

Jones is different from some of the other guys on this list. He's very intense when he plays, always focused on maximizing his performance. He plays hard, running out every grounder, every fly ball. Off the field, he doesn't take himself too seriously. He's regularly seen photobombing TV spots of teammates. And he's popular. Buck Showalter once told ESPN writer Tim Kurkjian that Jones could run for mayor of Baltimore when he's done playing baseball.

But what separates Jones is his willingness to speak his mind. He's thoughtful and brutally honest. When asked by *USA Today* about Colin Kaepernick's protest of the National Anthem, Jones said "Baseball is a white man's sport." While the quote certainly jumps off the page, it was rooted in reason rather than emotion. In a sport that tends to skew conservative politically, Jones was unafraid of the backlash that came with a lightning bolt of a quote.

Off the field, Jones also likes to impersonate his manager, something that is known to send Showalter into a fit of belly laughter. And when Tim Tebow announced he was going to pursue a baseball career, Jones responded on Twitter. "After this @MLB season, I'm going try out for the @NFL this offseason. I haven't played since HS but I've played in a few Turkey Bowls since!!"

Bartolo Colón

What more can even be written about Bartolo Colón? His first career home run took over the internet. It was one of the best moments of the baseball season. A lot has been written about the cult supporting Colón. He's a round dude who is 43 years old and still performing at a relatively high level.

Beyond his figure, Colón is a pretty fascinating pitcher. At his age, Colón is still starting at the major league level while also throwing a remarkable number of strikes while also throwing mostly fastballs (89.5 percent). After winning a Cy Young Award with the Angels in 2005, it's pretty remarkable that he remains a relatively effective pitcher more than a decade later

There's a lot to love here. Colón has picked off a runner unassisted, he makes behind-the-back flips to the first basemen, and he makes acrobatic catches coming off the mound. He's one of 34 pitchers who weighed more than 265 pounds and pitched at least 25 innings in the majors. He reportedly can do splits; despite his size, he is freakishly athletic.

For all the love Colón receives from "Baseball Twitter," it's kind of amusing that we don't really know how he feels about it. Whenever Bartolo Colón is pitching during the season, it's hard not to be aware of it. And of course, when he's not pitching in the playoffs, he could livestreaming himself watching baseball while in a pool.

I hope Bartolo Colón pitches forever. Long live Big Sexy.

Thinking about Fernández's passing is a tough exercise. There are so many questions left unanswered about his potential impact on the game. In my relatively short time on this earth, Fernández is one of the most electric exciting pitchers I've ever seen from a raw stuff standpoint. His youth could only feed into the engine of thinking about his potential impact on the game from a statistical standpoint. Lots of phenoms burn out, and Fernández certainly had his injury history, but it didn't feel ludicrous to imagine him putting together an 18-year career in the major leagues before being enshrined to Cooperstown.

Many in years past embodied the excitement and eccentricity that Fernández displayed on the field. In recent years, guys like Brian Wilson, Nyjer Morgan, Omar Vizquel and David Ortiz embodied this same passion for the game. And while I'm not old enough to remember them playing, players like Ernie Banks, Willie Mays, Dave Parker, Fred Lynn, Luis Tiant, Sean Casey, Kenny Lofton, Ozzie Smith, Tony Gwynn, and of course, Pedro Martínez, seemed to as well.

But what most excited me about Fernández's future was his potential to be a major ambassador for the game for the next generation. Millions of kids would see Fernández on the mound, representing the best the game had to offer. But they also would see his smile, see how much fun he had while on the mound. Fernández was going to help make baseball fun again.

Fernández's potential, I have no doubt, will live on as one of the greatest "what-ifs" in major league history. Even in his short time pitching professionally, Fernández made more of an impact on the game than most can even dream of making. Lots of legends die young, and the potential of what could have been only makes the loss harder.

An award rewarding those living through his spirit only feels appropriate.

References & Resources

- S.L. Price, *Sports Illustrated*, "José Fernández's death hit hard for the Marlins, baseball and Cuban-Americans," *si.com/mlb/2016/10/12/jose-fernandez-miami-marlins-death*

- Jean-Jacques Taylor, ESPN, "Play hard, laugh hard is the essence of Adrián Beltré," *espn.com/mlb/story/_/id/17715167/play-hard-laugh-hard-essence-texas-rangers-adrian-beltre*

- Blair Johnson, Yahoo Sports, "Munenoris Kawasaki interview a classic," *sports.yahoo.com/blogs/yahoo-sports-minute/munenori-kawasaki-interview-classic-074827571.html*

- Bob Nightengale, *USA Today*, "Adam Jones on MLB's lack of Kaepernick protest: 'Baseball is a white man's sport'," *usatoday.com/story/sports/mlb/columnist/bob-nightengale/2016/09/12/adam-jones-orioles-colin-kaepernick-white-mans-sport/90260326*

- Joon Lee, Over the Monster, "Mookie Betts is great at every sport he's ever played," *overthemonster.com/2015/6/30/8422417/mookie-betts-dunking-basketballs-and-being-generally-awesome*

History

The Sultan of Swat Award/ Babe Ruth Crown: A Widely Forgotten Trophy

by Sarah Wexler

It was one of Mickey Mantle's most cherished prizes. Joe DiMaggio once called it "the greatest award in baseball." Willie Stargell declared that he'd "never seen an award so pure" as this. Jesse Barfield boasts of winning it in his Twitter biography. Ted Williams' sold at auction for $200,000. Three of them are on display at the Baseball Hall of Fame.

Now, after a hiatus of almost two decades, the Babe Ruth Crown, originally known as the Sultan of Swat Award, is coming back.

I first spotted one of these trophies at the "Chasing Dreams: Baseball and Becoming American" exhibit, which originated at the National Museum of American Jewish History in Philadelphia before heading to the Skirball Cultural Center in Los Angeles. It's impossible to miss—a bejeweled, red-velvet-lined, golden crown, ornate without being ostentatious. The one I saw bore the following inscription:

Babe Ruth
Sultan of Swat Award
Presented to
Hank Greenberg
For outstanding batting achievement
1938
Maryland Professional Baseball Players' Association

It's difficult to find information about this award, save for scattered references in baseball encyclopedias and old auction house listings. This article aims to fill in some gaps about the history of the award, including a list of all of the prize's recipients, and a list of who would have won the prize for each season after its cessation.

The History of the Sultan of Swat/Babe Ruth Crown

The Sultan of Swat Award was first given by the Maryland Professional Baseball Players' Association in 1957, at its fourth annual Tops in Sports Banquet. The MPBPA was an organization whose purpose was to "get together all professional baseball players who played in Maryland," according to former president Frank Sliwka. Its membership was open to anybody associated with the state of Maryland who had played baseball professionally for at least one year, or was otherwise connected with professional baseball (e.g., as a general manager, coach, etc.).

Tony Armas' Babe Ruth Crown, which he received at the January, 1985 banquet. (photo courtesy of Babe Ruth Museum)

The Tops in Sports Banquet was the MPBPA's premier event. Proceeds from the banquet went to Johns Hopkins Children's Center for cancer research. The function celebrated several athletes from a variety of sports, not just baseball, and from throughout the country, not just Maryland. For instance, in 1956, Texan Olympic sprinter Bobby Morrow was also honored. Some of the awards given at the Tops in Sports Banquet throughout the years included the Major League Manager of the Year, Most Valuable Oriole, and Star of the Future. However, the Sultan of Swat Award/Babe Ruth Crown was always the evening's biggest honor.

Louis Grasmick, the banquet's founder, was also responsible for the conception of the Sultan of Swat Award. The life-sized, wearable crown's value was estimated at $3,800 in 1956 ($33,268 in 2016 dollars). In addition to the crown, the award came with a trophy that featured "a figural brass batter atop of a red velvet king's crown having inset colored 'gems'" mounted on a mahogany base.

For the first seven years of the Sultan of Swat Award's existence, a crown was given to one top offensive performer from the prior baseball season. For the first three years, the winners were simply nominated without any particular criteria. That changed in 1960, when Sliwka devised the following point system to determine who would receive the award, weighting the three Triple Crown stats across all of baseball:

- Four points for leading MLB in home runs
- Three points for leading MLB in RBI
- Two points for leading MLB in batting average
- Tiebreaker: One point for total bases

Sliwka takes pride in this methodology because it is so straightforward. Under this weighting system, the home run leader usually took the prize, though there were seasons where exceptionally productive batters prevailed over the leading sluggers. The resulting list of Babe Ruth Crown winners is both illustrious and fascinating, featuring many players who wound up being inducted into the Hall of Fame, and several others who had respectable careers but only a few especially noteworthy seasons.

The first winner of the Sultan of Swat Award was Mickey Mantle, in 1956; he also won a second crown that year: the American League triple crown. Three other men would receive the award the year they won the triple crown: Frank Robinson (1966), Carl Yastrzemski (1967), and Joe Medwick (1937, awarded retroactively in 1968). Jimmie Foxx received the retroactive Babe Ruth Crown for his 1932 season, while he won the Triple Crown in 1933.

In 1964, the MPBPA began awarding a retroactive Sultan of Swat Award in addition to the active player crown. That year, the organization recognized Joe DiMaggio's 1939 season. The retroactive Sultan of Swat Award was given for specific seasons through 1971, and then became a lifetime achievement award.

In 1967, the title of the prize officially changed from the "Sultan of Swat Award" to the "Babe Ruth Crown" (although the two titles were still used interchangeably by the press for some time). Sliwka explained that while most baseball fans are familiar with "Sultan of Swat" as a nickname for Ruth, the MPBPA felt that having the Babe's name in the award title was a better way of putting the focus on Ruth himself and on his Maryland upbringing. Babe Ruth's widow, Claire, presented three awards at the banquet that year—though interestingly, not the Babe Ruth Crown.

Thirteen men received multiple Sultan of Swat Awards/Babe Ruth Crowns, either active or retroactive. Chronologically from their first award, they are:

- Mickey Mantle: 1956, 1986 (retroactive)
- Eddie Mathews: 1959, 1987 (retroactive)
- Roger Maris: 1960, 1961
- Willie Mays: 1962, 1965
- Hank Aaron: 1963, 1978 (retroactive)
- Harmon Killebrew: 1964, 1969, 1988 (retroactive)

- Frank Robinson: 1966, 1982 (retroactive)
- Johnny Bench: 1970, 1972, 1996 (retroactive)
- Willie Stargell: 1973, 1991 (retroactive)
- Mike Schmidt: 1974, 1976, 1980, 1981
- Jim Rice: 1978, 1983, 1993 (retroactive)
- Cecil Fielder: 1991, 1992
- Juan Gonzalez: 1993, 1994

Four men won the Sultan of Swat Award/Babe Ruth Crown in consecutive seasons: Roger Maris (1960, 1961), Mike Schmidt (1980, 1981), Cecil Fielder (1991, 1992), and Juan Gonzalez (1993, 1994).

Two teams are tied with the most active Babe Ruth Crown recipients, at five: the Phillies (four times by Mike Schmidt) and the Red Sox. The Yankees and Giants had four active winners, and the Cubs, Rangers/Senators and Reds had three apiece. Twelve teams never had a winner.

At its 1985 Tops in Sports Banquet, the MPBPA honored Sadaharu Oh's legendary career by awarding him a Babe Ruth Crown, making him the first and only non-MLB recipient of the prize.

Almost every recipient of the Babe Ruth Crown attended the banquet—generally held in mid-January, though I could not confirm the date of every banquet—to receive his award, though there were a few exceptions. Willie Mays missed the 1966 banquet due to a fever. Illness prevented Jimmie Foxx from claiming his retroactive crown in 1967. In 1973, Johnny Bench's parents accepted his crown on his behalf while Bench was recovering from lung surgery. Inclement weather postponed the 1996 banquet, which kept that year's recipient, Albert Belle, from attending.

The absent attendee who left Sliwka the most ired, though, was Jose Canseco, in 1989. "He was terrible," Sliwka recalls. "I went down to the airport to pick him up, and he told me the night before to send him first-class airplane tickets from Miami to Baltimore for his girlfriend, his father and his brother...and he didn't show up!" After a series of communications with Canseco's agent that involved more requests from Canseco for first class tickets, Sliwka discovered that Canseco had been cashing in the plane tickets and had no intention of ever attending the banquet.

In the January following the strike-shortened 1994 season, the MPBPA decided, after some deliberation, to hold its annual banquet, but not to award an active player crown. The organization awarded just a retroactive crown that year, to Lee May.

The final year the award was given was 1997. According to the program for the 1998 Tops in Sports Banquet, no Babe Ruth Crown was given that year. The Tops in Sports Banquet ran until 1999, when the event was canceled due to a conflict with the Orioles.

The Maryland Professional Baseball Players' Association

The Maryland Professional Baseball Players' Association's founders were three former professional baseball players: Herb Armstrong, Johnny Neun and Eddie Rommel.

Armstrong, born in Cambridge, Mass. in 1893, played seven seasons of minor league ball, and later served as business manager for the Orioles. He lived in Baltimore until his death in 1984 at the age of 91.

Neun and Rommel were both Baltimore natives. Born in 1900, Neun played professionally from 1920 through 1937. The switch-hitting Neun served as backup first baseman for the Detroit Tigers from 1925 through 1928, and then for the Boston Braves from 1930 to 1931. Neun is perhaps best remembered for completing an unassisted triple play, which ended the Tigers' May 31, 1927 match against Cleveland. He died in Baltimore in 1990, at the age of 89.

Rommel, born in 1897, today is regarded as the father of the modern knuckleball. He spent his entire 13-year career, which spanned from 1920 until 1932, with Connie Mack's Philadelphia Athletics. Rommel's 27 wins in 1922 earned him second place in MVP voting, behind George Sisler. He holds the record for most batters faced in relief in a game, at 87. Rommel would later become a professional umpire. He died in Baltimore in 1970, at the age of 72.

The MPBPA had its first meeting in the executive room at Churchill Limited, a whiskey distribution plant in South Baltimore. The organization soon decided to dedicate itself to recognizing and honoring sports figures that were either from Maryland or associated with Maryland sports teams. One of the association's projects was the creation of the Maryland Shrine of Immortals, which commemorated the achievements of notable baseball players hailing from the state.

Banquet founder Grasmick, who passed away in May of 2016 at the age of 91, was a former Philadelphia Phillies farmhand. Sliwka, signed by the Boston Braves in 1952, played minor league ball for a year.

The MPBPA disbanded in 2004 when Sliwka was appointed a state judge, and "there was no one to lead the organization anymore." Sliwka, now retired, still resides in Maryland.

Recipients of the Sultan of Swat Award/Babe Ruth Crown

Here is a complete list of the award's winners, including their batting stats, along with some additional notes about the prize and the Tops in Sports Banquet. Though most of the winners do meet the criteria specified by Sliwka, there are a few instances where, for whatever reason, that's not the case; such instances are denoted below. The active year winners are in the first table, with a table for the retroactive winners following it.

Banquet Year	Winner	Stats	Notes
		Babe Ruth Sultan of Swat Active Winners, by Year	
1957	Mickey Mantle (Yankees, 1956)	52 HR, 130 RBI, .353 AVG	Mantle's 1956 Triple Crown season earned him the title of AL MVP. He would win MVP again the following season.
1958	Ted Williams (Red Sox, 1957)	37 HR, 87 RBI, .388 AVG	Williams led MLB in AVG and OPS (1.257). He finished second in the AL MVP voting to Mantle. He was crowned at the banquet by that year's NL batting champ, Stan Musial.
1959	Ernie Banks (Cubs, 1958)	47 HR, 129 RBI, .313 AVG	Banks, the 1958 (and 1959) NL MVP, led MLB in HR and RBI. He also led the NL in SLG (.614).
1960	Eddie Mathews (Braves, 1959)	46 HR* (4 points), 114 RBI, .306 AVG	Mathews's 46 home runs led MLB. He finished second that season in NL MVP voting to Banks.
1961	Roger Maris (Yankees, 1960)	39 HR, 112 RBI, .283 AVG	Maris was the first winner of this award to have batted below .300. He did, however, lead the AL in RBI, and in SLG (.581). He was the 1960 AL MVP. The winner, according to the provided points system, should have actually been Ernie Banks, that year's MLB home run leader.
1962	Roger Maris (Yankees, 1961)	61 HR* (4 points), 141 RBI, .269 AVG	Maris hit his then record-breaking 61 home runs that year. He became the first two-time Sultan of Swat Award winner, and the first to take home the prize in consecutive years. He was the 1961 AL MVP.
1963	Willie Mays (Giants, 1962)	49 HR* (4 points), 141 RBI, .304 AVG	Mays led MLB in home runs. He finished second in the NL MVP voting to Maury Wills. He missed the banquet that year due to a fever.
1964	Hank Aaron (Braves, 1963)	44 HR, 130 RBI* (3 points), .319 AVG	Aaron tied to lead the NL in home runs with Willie McCovey. Aaron led MLB in RBI and OPS (.977). The winner, according to the provided points system, actually should have been Harmon Killebrew, that year's MLB home run leader. This was the first time the Crown was awarded retroactively.
1965	Harmon Killebrew (Twins, 1964)	49 HR* (4 points), 111 RBI, .270 AVG	Killebrew's 49 home runs in 1964 led MLB.
1966	Willie Mays (Giants, 1965)	52 HR* (4 points), 112 RBI, .317 AVG	This was Mays' second Sultan of Swat Award. He led MLB in home runs and OPS (1.043), and.was that year's NL MVP.
1967	Frank Robinson (Orioles, 1966)	49 HR* (4 points), 122 RBI, .316 AVG	Not only did Robinson win the Triple Crown for his 1966 season, he also led MLB in OPS (1.047) and was named AL MVP.
1968	Carl Yastrzemski (Red Sox, 1967)	44 HR* (4 points), 121 RBI* (3 points), .326 AVG	Yastrzemski, the 1967 AL MVP, led MLB in HR, RBI and OPS (1.040).
1969	Frank Howard (Senators, 1968)	44 HR* (4 points), 106 RBI, .274 AVG	Howard led MLB in HR and SLG (.552), and was an All-Star that season.

1970	Harmon Killebrew (Twins, 1969)	49 HR* (4 points), 140 RBI* (3 points), .276 AVG	This was Killebrew's second time winning the award. That year's AL MVP, he led MLB in HR and RBI, and led the AL in OBP (.427), in part due to his league-leading 145 walks.
1971	Johnny Bench (Reds, 1970)	45 HR* (4 points), 148 RBI* (3 points), .293 AVG	Bench, the 1970 NL MVP, led MLB in HR and RBI.
1972	Joe Torre (Cardinals, 1972)	24 HR, 137 RBI* (3 points), .363 AVG* (2 points)	Torre led MLB in RBI and AVG.
1973	Johnny Bench (Reds, 1972)	40 HR* (4 points), 125 RBI* (3 points), .270 AVG	Bench, the 1972 NL MVP, led MLB in HR and RBI. This was Bench's second time receiving the Babe Ruth Crown. He could not attend the banquet due to lung surgery. His parents accepted on his behalf.
1974	Willie Stargell (Pirates, 1973)	44 HR* (4 points), 119 RBI* (3 points), .299 AVG	Stargell led MLB in HR, RBI, and OPS (1.038). He was second in MVP voting, losing to Pete Rose.
1975	Mike Schmidt (Phillies, 1974)	36 HR* (4 points), 116 RBI, .282 AVG	Schmidt led MLB in HR, and he led the NL in SLG (.546).
1976	Greg Luzinski (Phillies, 1975)	34 HR, 120 RBI* (3 points), .300 AVG	Luzinski, that year's MLB RBI leader, was a 1975 All-Star and the NL MVP runner-up. The winner, according to the provided points system, actually should have been Mike Schmidt, that year's MLB home run leader.
1977	Mike Schmidt (Phillies, 1976)	38 HR* (4 points), 107 RBI, .262 AVG	This was Schmidt's second Babe Ruth Crown. For the third season in a row, he led MLB in HR. Thomson, known best for his pennant-clinching "shot heard 'round the world" in 1951, was a three-time All-Star.
1978	George Foster (Reds, 1977)	52 HR* (4 points), 149 RBI* (3 points), .320 AVG	Foster, the 1977 NL MVP, led MLB in HR and RBI, and led the NL in OPS (1.013).
1979	Jim Rice (Red Sox, 1978)	46 HR* (4 points), 139 RBI* (3 points), .315 AVG	Rice, the 1978 NL MVP, led MLB in HR and RBI, and led the NL in OPS (.970). He also led MLB in hits (213).
1980	Dave Kingman (Cubs, 1979)	48 HR* (4 points), 115 RBI, .288 AVG	Kingman led MLB in HR, and led the NL in OPS (.956).
1981	Mike Schmidt (Phillies, 1980)	48 HR* (4 points), 121 RBI, .286 AVG	This was Schmidt's third Crown, making him the first (and only) player to receive the prize for active players more than twice. He led MLB in HR, and led the NL in RBI and OPS (1.004). He was that year's NL MVP.
1982	Mike Schmidt (Phillies, 1981)	31 HR* (4 points), 91 RBI, .316 AVG	This was Schmidt's fourth Crown. He led MLB in HR, RBI, and OPS (1.080), and was the NL MVP for the second year in a row.

1983	Gorman Thomas (Brewers, 1982)	39 HR* (4 points), 112 RBI, .245 AVG	Thomas led MLB in HR in 1982. This Tops in Sports Banquet was notable because Joe Altobelli, who would be the Orioles manager in 1983, fell off the stage while presenting an award and had to be taken to the hospital.
1984	Jim Rice (Red Sox, 1983)	39 HR, 126 RBI* (3 points), .305 AVG	Rice led the NL in home runs, and MLB in RBI. This was Rice's second Babe Ruth Crown. The winner, according to the provided points system, actually should have been Mike Schmidt, that year's MLB home run leader.
1985	Tony Armas (Red Sox, 1984)	43 HR* (4 points), 123 RBI* (3 points), .268 AVG	Armas led MLB in HR and RBI in 1984.
1986	Don Mattingly (Yankees, 1985)	35 HR, 145 RBI* (3 points), .324 AVG	Mattingly, the 1985 AL MVP, led MLB in RBI. The winner, according to the provided points system, actually should have been Darrell Evans, that year's MLB HR leader.
1987	Jesse Barfield (Blue Jays, 1986)	40 HR* (4 points), 108 RBI, .289 AVG	Barfield led MLB in HR, and received a Silver Slugger Award. Mathews was a 12-time All-Star. He twice led MLB in home runs.
1988	Andre Dawson (Cubs, 1987)	49 HR* (4 points), 137 RBI* (3 points), .287 AVG	Dawson, the 1987 NL MVP, led MLB in HR and RBI in '87. He also received a Silver Slugger Award.
1989	Jose Canseco (Athletics, 1988)	42 HR* (4 points), 124 RBI* (3 points), .307 AVG	Canseco, the 1988 AL MVP, led MLB in HR, RBI, and SLG (.569). He also received a Silver Slugger Award. Canseco caused quite a stir when he backed out of his commitment to attend the banquet.
1990	Kevin Mitchell (Giants, 1989)	47 HR* (4 points), 125 RBI* (3 points), .291 AVG	Mitchell, the 1989 NL MVP, led MLB in HR, RBI, and OPS (1.023).
1991	Cecil Fielder (Tigers, 1990)	51 HR* (4 points), 132 RBI* (3 points), .277 AVG	Fielder, the 1991 AL MVP runner-up, led MLB in both HR and RBI.
1992	Cecil Fielder (Tigers, 1991)	44 HR* (4 points), 133 RBI* (3 points), .261 AVG	Fielder led MLB in RBI in 1992.
1993	Juan Gonzalez (Rangers, 1992)	43 HR* (4 points), 109 RBI, .260 AVG	Gonzalez led MLB in HR in 1992.
1994	Juan Gonzalez (Rangers, 1993)	46 HR* (4 points), 118 RBI, .310 AVG	Gonzalez led MLB in HR in 1993, and led the AL in SLG (.632). He was the final consecutive-season Babe Ruth Crown recipient.
1995	n/a	n/a	There was no active winner crowned this year due to the 1994 MLB strike.
1996	Albert Belle (Cleveland, 1995)	50 HR* (4 points), 126 RBI, .317 AVG	Belle, the 1992 AL MVP runner-up, led MLB in HR and SLG (.690), and led the AL in RBI. He also received a Silver Slugger Award. The Banquet, usually hosted in January, was postponed until February this year due to inclement weather. Belle did not attend.
1997	Mark McGwire (Athletics, 1996)	52 HR* (4 points), 113 RBI, .312 AVG	McGwire led MLB in HR, SLG and OPS in 1996.

Babe Ruth Sultan of Swat Retroactive Winners, by Year

Banquet Year	Winner	Stats	Notes
1964	Joe DiMaggio (Yankees, 1939)	30 HR, 126 RBI, .381 AVG	This was the first time the Crown was awarded retroactively. DiMaggio's .381 AVG in 1939 was the best of his career, and he won the MVP for his efforts that season.
1965	Hank Greenberg (Tigers, 1938)	58 HR, 147 RBI, .315 AVG	In 1938, Greenberg fell two home runs short of tying Babe Ruth's single-season record of 60.
1966	Johnny Mize (Giants, 1947)	51 HR, 138 RBI, .302 AVG	Mize led MLB in home runs and RBI in 1947.
1967	Jimmie Foxx (Athletics, 1932)	58 HR, 169 RBI, .364 AVG	Foxx, the 1932 AL MVP, led MLB in HR, RBI and OPS (1.218) that season. He could not attend the banquet due to illness.
1968	Joe Medwick (Cardinals, 1937)	31 HR, 154 RBI, .374 AVG	Medwick won the 1937 NL MVP award and triple crown.
1969	Bill Dickey (Yankees, 1937)	29 HR, 133 RBI, .332 AVG	Dickey was an 11-time All-Star, including in 1937.
1970	Charlie Gehringer, (Tigers, 1924-1942)	184 HR, 1,427 RBI, .320 AVG	Gehringer, the 1937 AL MVP, was a six-time All-Star. I could not pinpoint a specific year for which Gehringer received the award. The Associated Press story about the event identified the award as being for Gehringer's "hitting feats of the past."
1971	Bill Terry (Giants, 1930)	23 HR, 129 RBI, .401 AVG	Terry was the last National Leaguer to hit .400. He led MLB with hits in 1930, with 254.
1972	Frankie Frisch (1919 - 1937)	105 HR, 1,244 RBI, .316 AVG	At this point, the retroactive Babe Ruth Crown appears to be given based on lifetime achievement. Frisch was a three-time All-Star who won the NL MVP in 1931.
1973	Stan Musial (Cardinals, 1941-1963)	475 HR, 1,951 RBI, .331 AVG	Musial was a 24-time All-Star (across 20 seasons—some years had two All-Star Games), and a three-time MVP. He missed 1945 due to military service.
1974	Ralph Kiner (1946-1955)	369 HR, 1,015 RBI, .279 AVG	Kiner was a six-time All-Star, who started off his career by leading the NL in HR for six consecutive seasons.
1975	Yogi Berra (Yankees, 1946-1963, 1965)	358 HR, 1,430 RBI, .285 AVG	Berra was an 18-time All-Star, and a three-time MVP.
1976	Ted Kluszewski (1947-1961)	279 HR, 1,028 RBI, .298 AVG	Kluszewski was a four-time All-Star, and the 1954 NL MVP runner-up, when he also led the majors in HR.
1977	Bobby Thomson (1946-1960)	264 HR, 1,026 RBI, .270 AVG	Thomson, known best for his pennant-clinching "shot heard 'round the world" in 1951, was also a three-time All-Star.
1978	Hank Aaron (1954-1976)	755 HR, 2,297 RBI, .305 AVG	Aaron was a 25-time All-Star and the 1957 NL MVP. At the time, Aaron's career 755 home runs was the record. His 2,297 RBI are still the MLB record.
1979	Duke Snider (1947-1964)	407 HR, 1,333 RBI, .295 AVG	Snider was an eight-time All-Star, and one of the original Boys of Summer.

1980	Al Kaline, (1953-1974)	399 HR, 1,582 RBI, .297 AVG	Kaline, an 18-time All-Star, led MLB with 41 HR in 1961.
1981	Brooks Robinson (1955-1977)	268 HR, 1,357 RBI, .267 AVG	Robinson, the 1964 AL MVP, was an 18-time All-Star.
1982	Frank Robinson (1956-1976)	586 HR, 1,812 RBI, .294 AVG	Robinson was the Rookie of the Year, a two-time MVP, and a 14-time All-Star.
1983	Willie McCovey (1959-1980)	521 HR, 1,555 RBI, .270 AVG	McCovey, the 1959 NL Rookie of the Year and 1969 NL MVP, was a six-time All-Star.
1984	Boog Powell (1961-1977)	339 HR, 1,187 RBI, .266 AVG	Powell was the 1970 AL MVP, and a four-time All-Star. He played all 17 seasons of his career for the Orioles.
1985	Billy Williams (1959-1976); Sadaharu Oh (1959-1980)	Williams: 426 HR, 1,475 RBI, .290 AVG; Oh: 868 HR, 2,170 RBI, .301 AVG	Williams was the 1961 Rookie of the Year, and a six-time All-Star. Sadaharu Oh, the Nippon Professional Baseball League's career home run king, is the only non-MLB player to be given this honor.
1986	Mickey Mantle (1951-1968)	536 HR, 1,509 RBI, .298 AVG	Mantle was a three-time MVP and a 20-time All-Star. He was the first recipient of the active player crown.
1987	Eddie Mathews (1952-1968)	512 HR, 1,453 RBI, .271 AVG	Mathews was a 12-time All-Star. He twice led MLB in HR. Mathews received an active player crown in 1959.
1988	Harmon Killebrew (1954-1975)	573 HR, 1,584 RBI, .256 AVG	Killebrew, the 1969 AL MVP and an 13-time All-Star, won two active Babe Ruth Crowns.
1989	Pete Rose (1963-1986)	135 HR, 1,314 RBI, .303 AVG	Rose, the 1963 NL Rookie of the Year, 1973 MVP, a 17-time All-Star, and, of course, the all-time MLB hits leader, may not be in the Hall of Fame, but he does have this honor.
1990	Joe Morgan (1963-1984)	268 HR, 1,133 RBI, .271 AVG	Morgan was a two-time MVP and 10-time All-Star.
1991	Willie Stargell (1962-1982)	475 HR, 1540 RBI, .282 AVG	Stargell, a six-time All-Star and the 1979 NL MVP, had previously received the active Sultan of Swat Award, for his 1973 season.
1992	Rocky Colavito (1955-1968)	374 HR, 1,159 RBI, .266 AVG	Colavito was a six-time All-Star, and three times he finished in the top five in the AL MVP voting.
1993	Jim Rice (1974-1989)	382 HR, 1,451 RBI, .298 AVG	Rice, an eight-time All-Star and the 1978 AL MVP, received the active Babe Ruth Crown twice.
1994	Tony Perez (1964-1986)	379 HR, 1,652 RBI, .279 AVG	Perez was a seven-time All-Star.
1095	Lee May (1965-1982)	354 HR, 1,244 RBI, .267 AVG	May, a three-time All-Star, spent six seasons with the Orioles.
1996	Johnny Bench (1967-1983)	389 HR, 1,376 RBI, .267 AVG	Bench, a 14-time All-Star and two-time MVP, received the active Babe Ruth Crown twice.
1997	Dale Murphy (1976-1993)	398 HR, 1,266 RBI, .265 AVG	Murphy was a seven-time All-Star and two-time MVP.

Who Would Have Won?

Since the system for awarding the Babe Ruth Crown is so straightforward, it's easy to determine who would have won the active player award from 1998 through 2015. Just for fun, here's that list.

Year	Player	Stats
Prospective Babe Ruth Crown Winners		
1998	Mark McGwire (A's/Cardinals, 1997)	58 HR* (4 points), 123 RBI, .274 AVG
1999	Mark McGwire (Cardinals, 1998)	70 HR* (4 points), 147 RBI, .299 AVG
2000	Mark McGwire (Cardinals, 1999)	65 HR* (4 points), 147 RBI, .278 AVG
2001	Todd Helton (Rockies, 2000)	42 HR, 147 RBI* (3 points), .372 AVG* (2 points)
2002	Barry Bonds (Giants, 2001)	73 HR* (4 points), 137 RBI, .328 AVG
2003	Alex Rodriguez (Rangers, 2002)	57 HR* (4 points), 142 RBI* (3 points), .300 AVG
2004	Alex Rodriguez (Rangers, 2003)	47 HR* (4 points), 118 RBI, .298 AVG
2005	Adrián Beltré (Dodgers, 2004)	48 HR* (4 points), 121 RBI, .334 AVG
2006	Andruw Jones (Braves, 2005)	51 HR* (4 points), 128 RBI, .263 AVG
2007	Ryan Howard (Phillies, 2006)	58 HR* (4 points), 149 RBI* (3 points), .313 AVG
2008	Alex Rodriguez (Yankees, 2007)	54 HR* (4 points), 156 RBI* (3 points), .314 AVG
2009	Ryan Howard (Phillies, 2008)	48 HR* (4 points), 146 RBI* (3 points), .251 AVG
2010	Albert Pujols (Cardinals, 2009)	47 HR* (4 points), 135 RBI, .327 AVG
2011	José Bautista (Blue Jays, 2010)	54 HR* (4 points), 124 RBI, .260 AVG
2012	José Bautista (Blue Jays, 2011)	43 HR* (4 points), 103 RBI, .302 AVG
2013	Miguel Cabrera (Tigers, 2012)	44 HR* (4 points), 139 RBI* (3 points), .330 AVG
2014	Chris Davis (Orioles, 2013)	53 HR* (4 points), 138 RBI* (3 points), .286 AVG
2015	Nelson Cruz (Orioles, 2014)	40 HR* (4 points), 108 RBI, .271 AVG
2016	Chris Davis (Orioles, 2015)	47 HR* (4 points), 117 RBI, .262 AVG
2017	Mark Trumbo (Orioles, 2016)	47 HR* (4 points), 108 RBI, .256 AVG

The Future of the Babe Ruth Crown

Though it hasn't been issued since 1997, the Babe Ruth Crown's story has not reached its end. When I contacted the Babe Ruth Museum in Baltimore for information about the award, I learned from the museum's curator, Michael Gibbons, that he plans to bring the Babe Ruth Crown back. Gibbons met with Sliwka "seeking his approval to renew the award under the auspices of the Babe Ruth Museum." Sliwka granted his approval, and provided Gibbons with the prototype for the award. Interestingly, for the past four years, the winner of the Babe Ruth Crown would have been a member of the Baltimore Orioles. It would be an especially triumphant return—and a great way to involve the local community—if the Babe Ruth Museum honored Chris Davis, Nelson Cruz and Mark Trumbo with crowns of their own.

The Babe Ruth Museum plans to use the "same basic criteria" in bestowing the prize that Sliwka and the MPBPA used, although the museum will not be providing additional hardware besides the crown itself. Gibbons says the Babe Ruth Museum hopes to soon begin presenting the award at the museum's annual gala. The gala is a celebration of the Babe's birthday, and usually takes place in February, though the event has been placed on hold for 2017 due to a period of change at the museum. But it's only a matter of time before the top major league sluggers begin receiving these crowns again. Like so many stars of the past, the stars of today will likely cherish this prize as one of the finest out there.

Reference and Resources

- Frank Sliwka, personal interview, July 25, 2016
- Michael Gibbons, personal interview, July 25, 2016
- *Guernsey's*, Mickey Mantle Auction Addendum, 2. *guernseys.com/Guernseys%20New/images/mantle/mantle_addendum.pdf*
- Hunt Auctions, Lot Number: 989. *huntauctions.com/live/imageviewer_online.cfm?auction_num=27&lot_num=989&lot_qual=*
- Newspapers.com
- Baseball-Reference
- Society for American Baseball Research, *sabr.org*
- Wikipedia
- Jesse Barfield's profile, Twitter, *twitter.com/JesseBarfield29*

Kansas City (though, as we'll see, they wouldn't stay long). Still, the sense that the A's were ever-ready to accommodate the Yankees was amplified.

The Swingin' A's

Whatever the Athletics' frantic wheeling-and-dealing achieved, it wasn't an improved ball club. The 1955 team finished at 63-91, in '56 they went 52-102, and the 1957 version would slog in at 59-94. But the interesting aspect of the constant turnover was an extremely oddly assembled roster in '57, yielding one of the most peculiar statistical profiles in major league history.

The 1957 Athletics led the American League in home runs, with 166, and they led by a wide margin. The second-best team hit 153, and the average of the seven other teams in the league was 123. Yet the A's were dead last in the league in runs scored, with 563, and by a wide margin. The next-to-worst offense scored 597, and the average of the seven other teams in the league was 664.

How exactly does a team pull that off? Well, like this:

1. Their team batting average of .244 was quite low, tied for last in the league.
2. They drew just 363 walks, an astonishingly low total, one of the lowest totals in modern major league history.
3. This combination of low batting average and extremely scarce walks yielded a dismal team on-base percentage of just .295.

And because of that:

1. The 1957 A's plated just 397 runs that weren't scored by home run hitters themselves. There have been a few lower totals in history, but not many, and not by much.
2. The percentage of A's "home run runs" (166) divided by their total runs scored (563) was 29.5, one of the very highest such proportions ever presented.

This bizarre arrangement was the result of a roster and lineup gathered opportunistically, almost randomly, without any coherent plan. The A's were just the talent currently available to the A's. And in 1957 it took the form of a dense accumulation of modestly capable free-swinging power hitters with little ability to hit for average.

And that's just one of the weird things about them.

A Collaborative Pitch

Taking a look at the 1957 Athletics' cobbled-together pitching staff, we find no one who qualified for the league earned run average title, pitching at least one inning per scheduled game (154 innings). This was the first time in major league history such a thing had happened, and it wouldn't happen again for another 40 years (when achieved by, interestingly, the 1997 Oakland A's).

The top A's starter (veteran Ned Garver, recovering from arm trouble) made 23 starts and handled 145 innings. The team deployed 11 different pitchers in six or more starts. And this wasn't a function of midseason roster shuffles. In their first 17 games of the season, the Athletics used nine different starting pitchers. At no point did managers Lou Boudreau (fired in early August with the team at 36-67) or Harry Craft fashion a rotation of regular starters and stick with it.

Nor did all those A's starters stick around very long. The 1957 A's had just 26 complete games, the lowest total in major league history up to that time. Yet just like the starting staff, the Athletics' bullpen was a free-for-all. Despite the high frequency of relief stints, only one A's pitcher made as many as 40 relief appearances (40-year-old Virgil Trucks, with 41). Only one other Athletic made as many as 30 (Tom Morgan, with 33). Every single one of the 20 pitchers the team employed that season worked at least once in relief. No pitcher among the 13 who worked in more than 10 games for the A's that season worked exclusively as a starter or reliever.

Irregularity

Just as the pitching was all-hands-on-deck, so was the situation among position players. The 1957 Athletics presented nothing resembling a standard, regular line-up. No Athletic played in more than 135 games or received as many as 500 plate appearances.

Light-hitting shortstop Joe DeMaestri was the only fellow who played in more than 113 games at any single position. Seven different defenders saw action at three or more positions. No one played more than 90 complete games in the outfield, with six players making starts in left field, and eight in right.

One of the principal members of that outfield shuffle was Lou Skizas, who also played 32 games at third base, where the primary incumbent, Héctor López, also played some in the outfield—why not? After picking up Billy Martin in the June trade, the A's declined to deploy him full-time at second base (where they had no one else who batted higher than .191), yet felt it necessary to use Martin in 20 games at third base, too.

The chaos wrought havoc with the batting order, of course. Veteran slugger Gus Zernial started 109 games batting third, and no other Athletic made more than 87 starts at any slot in the order. At leadoff, the A's tried seven different starters, and that was their fewest sharing any spot. In the high spirit of mixing it up, Boudreau batted his starting pitcher in the eighth position for the first 56 games of the season—something he'd never done before in 14 previous years as a big league manager—before abandoning that idea and never doing it again.

But with all of the frenetic lineup-juggling, another peculiarity was that in an era in which a third-string catcher was a given on nearly every roster, for the 1957 Athletics, all season long, no one other than Hal Smith or Tim Thompson spent a single inning behind the plate.

Wheel Spinning

It was a furious ride to nowhere. The A's still wound up losing 94 games, and the thrill was wearing off for Kansas City fans, as attendance in 1957 declined again by more than 100,000 spectators.

To be sure, the organization Johnson had purchased in late 1954 included minimal talent, on the major league roster or in the minor league system. So it's no surprise the new ownership was unable to achieve improved results within the first few years. What's striking about the A's of this era isn't that they were a bad team, but rather that Johnson's management demonstrated no discernable strategy for improvement.

Consider the minors. The six farm clubs comprising the minor league system of the Philadelphia Athletics in 1954 combined for a winning percentage of .475 (377 wins versus 416 losses). That result was 14th worst among the 16 farm systems in baseball. The only chains performing more badly were those of the threadbare Washington Senators organization and the rock-bottom Baltimore Orioles, in their first season removed from the woebegone St. Louis Browns. Johnson didn't dismantle the A's system, but neither did he grow it, nor did he succeed in improving the overall quality of its talent. In no season in his 1955-1960 ownership tenure would the Kansas City organization's minor league record reach the .500 mark. That lackluster system, unsurprisingly, delivered precious little help to the big league roster.

And at the major league level, the chronic flurry of trades seemed guided by no objective beyond turnover for its own sake. The A's didn't endeavor to incrementally make their roster younger, or focus on pitching or speed or defense or power or anything in particular on a sustained basis. It wasn't so much that their trading record was poor in terms of talent-expended-for-talent-received (though they did pull off some head-scratchers) as it was purposeless.

Among the handful of good young players within the organization at the time of Johnson's purchase were first baseman-outfielder Vic Power and infielder-outfielder López. Both would blossom in Kansas City in 1955 and continue to perform well. But rather than recognize them as foundational assets around which the roster could be constructed, the Athletics would soon expend both in trades.

It was in June of 1958 that Power, along with Woodie Held—one of the impressive young players acquired from the Yankees alongside Billy Martin in June of '57—was traded to Cleveland for a package whose key talent was 23-year-old power-hitting center fielder Roger Maris. Just 18 months later, the Athletics would trade Maris to (who else?) the Yankees, in a deal in which the key player coming to Kansas City was outfielder-first baseman Norm Siebern, a fine young player but not as good as Maris, and certainly no better than the combination of Power and Held.

And it was in May of 1959 that López was traded to (who else?) the Yankees, alongside Ralph Terry, the *other* impressive young player acquired in the Martin deal. This time the A's netted Jerry Lumpe, a fine young infielder, but not better than the combination of López and Terry.

Indeed, if any purpose could be detected within the fog of frenzied Kansas City trades in these years, it wasn't to fill the needs of the Athletics as much as the needs of the Yankees. That odious notion prompted baseball historian Joe Reichler, in his epic 1984 compendium *The Baseball Trade Register*, to describe Arnold Johnson's A's as "The Strange Case of the Major League Farm Club."

Moving on

It was on Aug. 8, 1957 that Walter O'Malley announced the Brooklyn Dodgers would be relocating to Los Angeles. It was 11 days later that Horace Stoneham revealed the Giants would be leaving New York as well, and moving to San Francisco. Kansas City's brief prominence as the westernmost location in major league baseball was over.

Like the Braves' 1953 Boston-to-Milwaukee shift, these migrations were nothing unique to baseball. Westward and southward movement was an overriding current in the United States of that era, as the Sun Belt boomed and much of the Northeast and upper Midwest stumbled toward the Rust Belt period.

Transformation was afoot within the cities themselves, as well. Rapid expansion of freeway systems contributed to explosive development of suburban housing tracts and "white flight" population transfers out of inner cities. Kansas City was no exception. The rapid growth and vitality that had characterized the area for decades slowed in the 1950s and '60s, even as its sprawling suburbs expanded. Kansas City's population would peak at just over 500,000 in the 1970 census and then would decline for more than 20 years before leveling off.

The racial demographics of the area dramatically changed. The hollowed-out interior of Kansas City became grim, poor and predominantly African-American. Simmering resentments would explode in April of 1968 following the assassination of Dr. Martin Luther King Jr., as Kansas City became one of many American cities to suffer intense rioting, resulting in five fatalities, dozens of injuries and hundreds of arrests. It would take decades for most downtown Kansas City neighborhoods to regain economic strength.

And Here Come the '60s

It was on Oct. 4, 1957, that the Soviet Union launched Sputnik I, the first artificial Earth satellite. Its success would be shocking, frightening and threatening to the United States military and political establishments and would set in motion the space race and heightened Cold War anxieties.

It was on Dec. 20, 1957, that the Boeing 707 first flew. It would become the first commercially successful jet airliner and usher in the Jet Age worldwide.

It was on July 6, 1957, that 16-year-old John Lennon met 15-year-old Paul McCartney and invited him to join his skiffle band, The Quarrymen.

Arnold Johnson's Kansas City Athletics would never rise above seventh in the standings, and A's attendance would never again approach the giddy heights of 1955. In March of 1960, Johnson would die unexpectedly of a cerebral hemorrhage at 53. Several months later, his estate would sell the Athletics to insurance millionaire Charles O. Finley.

The KC-to-NY shuttle dynamic had been infuriating to Athletics' fans, a point not lost on Finley. His first publicity stunt upon purchasing the franchise was to find an old bus, have "Shuttle Bus to Yankee Stadium" painted on its side, and invite the Kansas City press to watch him, yes, set it on fire.

However, the GM Finley hired was none other than Frank "Trader" Lane, famous as the most prolific wheeler-dealer in the business in stints with the White Sox, Cardinals and Cleveland. (It was Lane who'd traded Maris to Kansas City in 1958). Apparently Lane didn't get the memo about the bus, because in June of 1961 he traded the Athletics' most accomplished pitcher, Bud Daley, to the Yankees in exchange for a now-washed-up Art Ditmar and a prospect (Deron Johnson). Whatever the merits of this deal, it definitely indicated a rescheduling of the shuttle.

Kansas City fans howled, and an embarrassed and infuriated Finley quickly fired Lane. Finley would never again allow a transaction to be executed without his personal approval (eventually he would just give up any pretense and officially serve as his own general manager), and the shuttle was indeed cancelled, with no more deals with the Yankees until 1965.

Finley wasn't just serious about not being subservient to the Bronx Bombers. He was genuinely devoted to improving the competitiveness of the Athletics. He had a keen eye for talent, and following Lane's dismissal, the transactions his organization undertook presented a pattern and method absent in the Johnson era: the A's were scavenging underused, undervalued talent available at bargain rates and seeking to build a foundation based on pitching, speed and defense. In 1962 and 1963, the A's were incrementally improving.

Finley would then commit a significant blunder. In November of 1963, he made big trades for slow-footed, past-their-peak power hitters Rocky Colavito and Jim Gentile, and then moved the Kansas City outfield fences far inward. The gambit bombed, as the 1964 A's surrendered a record 221 home runs and lost 105 games. To his credit, Finley immediately recognized his error, dumped Colavito and Gentile, moved the fences back, and re-focused on his run-prevention strategic direction. But the team's inching progress had been set back at least a year.

More importantly, what Finley had been doing all along was investing in high-quality scouts and building a productive farm system. Such an endeavor necessarily requires a long-term perspective, and it took years to pay off. But pay off it did. By the mid-1960s, youngsters with names such as Bert Campaneris, Catfish Hunter, Rick Monday, Sal Bando, and Reggie Jackson were debuting with the Kansas City Athletics.

Westward Ho

Alas, the bounty would ripen in Oakland. Finley stuck it out in Kansas City for seven losing seasons before heading further westward in 1968, just as the team was ready to be competitive.

Along with a brilliant baseball mind, Finley readily displayed a detestable personality. U.S. Sen. Stuart Symington of Missouri, exasperated in his attempts to persuade Finley to stay in Kansas City, memorably described Oakland as "the luckiest city since Hiroshima."

The Athletics' tenure in Kansas City lasted just 13 frustrating years, never featuring anything close to a winning season. Indeed, as boyhood fan Bill James elaborated in a poignant 1986 essay, "A History of Being a Kansas City Baseball Fan," the Kansas City A's posted losing records in 69 or their 78 months of seasonal existence. The dreary experience amounted to little more than a cynical insult to the eager-beaver local fan base. Altogether, the Kansas City Athletics lurk among the most forlorn episodes in baseball history and never with a stranger manifestation than that of 1957.

References & Resources

- Joseph L. Reichler, *The Baseball Trade Register*, 1984, p. 349.
- Bill James, *The Bill James Baseball Abstract 1986*, 1986, pp. 39-50.

The World Series of Love: The Rolling Stones at Shea Stadium

by Dan Epstein

For most baseball fans, a road trip involving visits to 14 current and former major league stadiums would be something of a dream come true. But for the Rolling Stones in the late summer and fall of 1989, such an expedition was strictly business—or, as they themselves might have put it, only rock n' roll.

It had been eight years since the Stones last performed in North America, and the demand for tickets to their blockbuster Steel Wheels tour was so intense that the band was able to easily sell out gigantic sports facilities in most of the cities they visited. Of the 33 North American venues the band hit between Aug. 31 and Dec. 20, nearly half were (or had previously been) home to major league baseball teams: Philadelphia's Veterans Stadium, Toronto's CNE Stadium and SkyDome, Pittsburgh's Three Rivers Stadium, Riverfront Stadium in Cincinnati, Busch Stadium in St. Louis, RFK Stadium in Washington DC, Cleveland's Municipal Stadium, New York's Shea Stadium, the Los Angeles Memorial Coliseum, the Oakland-Alameda County Coliseum, the Houston Astrodome, the Hubert H. Humphrey Metrodome in Minneapolis and Olympic Stadium in Montreal.

The band's four October 1989 dates at LA's Memorial Coliseum—home to the Los Angeles Dodgers from 1958 through 1961—drew more than 360,000 fans, grossed more than $9 million and garnered the most national press, thanks to the controversial addition of the then up-and-coming Guns N' Roses to the bill. But the Stones' six October concerts at the home of the New York Mets really underscored just how massive the once-notorious band had become in the 27 years since its original formation. The band sold 387,737 tickets for the Shea shows, earning the Stones a reported $11,607,452 (or $22,352,021 in 2016 money), but the six-night stand was also a symbolic success: No band, not even the Beatles, had ever headlined the Flushing Meadows ballpark more than twice. Whatever you thought of their current music, or how well the musicians had aged—other than Ronnie Wood, who'd turned 42 that June, they were all in their mid-to-late 40s—the Stones' stature on the rock n' roll playing field was clearly unequaled.

"It was like a residency," is how Jason Kassin remembers the Stones' Shea concerts, "but in a stadium instead of a club." The co-founder of FilmTrack, Inc., a Los Angeles-based software company, Kassin was a senior at Vassar College when he attended four of the band's six Shea shows. An obsessive Stones fan who'd grown up in Brooklyn, Kassin also caught three other shows on the Steel Wheels tour—in Philadelphia, Syracuse and Atlantic City—but recalls the Shea shows as having a definite "homecoming" vibe. "The Stones were such a New York band, in a weird way," he says. "Mick Jagger and Keith Richards were basically New Yorkers at that point; Keith was actually living above Tower Records in the Village. So even though they were English, they felt like *our* band."

Indeed, Jagger and Richards had maintained residences in New York City since the 1970s, and their affection for the Big Apple and its vibrant culture had come through loud and clear in such Stones songs as "Miss You" and "Shattered" (from 1978's *Some Girls* LP), while "Neighbors" (from 1981's *Tattoo You*) was inspired by Richards' difficulties in finding a Manhattan apartment where he could jam long into the night without getting the police called on him. And then there was the video clip for "Waiting On a Friend" (also from *Tattoo You*), which showed Jagger and Richards looking far more at home on New York's funky St. Marks Place than they would have been in early-'80s London.

Thus, it made perfect sense that the Stones should announce the Steel Wheels tour (as well as the impending new album that gave the tour its name) with a press conference at New York's Grand Central Station. Held on July 11, 1989, the event—attended by over 300 members of the media, with hundreds of fans thronging outside—began with Jagger, Richards, bassist Bill Wyman, drummer Charlie Watts and guitarist Ronnie Wood chugging into the station on an antique caboose. The absurd nature of their entry, along with the apparent good-humored looseness of the five musicians (who hadn't even appeared together in public since 1982), seemed to sharply rebut the breakup rumors that had been swirling about the band for years. The Stones hadn't toured behind their previous two albums, 1983's *Undercover* and 1986's *Dirty Work*, while the release of two Jagger solo albums (1985's *She's The Boss* and 1987's *Primitive Cool*) and one by Richards (1988's *Talk Is Cheap*) had led many to believe the band was dissolving. But at Grand Central, the Stones seemed enthusiastic about being—and touring—together again. "We don't have fights," Jagger told the assembled press while theatrically draping a sinewy arm around Richards. "We just have disagreements."

"It was super-cool, but also goofy," says Kassin, who managed to sneak into the press conference along with his girlfriend. "It was kind of the Ron Wood show, in a way; somebody asked, 'Are you doing it for the money?' And he said, 'No, that's the Who!'" Wood's crack was at the expense of the surviving members of the Who, who had recently reunited for a 25th anniversary tour, and who had played two nights at Shea in October 1982 as part of their previous "farewell tour." Jagger, when asked, sniffed at the suggesting that the Stones would be doing a similar sort of "historical" set on their upcoming trek. "I don't see it as a retrospective or a farewell or anything like that," he said. "It's the Rolling Stones in 1989."

Unlike the Who, the Stones actually had a new album to promote. Jagger treated the press to "a free sample" of the forthcoming *Steel Wheels* LP by holding a portable cassette player up to the microphone as "Mixed Emotions," the album's first single, echoed throughout the room in a distinctly lo-fi fashion. "They were up there with a boom box, playing 'Mixed Emotions' through the mic, and it sounded *terrible*," Kassin laughs. 'Ron Wood was like, 'Listen to the new song—doesn't it sound good?' But it was completely distorted!"

A decent sound system wasn't the only thing noticeably absent from the Grand Central press conference: There was also no mention of any New York City tour dates. Canadian promoter Michael Cohl (who had lured the Stones away from their long-standing relationship with American promoter Bill Graham by offering them a then-unheard-of guarantee of $70 million) told the press that stops in 27 North American cities had been confirmed for the MTV-sponsored tour; but it wouldn't be until Aug 16, over a month after the Grand Central tour announcement, that NYC dates for the Steel Wheels tour were officially revealed. New York City Parks Commissioner Henry J. Stern and local promoter Ron Delsener—who was working with Cohl on the NYC dates—held a joint press conference to announce that the Stones would perform two shows at Shea Stadium, on Oct. 26 and Oct. 28. Tickets, at $30 a pop, would go on sale via Ticketmaster at 9 a.m. on Saturday, Aug. 19, with a limit of eight tickets per buyer.

Though anyone born in the last quarter-century may have difficulty imagining it now, obtaining concert tickets—especially for big-name acts—in the pre-Internet age generally required more effort than just refreshing your browser. You could try repeatedly dialing various local Ticketmaster outlets from your home or work phone, praying you could get through to an operator before all the tickets sold out (or an important call came in); but if you were serious about snagging tickets, you had to stake out a store that housed an actual Ticketmaster desk, and line up hours (or even days) before the show went on sale.

Marty Walsh, now a mobile crane operator for Metro North railroad in Croton-On-Hudson, N.Y., was 25 years old and working as a dairy manager at a Croton A&P when the Stones' first two Shea shows went on sale. He and a friend decided to buy their tickets from a Ticketmaster outlet located in a TSW toy store in nearby Yorktown Heights. He remembers showing up the Friday afternoon before the tickets went on sale in order to snag two of the 250 individually numbered wristbands that were handed out ahead of time to prevent people from camping out overnight (or cutting in line on the day of the sale). "It didn't matter which numbered band we received, because the store would pick a random number to be the first on line," Walsh explains. "Even if someone had wristband #001, if #120 was the number pulled, [the customer with the #120 wristband] would be first in line to purchase the tickets, with subsequent numbers 121, 122, 123, etc., being the next in line."

When Walsh and his friend returned to the store the following morning, they were disappointed to learn that their wristband numbers were fairly low in the lineup, and they watched dejectedly as the tickets for the Oct. 26 show quickly disappeared. "We were lucky to score nosebleeds moments before the second show sold out," Walsh remembers. "But I was really excited, as I had missed out on seeing the Stones the last time they toured, in 1981, and for all we knew this could very well be their last tour, so I was extra-determined to see them at least once."

Walsh and his friend were walking back to his car with their tickets when a cry went up from the fans still remaining in line—a third show, for Oct. 25, had just been added. "We double-timed it back to the line, where we got better seats in the mezzanine level," he recalls. "Again we were going to leave, but a couple were asking if anybody had wanted to trade two tickets to the first show for two to the third; being as I had just bought the maximum eight tickets for the third show, I gladly made the swap. As we were completing the exchange a fourth show [for Oct. 29] was added, and we all returned to score more mezzanine seats. We lingered to see if a fifth show would be added, but it didn't come to pass."

Though the Mets were still very much in contention at this point—their 4-1 win over the Dodgers on Aug. 19 pulled them within 2.5 games of the National League East-leading Cubs, and kept them a half-game ahead of the third-place Expos—there were no worries about the Stones possibly having to share Shea with the Mets during the World Series. Even with the 1985 expansion of the League Championship Series to a best-of-seven format, the baseball postseason rarely stretched past mid-October in the pre-Wild Card era. And since the ballpark was owned by the city and not the team, the Mets organization was absolved from any involvement in the promotion or logistics of the concerts. "Honestly, I have absolutely no memory of anything about those shows," says legendary Mets PR man Jay Horwitz, who has worked for the team since 1980. "They happened after the season was over."

"I've seen the Stones 15 times, but I wasn't at the [Shea] shows," says Ron Darling, who went 14-14 with a 3.52 ERA in 33 starts for the '89 Mets. "When I was with the Mets, whenever we didn't make the playoffs, I always went away for a month to Europe. I hate when I miss them, but I have seen them all over." Darling, who grew up in the blue-collar town of Millbury, Mass., says he always identified with the Stones' working-class vibe. "They were my band when I was a kid. The Beatles were just too pretty for where I was from. The Rolling Stones were more like the people I knew—tough kids, tough language, tough music."

The Mets inadvertently gave the Stones an assist on Sept. 25, when a 2-1 loss to the Phillies officially eliminated the team from postseason contention. The Davey Johnson-led squad would finish the season in second place with a 87-75 record, six games behind the Cubs. "It was another one of those disappointing post-'86 teams where they could have won it all, but they didn't," remembers music publicist Jim Merlis. A diehard Mets fan since childhood, Merlis was 23 years old and working as an assistant publicist at Columbia Records, the Stones' label, when the band came to Shea. "There were several years in a row after 1986 where it was like, 'This is a good team…so why aren't we playing up to our capacity?' They were in second the whole season and never made their move; that seemed to happen a lot in those days."

But if the Mets couldn't use Shea Stadium in mid-October, the Stones certainly could. Four days after the team was eliminated, the Stones announced that a fifth date—Oct. 10—would be going on sale. When tickets to that one sold out within hours, a sixth concert on Oct. 11 was added. "I really lucked out this time," says Walsh, who managed to score tickets for both of these shows, in addition to the first four. "My kid brother's friend had just started working as a stock boy at the [TSW] store, and he told me to just let him know how many tickets I wanted for each show. I bought the maximum eight for one show and four for the other, as it was all I could afford at that point—[$30] was a steep price at the time for a concert ticket."

The new dates meant the Stones would have to play two nights at Shea, then transport the entire tour (including a gigantic post-modern stage set, which was designed and built by London architect Mark Fisher at an estimated cost of $18 million) to Los Angeles for four dates, then bring the whole thing back across the country for the final four shows at Shea. "Logistically, it must have been insane," says Merlis. "It was like, 'Okay, we're going to move this whole operation across the country, only to come back here with it in two weeks!'" But the extra $3.7 million pulled in by the additional dates—not to mention the cachet of selling out six shows at Shea—apparently made the massive endeavor more than worthwhile.

By the time Stones finally arrived in New York for their first pair of Shea dates, the buzz surrounding the concerts was practically inescapable. "Stonesmania had completely gripped the town," remembers attorney Michael B. Ackerman, who attended one of the shows as a guest of Living Colour, the New York funk-metal quartet who opened the concerts. "Everybody was like, 'Are you going to see the Stones? Which night are you going? How were they last night?' It was a big topic of conversation. I took the train from the Upper West Side down to Times Square to get the 7 train to Shea Stadium, and *everybody* on the 7 train was going to see the Stones."

"One of the great things about those concerts at Shea was that I could take the subway there," adds Kassin. "The Stones had felt so unreachable to me, so godlike— and here I was, taking the subway from my neighborhood to see them! There used to be a TV jingle for the subway train to JFK airport, which went 'Take the train to the plane/Take the train to the plane'—and me and my friends were on the train singing, 'Take the train to the Stones/Take the train to the Stones!'"

Ever mindful of his audience and surroundings, Jagger made sure to acknowledge the Mets during the first night of the Stones' six-show stand. "We're sorry the Mets didn't make it to the World Series," he told the audience from the stage, which had been built across the far reaches of the Shea outfield. "Too bad—but we're going to have the World Series of Love!" The band then kicked into a fiery version of

"Tumbling Dice," from 1972's classic *Exile On Main Street*. If there were any lingering bad feelings remaining in the house over the team's disappointing performance, they pretty much dissipated at this point. "It wasn't really bittersweet at all to be there in October without the Mets," laughs Merlis. "It was more like, 'Oh, cool—I'm seeing Shea Stadium in a different way!'"

Indeed, it was a World Series in which there would be no losers. Rather than offering a rote run-through of their greatest hits, the Stones—abetted by saxophonist Bobby Keyes, keyboardists Matt Clifford and Chuck Leavell, backing vocalists Bernard Fowler, Lisa Fischer and Cindy Mizelle, and the Uptown Horns, a Ray-Bans-wearing brass section featuring Arno Hecht, Crispin Cioe, Bob Funk and Paul Litteral—served up a muscular mixture of new material, classic tracks and deep cuts, including the psychedelic obscurity "2,000 Light Years From Home" from 1967's *Their Satanic Majesties Request*. Though several wags in the rock press had jokingly dubbed it the "Steel Wheelchairs Tour," the band was clearly still capable of going toe-to-toe with bands half their age.

"I'd seen the Stones at the Meadowlands in '81, and to be honest I didn't think they were very good," says Ackerman. "But in 1989, I was pleasantly surprised—the set list was great, the pacing was great, the band sounded great. I thought they were terrific."

"It really felt like I was seeing *the Stones*, compared to any of the times I've seen them since," adds Kassin. "It also felt like a reaction to some of what was going on musically in the '80s; it was the era of Milli Vanilli, but this was just a band out there singing and playing really well. The first night at Shea, they even brought on Eric Clapton to play 'Little Red Rooster' with them, which was cool."

For a Mets fan like Ackerman, getting to traverse the hallowed ground where his baseball heroes played was almost as cool as seeing his musical heroes perform. "My date and I had seats in the 18th row, and I remember walking to then, thinking, 'Wow, I'm walking past the pitcher's mound—this is amazing!' I turned around to look at home plate from the pitcher's mound, like, 'Oh, *that's* what [Tom] Seaver saw!'"

Ackerman got an unexpected treat when the skies opened up, forcing him and his date to find shelter. Concert security being significantly more lax than it would become in the '90s and beyond, the pair were able to briefly duck into the visitor's dugout. "I couldn't see the show very well from there," he says, "but I didn't care, because I was too busy looking at the bat rack, the water fountain, the cubbies, the tunnel to the clubhouse; I'm touching everything like a kid in an unguarded toy store! My date, who's Swedish, was like, 'What's wrong with you? What are you doing?' I explained to her that this was where the players sit during the baseball games, and she finally understood. We were there for two numbers before the cops came and made us leave. It was my one and only time in the dugout at Shea."

The Stones' six-show stand at Shea would ultimately represent the end of an era, and the beginning of another one. Those 1989 concerts would be the last time the band ever played New York with original bassist Bill Wyman, who opted to retire following the band's European leg of the tour in the summer of 1990. "That was really it, as far as the Stones bringing their 'A' game," says Merlis. "It was their last tour with Wyman, and after that it just became like a parody—I've seen them several times since Shea, and it's almost the Rolling Stones Las Vegas Show."

On the other hand, the Steel Wheels shows of 1989 effectively set the musical and financial template for the Stones' next 27 years of existence, one involving lavish stage sets, a multitude of backing musicians, and wheelbarrows full of money. The band took in a record $175 million from ticket and merchandise sales in 1989 and 1990; realizing that people would pay far more than $30 for Stones tickets, Michael Cohl and the band began jacking the prices of medium- and top-end tickets on their subsequent tours, with staggeringly lucrative results. Just five years later, their Voodoo Lounge tour would see them gross $320 million, a number they would surpass on 2005-2007's Bigger Bang tour, which set another industry record by grossing over $558 million. (A record that's been broken only by U2's 360 Tour of 2009-2011.)

Though several other major artists would perform at Shea Stadium before demolition of the ballpark began in October 2008—including Bruce Springsteen, who played three shows on his The Rising tour there in October 2003, and Billy Joel, who performed twice at Shea in the summer of 2008—no one would ever match the Stones' record of six Shea concerts. Nor, for that matter, has any band ever played as many shows at one major league ballpark on a single tour.

But for the fans who were there, the Stones' "World Series of Love" at Shea is warmly remembered as a magical event, as opposed to an impressive business feat. "Those six nights were as memorable for me as they were exciting," says Walsh. "While I would subsequently see the Stones 13 more times in later years with each performance being fantastic, none of those matched Shea."

"I felt personally validated by those shows," says Kassin. "I'd spent high school and college being such a fan of a band that almost didn't exist; people made fun of me for it, and people made fun of them. So if they'd been horrible at Shea, for me personally it would have been devastating. But they were phenomenal."

References & Resources

- Special thanks to David Laurila for interviewing Ron Darling.
- Baseball-Reference
- Patricia Leigh Brown, *The New York Times* (reprinted by *Ocala Star-Banner*), "The Rolling Stones' Touring Stage Is Transportable Architecture," *news.google.com/news papers?nid=1356&dat=19891008&id=6q5PAAAAIBAJ&sjid=sAYEAAAAIBA J&pg=6841,6162147&hl=en*

- Anthony DeCurtis, *Rolling Stone*, "Rolling Stones' Steel Wheels Tour Stutters, Then Rolls," *rollingstone.com/music/news/rolling-stones-steel-wheels-tour-stutters-then-rolls-19891019*

- Murry R. Nelson, *The Rolling Stones: A Musical Biography*, 2010

- Sheila Rogers, *Rolling Stone*, "Stones Set Tour Dates," *rollingstone.com/music/news/stones-set-tour-dates-19890824*

- Peter Watrous, *The New York Times*, "Reviews/Music; Icons Who Rock: The Stones Play Shea," *nytimes.com/1989/10/12/arts/reviews-music-icons-who-rock-the-stones-play-shea.html*

- *MaCentcon Chronicle-Herald*, "People in the News: Shattered at Shea," Aug. 18, 1989

- *The New York Times*, "The Rolling Stones Add Fifth Concert at Shea," *nytimes.com/1989/09/28/arts/the-rolling-stones-add-fifth-concert-at-shea.html*

- YouTube, "Rolling Stones 1989 Steel Wheels Tour Announcement NYC," *youtube.com/watch?v=jHk1v32C3CY*

- CenterfieldMaz.com, "History of Concerts at Shea Stadium (Part 2)," *centerfield-maz.com/2008/07/history-of-concerts-at-shea-stadium.html*

- Richard Metzger, Dangerous Minds, "The Rolling Stones' 1989 'Steel Wheels' Tour Was Only Rock & Roll, But I Liked It," *dangerousminds.net/comments/the_rolling_stones_steel_wheels_tour_was_only_rock_roll*

- Jack Doyle, The Pop History Dig, "Stones Gather Dollars," *pophistorydig.com/topics/tag/rolling-stones-at-shea-stadium*

- Wikipedia, "Steel Wheels/Urban Jungle Tour," *en.wikipedia.org/wiki/Steel_Wheels/Urban_Jungle_Tour*

Branch Rickey and the History of Farming

by Adam Dorhauer

B ranch Rickey's Hall of Fame plaque in Cooperstown lists two accomplishments. One, of course, is what everyone knows him for: "Brought Jackie Robinson to Brooklyn in 1947."

That line, tacked on the end of his career summary, is as far as it goes into his role in what is probably baseball's single most important contribution to American history. The rest, save for the list of teams he worked for, is devoted to his role in developing baseball's farm system. In full, the plaque reads:

> *Founder of farm system which he developed for St. Louis Cardinals and Brooklyn Dodgers. Copied by all other Major League Teams. Served as executive for Browns, Cardinals, Dodgers and Pirates. Brought Jackie Robinson to Brooklyn in 1947.*

Granted, there's not a lot of room on the plaque. The point is very much to be succinct. Heck, they don't even use full sentences to save space. The assumption was probably that anyone visiting the Baseball Hall of Fame knows exactly why bringing Jackie to Brooklyn was such a big deal, so better to use that space to explain why creating the farm system was so big—"copied by all other Major League Teams"— than to explain that something called the color barrier was involved in that other thing.

Putting aside the number of words devoted to each accomplishment, the point is that the farm system is a huge part of Rickey's legacy. Even if he had never had any role in breaking the color barrier, he would still be considered possibly the greatest executive in major league history, and the farm system is a big reason why.

Thomas Edison is kind of like Rickey, except with invention and industry instead of baseball. And the incandescent light bulb is basically the farm system of Edison's portfolio. Out of over 1,000 patents Edison held in the U.S. alone, the light bulb is the one thing every American schoolchild learns about his career, the one thing we all still use every single day.

There is, of course, more to the story. In 1802, nearly 80 years before Edison's patent, a British scientist named Humphry Davy created what could be considered the first incandescent light bulb, though it was of no practical use. Over the next several decades, dozens of scientists and inventors experimented with the concept Davy had demonstrated, slowly making improvements that paved the way for Edison's research in the late-1870s. After Edison's contribution, many more continued to refine the product, constantly improving its efficiency and practicality to develop what we use today.

Major innovations, even those commonly thought of as singular strokes of genius, tend to really be a culmination of several people gradually building on each other's work to evolve toward something usable. That doesn't mean Edison's contribution to creating the light bulb wasn't important, but popular history tends to simplify that long process into one groundbreaking, easily digestible event.

Such is the nature of Rickey's farm system.

The First Farm Team

On March 30, 1919, *The Houston Post* reported that Rickey, the newly appointed manager of the St. Louis Cardinals, had sent a group of players to the Houston Buffaloes training camp for the coming Texas League season. Some were established minor leaguers who had already debuted for St. Louis the year before. Some were amateur prospects Rickey had been scouting. A couple (including Joseph Doyle, who would become Houston's starting second baseman that year) were players Houston's management had never even heard of before Rickey sent them along.

This is generally regarded as the starting point for the modern farm system. The Cardinals purchased a minority stake in the Houston franchise that year, and a few years later increased their ownership to a controlling majority. Soon, Rickey had convinced owner Sam Breadon to begin investing in more and more minor league clubs. Over the next decade, other teams began experimenting with Rickey's system of affiliation, and by 1934, all 16 major league teams had at least one minor league affiliate.

That's the simplified version of how the farm system was born. If we dig deeper, though, we find the origins of the farm system are in fact quite a bit more complicated. For example, we have the 1903 National Agreement, the document that marks the beginning of cooperation between the American and National Leagues. The agreement reads, in part:

> *The practice of farming is prohibited. All right or claim of a major league club to a player shall cease when such player becomes a member of a minor league club, and no arrangement between clubs for the loan or return of a player shall be binding between the parties to it or recognized by other clubs.*
> *- 1903 National Agreement, Article VI, Section 4*

There, 16 years before Rickey began his farm system, is an explicit prohibition of farming, along with a pretty accurate description of what farming is, which doesn't make a whole lot of sense unless teams were farming players long before 1919.

In truth, what Rickey was doing, at least in 1919, wasn't unprecedented. The practice of farming in baseball is as old as the minor leagues themselves, and even without formal affiliations, teams had been loaning out players to lower levels for development for a good 40 years by Rickey's time.

Rickey was also not the first major league executive to come up with the idea of directly owning a minor league team to take control of its development resources. Brooklyn owner Charles Ebbets, for example, bought Newark's International League team in 1912. In fact, dual ownership was already fairly common in the 19th century as well.

Rickey undoubtedly played a critical role in the evolution of the farm system into what it is today, but that role falls within a broader context spanning several decades. To really understand where the farm system came from and what role Rickey played, we first need to first explore that context.

Farming Before the 1903 National Agreement

We can divide the pre-Rickey history of farming into two distinct periods, with the 1903 National Agreement as the dividing line. Following the agreement, the National Commission—a three-person committee made up of the presidents of the American and National Leagues along with a neutral chairman that held authority over the two major leagues—and the National Association, a similar organization governing the minors, closely monitored and regulated farming. Before that, however, teams essentially had the freedom to do what they wanted with players.

This freedom meant farming was pretty common. Loans could be short-term, long-term or open-ended. Players could be sold to another team with an option for the original team to purchase the player back at a later date. Owners who controlled multiple teams could transfer players between their organizations at will. It wasn't unheard of, at least in the early days of professional baseball, for a player to even be loaned between two NL teams.

As we might expect, this early history of unchecked farming, especially among owners of multiple teams, is pretty closely related to the farming prohibition in the 1903 National Agreement.

One of these dual owners was John T. Brush, a businessman from Indianapolis who had purchased the National League's St. Louis Maroons in 1887 and moved them to his hometown as the Hoosiers. (The Browns, who would later become the Cardinals, were still in the American Association at the time.) After just three years in Indianapolis, the team folded and sold its player assets to New York, where Brush became a minority owner.

Within a few years, Brush was back as a majority owner, having purchased both the Cincinnati team that had replaced his Hoosiers in the NL and a new Indianapolis team in the Class A (at the time, the highest level of the minors) Western League. Like most dual owners, Brush sometimes would use the Indianapolis team to develop prospects for Cincinnati.

What was somewhat more unusual was that Brush also sometimes funneled talent the other way. Take, for example, the pennant-winning 1895 Indianapolis team. On July 23, Indianapolis held just a half game lead over Kansas City with about 50 games left in the WL season. Cincinnati wasn't exactly out of contention for the NL pennant at 42-33, but was in fifth place, 4.5 games back of Cleveland for first.

That day, Brush told reporters for the Indianapolis Journal that he was considering sending reinforcements from Cincinnati, hinting that former Indianapolis outfielder George Hogriever could be headed back to the WL. Brush noted that fellow Indianapolis alums Bill Phillips (pitcher) and Bill Gray (third base) were too valuable to Cincinnati's bench to spare, but that he was interested in doing what he could to lift his Hoosiers to the pennant.

In fact, Brush ended up sending not only Hogriever, but Phillips as well. Following Brush's proclamation, Indianapolis went 36-15 and ran away with the pennant. Cincinnati went 24-31 and fell to eighth place.

Phillips was especially helpful to Indianapolis' cause, going 12-4 after getting sent down. He also epitomized the favoritism Brush sometimes showed toward his hometown team, because Brush didn't call him back up to Cincinnati. Instead, Phillips started 1896 back in Indianapolis, and while pitching statistics have not been compiled for the 1896 WL season, news accounts indicate Phillips was having another standout year as Indianapolis' ace when a knee injury ended his season that July.

He returned the following season to post a 28-13 record and lead Indianapolis to another pennant. Still, no call up came. He again spent the entire 1898 season in Indianapolis, going 29-8. Finally, in 1899, at age 30, Phillips returned to the majors.

The Bill Phillips saga shows what was wrong with farming in the 19th century. Players were at the mercy of the whims of their owners, and there wasn't really anything they could do to prevent abuse of the system. When the players began to unionize around the turn of the century, one of their demands was an end to the practice.

Those early unions didn't have a whole lot of leverage, and the union's objections by themselves didn't bring about the provision in Article VI, Section 4. On this particular issue, though, the players had a powerful ally.

The WL president at the time of Brush's machinations happened to be Ban Johnson, future president of the American League and one of the most powerful figures in baseball in the early 20th century (in fact, the WL itself was the future American League). And Johnson was not exactly thrilled with Brush affecting the outcome of pennant races by stocking his team with loaned-out major leaguers.

When Johnson decided to make his push to elevate the AL to major league status, one of his key tactics to lure players from the NL was to agree to their farming prohibition. Johnson wasn't the only person concerned about potential abuses of farming and dual ownership at the turn of the century either.

The Cleveland Spiders debacle of 1899—which involved Cleveland's owners buying a second NL team, transferring all of Cleveland's stars to their new team, and watching Cleveland go bankrupt, and which contributed to the sudden contraction of the NL from 12 to eight teams—helped convince a lot of other people there was a problem with owners being able to transfer players between teams however they wanted.

When the AL and NL negotiated the National Agreement a couple years later, Johnson's support and general concern over recent abuses was critical to getting the farming prohibition included.

Differences from the Modern System

Even with extensive farming and dual ownership, player development in the 19th century completely lacked the organizational infrastructure that underpins the modern farm system. Farming agreements were negotiated between teams as one-off arrangements, and even owners who controlled multiple teams frequently dealt with other teams from across the minors on a case-by-case basis.

During this period, teams and leagues were simply too volatile to make building a farming network practical. Most professional leagues founded before the turn of the century lasted only a year or two at most, with some not even making it through a full season before running out of money. Even the leagues that stuck around were constantly changing as teams went bankrupt or dropped out of the league and new ones formed or switched leagues to replace them.

This would have made it virtually impossible to create a multi-level system with any continuity. And unlike today, major league organizations of the time lacked the financial stability to prop these teams up. While they were more stable than the minor leagues, major league teams, and even leagues, also folded somewhat frequently in the 19th century. Investing in a wide array of minor league teams would have just risked putting more potential strain on a team's finances.

As a result, minor league affiliates were rarely run purely as a farm team for the parent club. Owners had to work to keep the minor league club viable as well, and neglecting its needs for those of the parent club increased the chances of bankrupting the farm team.

This volatility made the modern application of farming virtually unworkable, but it also created an opportunity for an alternative model of player acquisition. The same risk that meant running a farm team could see your efforts lost to bankruptcy also meant that you could simply wait for a team to go bankrupt and then buy out that team's roster for significantly less than it would cost to buy and run the team itself.

One of the most notable examples of this was the NL's Detroit Wolverines of the mid-1880s. After going 28-84 in 1884 and starting the 1885 season 7-32, Detroit was in danger of going bankrupt itself. During that season, however, the team bought out the bankrupt Indianapolis WL club (a predecessor to Brush's later expansion team), bolstering its roster enough to recover to a 48-60 record.

The following season, with new owners willing to spend more money on the team, Detroit bought out Buffalo's bankrupt NL franchise. Among the talent acquired in these two buyouts were future Hall of Famers Sam Thompson, Dan Brouthers and Deacon White. Just two years removed from its horrific 1884 campaign, Detroit finished the 1886 season 87-36.

The magnitude of Detroit's turnaround shows just how powerful the financial instability of the game was in the 19th century. The amount of talent that became available through bankruptcies was at times staggering, and the market for that talent was often a cheaper and more secure alternative to operating an actual farm team.

Farming in the National Commission Era

Things changed considerably after the 1903 National Agreement. There had been previous such agreements, but the professional game became significantly more organized with the alliance of the American and National Leagues. The National Commission centralized authority and coordinated with the National Association more efficiently than previous alliances, allowing them to impose order on inter-league transactions such as farming agreements.

The first and most glaring example of this order was the farming prohibition in Article VI, Section 4 of the National Agreement. This leads us to a fairly obvious question I've been ignoring up to now. If farming was banned in the 1903 National Agreement, how was Rickey able to begin his system at all?

The answer is actually pretty simple: The ban didn't last very long. Or rather, the text of Article VI, Section 4 remained, but exceptions quickly were added that reintroduced farming to the game.

A key phrase in the discussion over the farming prohibition was "allowing players to advance in their profession." That phrase, or some close variation, was used repeatedly by league executives, owners and journalists who advocated for the National Agreement. Cases like Bill Phillips' treatment under John Brush were bad not only because they affected pennant races, but because they unfairly prevented qualified players from competing at the top level.

(Of course, this language had a dual purpose. By emphasizing the rule as a defense of player rights, its advocates were presenting the National Commission as a neutral body charged with protecting the interests of players as well as owners, thus undercutting public support for a player-led labor movement. This, and other rules ostensibly designed to allow players to advance in their profession, were equally designed to allow owners to maintain near-total control over these players' careers.)

As long as these abuses could be held in check, most of the game's leaders had no real problem with farming. They saw the practice as having its place in the traditional player development model; it just needed some regulation to make sure teams were using it properly.

At some point over the next few years, language was added to the National Agreement that allowed for "optional assignments," which basically meant what it does today (sending players to the minors). Players could be optioned to the minors, but the clubs involved had to file paperwork and get prior approval from the National Commission, and players had to clear waivers before they could be optioned to ensure teams weren't farming players who were already at a major-league skill level.

There were also further restrictions limiting the timing and volume of these transactions. Teams that tried to get around these restrictions were fined, and players who were illegally farmed could be declared free agents or otherwise prevented from returning to the offending club.

With the National Commission monitoring the flow of players to and from the minors, the avenues for farming were reopened. While that largely restored the system of player development in place during the 19th century, there were still some key differences between this and the system Rickey developed in the 1920s and '30s.

As in the previous era, farming was mostly done via one-off agreements rather than specific affiliates, even as the financial landscape of the game began to settle down. Leagues and teams in the low minors could still struggle to stay afloat, but for the most part, the high minors, and especially the majors, were becoming much more stable than in the 19th century. However, the regulations introduced by the National Commission still presented obstacles to forming a modern farming network.

One of these obstacles was the implementation of the draft, another of the rules tagged with the purpose of allowing players to advance in their profession. The draft allowed teams to select players from the rosters of lower-level clubs at the end of each season, with the caveat that any player drafted had to remain with his new team for the entire next season or else be offered back to his original team. Basically, it worked just like the Rule 5 draft today, largely because this was in fact the Rule 5 draft, though no one called it that until after the Rule 4 (i.e. amateur) draft was created in 1965.

This meant that even if you controlled a minor league team's entire roster, other organizations still had access to that team's prospects through the draft. If you owned a farm team in the low minors, then you risked those players being drafted by teams from higher levels of the minors before you were ready to promote them.

The draft by itself wasn't necessarily a huge impediment, though. You could protect players from being drafted by promoting them during the season, and the rules restricted the number of players who could be drafted from one team. At most, you would lose one player per team per year, and even then it wasn't guaranteed to be that team's best prospect (for example, if multiple teams tried to draft different players from the same minor league club, there were years when the rules called for a random drawing to determine which player got drafted).

What was a significantly bigger obstacle was that the National Commission (of which Ban Johnson was a member) was still wary of dual ownership. Along with the National Association, the commission saw it as critical that the minor leagues be allowed to maintain their autonomy.

Minor league owners were becoming concerned that delegates appointed by major league owners who controlled minor league affiliates were gaining too much influence over National Association affairs. There were also concerns about how direct affiliation would affect the financial health of the minors, which relied heavily on open negotiations between leagues both to sell prospects and to add talent through optional assignments.

The National Commission also had to contend with legal issues with dual ownership. High-profile Supreme Court decisions from the early 20th century, such as Northern Securities Co. v. United States (1904) and Standard Oil Co. of New Jersey v. United States (1911), showed the Court's willingness to break up and fine companies found to be engaging in anti-competitive businesses practices such as collusion or monopolization. There were legitimate concerns that owners operating a network of teams, all of which were ostensibly supposed to be acting as independent businesses, in coordination to produce talent for one major league club could be seen as a violation of the same antitrust laws used in those cases.

This didn't mean dual ownership immediately stopped once the National Commission came into power. Recall, for example, that in 1912 Charles Ebbets owned a minor league team in addition to the Dodgers. In 1913, however, Ebbets suddenly sold his share of the Newark club. The National Commission had decided the potential risks of dual ownership were not worth dealing with and ordered that all major league owners dispose of any holdings in minor league clubs as soon as possible.

Paving the Way for the Modern System

That brings us up to Branch Rickey. When Rickey took over running the Cardinals in 1919, the team had Rogers Hornsby and not a whole lot else. Even with arguably the best player in the National League, the team still had finished last in 1918, and the 1919 team didn't fare much better.

To make matters worse, the Cardinals were roughly $150,000 in debt. They were the last major league team still playing in a primarily wooden (read: flammable) ballpark. At a time when the top prospects from the upper minors were fetching five-digit sums, the poorly funded Cardinals had little choice but to restock their roster by scrounging the low minors for bargains. Even Hornsby had originally come to the Cardinals from a Class D team for $600.

When asked later in his life how he had come up with the idea for his farm system, Rickey pointed to these conditions. It was a case of simple necessity. He didn't have the resources to do things the way other teams did, so he had to find something cheaper.

The problem was the National Commission. Rickey was well aware of the obstacles presented by the commission's regulations. For example, at the 1917 winter meetings, he had explicitly campaigned to make waivers revocable (meaning a team could pull a player back off waivers once he's been claimed instead of automatically losing him) to remove one of the major risks involved in farming.

(It's not really clear how well Rickey's campaigning worked—the waiver rule switched back and forth between revocable and non-revocable over the ensuing years, including some years during which the AL had it one way and the NL the other.)

Then, of course, there was that pesky ban on major league teams owning minor league affiliates, which put Rickey's ideas for a farm system slightly out of the question. Fortunately for Rickey, however, his emergence as an executive coincided almost perfectly with the close of National Commission era.

Three key changes that closely overlapped during this period changed the nature, or at least the potential, of farming: the withdrawal of the minor leagues from the National Agreement, the dissolution of the National Commission, and the antitrust exemption.

The first two changes are somewhat related. In the late 1910s, tensions between the minor and major leagues were growing. In 1917, the National Association nearly pulled out of the National Agreement, and the agreement had to be rewritten to maintain unity. Two years later, tensions once again boiled over, and the minor leagues collectively withdrew from the National Agreement.

In the short term, this meant an end to the draft, which somewhat increased the benefits of dual ownership. This lasted for two years before the draft was partially reinstated, on the condition that individual leagues were free to withdraw from the draft, as most leagues at the top level of the minors did. It also threw the various other rules pertaining to the minors into question, as the minors themselves no longer recognized those rules.

More importantly, this rift exacerbated existing tensions over the future of the National Commission (the NL, for example, had become increasingly skeptical of commission chairman August Herrmann as a neutral third party), and some owners began to lose confidence in the National Commission's ability to govern the game. Herrmann resigned after the 1919 season and was never replaced. When the Black Sox scandal broke the following year, the National Commission was essentially done, and the owners began seriously discussing plans for a new hierarchy to replace it.

The weakened authority of the National Commission, along with the minors no longer recognizing the National Agreement, contributed to Rickey being able to invest his owner's money in the Houston franchise, but this alone was probably not enough to fully eliminate the obstacles to modern farming. After all, incoming Commissioner Kenesaw Mountain Landis, who replaced the National Commission as MLB's central authority following the 1920 season, had similar reservations about dual ownership.

The third change, however, cemented the changing landscape that allowed for Rickey's system to flourish.

The Federal League attempted to form a third major league in 1914. When it did so, it filed a lawsuit against the American and National Leagues claiming their 16 teams, along with the National Commission, were in violation of antitrust laws by colluding to monopolize the baseball industry. Following the collapse of the Federal League in 1915, most of the league's teams accepted a settlement and dropped the antitrust suit, but the Baltimore Terrapins refused and filed a new suit in 1917.

The initial trial ruled in favor of Baltimore, but this was reversed on appeal based on the court's opinion that baseball was not engaged in interstate commerce and was therefore exempt from federal antitrust law. The Supreme Court upheld this decision in 1922.

As this had been a central concern in the National Commission's ban on dual ownership, Landis lacked the same grounds to renew the commission's ban whether he wanted to or not, and the ruling essentially guaranteed the courts wouldn't break up a farming network on antitrust grounds. (Coincidentally, Landis actually had a chance to influence this much earlier, as he was the judge presiding over the original Federal League suit, but he ended up just putting it off until the Federal League went bankrupt and agreed to a settlement.)

Branch Rickey's Farm System

The impact of these changes was felt pretty quickly, and not just by Branch Rickey. The same year Rickey first purchased a stake in the Houston franchise, Detroit worked out a similar agreement to affiliate with Fort Worth, another Texas League team.

What set Rickey's approach apart was how far he pushed the system of affiliation. He saw its latent potential, especially with the National Commission's regulations and antitrust concerns out of the way, in ways his rivals didn't. Rickey's ambitions already started showing in the contrast between St. Louis' and Detroit's affiliations with Houston and Fort Worth.

According to the record of transactions in the 1920 Reach baseball guide, St. Louis sold or farmed 11 players to the minors during the 1919 season. Five of them were to Houston, and that's not including any of the players from the Houston Post report mentioned earlier, all of whom had been sent before the season started. St. Louis also picked up pitchers Art Rienhart and Bill Bolden from Houston for brief stints in the NL that year.

Of the several players Detroit farmed out to minor league clubs in 1919 (including one to Texas League rival San Antonio), none were sent to Fort Worth. The only transaction between the two clubs was the transfer of catcher Larry Woodall from Fort Worth to Detroit following the close of the season. In fact, Fort Worth became known for running its team with remarkably low turnover, keeping a core of veterans intact for years rather than producing prospects to sell to the majors, which made Fort Worth a good baseball team (winning six straight Texas League titles from 1920-1925), but more-or-less useless as a farm team.

There was a reason Rickey depended more on his affiliates for farming than his contemporaries. Rickey realized there were benefits of affiliation over and beyond the simple purpose of farming, and that these were actually hugely important. And not only were they important, they could also stack by owning several affiliates, turning a relatively minor advantage into a substantial one.

For example, a team could gain a significant scouting advantage from owning an affiliate in the minors, helping it identify prospects before other teams or alerting it when a strong scouting report might be an aberration. Teams had certainly used this scouting advantage before, but it was especially important to Rickey, whose lack of funding left his Cardinals with an underdeveloped scouting network in addition to all its other woes.

By using the coaches on his affiliates as part of his scouting network, Rickey was able to get not only inside information on players in his own system, but also firsthand accounts of players from the teams the affiliates played. As his farm system grew more and more expansive, his scouting net grew along with it at no extra cost.

Rickey also realized that owning the teams that develop your prospects could give you greater control over that development. By owning your affiliates, you could control coaching hires and direct those coaches on how to develop players. You could control spring training workouts for every prospect in your system. You could coordinate coaches across different levels to make sure prospects got consistent instruction that reinforced what they learned at previous levels.

This type of organizational coordination and consistency is a hallmark of the current minor league structure. It's probably Rickey's single biggest contribution to the modern farm system.

Before Rickey could implement his system, however, he had to convince Cardinals owner Sam Breadon that buying up these minor league affiliates was a sound use of the team's limited resources. The biggest test came in 1922, when one of Rickey's amateur signings was having a breakout season with the Syracuse Stars, the top affiliate in Rickey's still fairly modest system. The Stars' team president, Earnest Landgraf (who still owned half the team after selling the other half to the Cardinals), was considering auctioning off the prospect to the highest bidder.

Rickey immediately headed to Syracuse to meet with Landgraf and work out an agreement to send the player to St. Louis without fielding bids from other teams. The meeting proved successful, and the prospect, Jim Bottomley (who was acquired for about $15,000, with roughly half of that going back to St. Louis for their share as part owners), became one of the first big successes of Rickey's farm system.

Breadon was convinced. The year after St. Louis called up Bottomley, Max Bishop sold for $20,000, Al Simmons went for $40,000 and Earle Combs for $50,000. With prices for prospects escalating (and it wasn't just sure-fire prospects bringing in that kind of money either: Rube Yarrison and Paul Strand sold that season for $20,000 and $32,500, respectively, and neither lasted more than a year with their new clubs before being sold or traded back to the minors), the returns on Rickey's investments were already starting to save money.

Rickey's solution to overcoming St. Louis' limitations was rooted in the old system of farming, but he found new ways to exploit that system and push it beyond the limits of how it had been previously used. What started as a single affiliate in Houston eventually stretched to include dozens of teams and hundreds of prospects scattered across every level of the minors. Other teams soon began copying Rickey's system, but it would be decades before they would fully catch up to the strides he had made. In 1926, Rickey's Cardinals, boosted by the fruits of his farm system, won their first World Series and would remain an NL power for years to come.

Development Beyond Rickey

Rickey would continue to grow and refine his system over the ensuing decades. Even at the end of his career in the mid-1950s, though, after his system had spread across major league baseball, the modern system was still not fully developed. Several of the top minor league teams in the country remained independent. The affiliations between major and minor league clubs were looser than they are today, and minor league affiliates maintained more autonomy and control over roster decisions than they do today.

This was especially apparent in the Pacific Coast League, which had long been the top minor league in the country due to its dominance of the markets in the Western United States. While some of the league's clubs were owned or partially owned by major league teams, overall the league remained largely independent throughout Rickey's career.

Around the time Rickey's career was ending, the PCL was pushing to become a third major league. In 1952, the PCL was elevated to Open classification, a step higher than Triple-A. A couple of major league teams still owned stakes in PCL affiliates, but officially the PCL terminated any existing working agreements with MLB. In 1953, the PCL instituted a new rule prohibiting its teams from accepting players on optional assignment from major league teams.

These efforts were short-lived, however. Even as the PCL was attempting to distance itself from the notion that it was a farm league, its teams continued to rely on selling contracts to big league teams to remain profitable. The Hollywood Stars, a former Brooklyn affiliate that had switched over to Pittsburgh along with Rickey in 1950, sold 27 players to the Pirates for a total of $116,550 between 1952 and '53. These sales accounted for roughly 12 percent of Hollywood's overall revenue in those years.

In 1954 alone, Hollywood's sales to Pittsburgh jumped to 35 players totaling $123,000. The PCL was quickly reverting to its previous level of reliance on Major League Baseball. The league gave up on the no-option rule after one year, having struggled to replace the talent major league teams normally provided through optional assignments.

The PCL's final hopes of remaining independent disappeared for good when the Dodgers and Giants moved west in 1958. The PCL dropped back down to Triple-A, and its teams quickly aligned themselves with major league parent clubs. Soon, the league became fully affiliated as a permanent part of major league teams' farm systems.

Still, we can see evidence in this realignment that the farm system had not yet reached its current form. Take, for example, the 1956-57 Los Angeles Angels, whose sale from the Cubs to the Dodgers prompted major league baseball's move into the Pacific market.

At the time, the Angels were a mix of prospects and roster depth the Cubs had assigned to LA and players the Angels controlled themselves. When Chicago sold the team to the Dodgers, the Chicago players were transferred to Portland, which affiliated with Chicago following the sale. The LA players remained in LA Of the players who returned to the PCL in 1957, five stayed with LA, and eight shifted to Portland.

Compare that to the 2015 Sacramento River Cats, who switched their affiliation from Oakland to San Francisco after the 2014 season. Sacramento itself didn't own the rights to anyone on its roster, and not a single player from the 2014 team returned to Sacramento for the 2015 season.

This continued evolution was heavily driven by the financial relationship between the majors and minors. As westward expansion and national TV coverage made major league baseball accessible to more and more fans, it become more difficult for minor league teams to compete. Eventually, it reached a point where it was virtually impossible for a league to survive without support from MLB. This, in turn, led the minors to cede increasingly more control over their operations to MLB in order to stay afloat.

In the modern game, the parent club now signs, pays and controls the contract of every player in its minor league system. Players can be promoted, demoted, sold or traded without any input from the minor league teams involved. Minor league GMs don't even negotiate with players anymore since roster construction is no longer part of their job, and instead focus solely on the day-to-day business side of running the team.

Just as Branch Rickey wasn't the beginning of farming in major league baseball, neither was he the endpoint in its development—the farm system was very much still evolving when he left baseball.

The farm system we know today is a mixture of farming practices dating back to the 19th century, changes to the rules and power structure in MLB, the gradual expansion of farming networks, and the eventual concession of roster control from the minors to MLB in exchange for financial security. These factors all contributed to a development that spans most of major league history, spurred on by a powerful catalyst: the mind of Branch Rickey.

References & Resources

- Baseball-Reference
- Retrosheet transaction logs
- Sean Lahman, SeanLahman.com, "Index of Online Baseball Guides," *seanlahman.com/2014/08/index-of-online-baseball-guides/#Reach*
- Various *Reach Baseball Guides*, 1903-1921
- Doug Pappas, Society for American Baseball Research's (SABR) Roadside Photos, "1903 National Agreement for the Government of Professional Base Ball Clubs," *roadsidephotos.sabr.org/baseball/1903NatAgree.htm*
- *Indianapolis Journal*, "May Get Hogriever: John T. Brush Speaks of a Transfer as a Probability," July 24, 1895, p. 5
- *Indianapolis Journal*, "Damon's Fine Pitching Was Hit Safely but Once in Seven Innings After Phillips Retired," July 26, 1896, p. 5
- *Indianapolis Journal*, "No Brass Band Met It, But the Champion Team Was Even Glad Enough to Get Home," Sept. 10, 1896, p. 3
- *Bridgeport Evening Farmer*, "The Ball Trust Bugaboo," Sept. 18, 1913, p. 14
- *The Day Book* (Chicago), "Sports of All Sorts," Oct. 23, 1913, p. 11
- *The Houston Post*, "Branch Rickey Sends on Menze, Larmore, Doyle and Miller to Help the Buffs," Mar. 30, 1919, p. 18
- Associated Press, *Spokane Daily Chronicle*, "Coast League, in New Status, to Open Tomorrow," Mar. 30, 1953, p. 12
- *The Tennessean*, "Dressen Signs 3-Year Contract With Oakland," Oct. 28, 1954, p. 24
- Leagle, "Hollywood Baseball Association v. Commissioner," *leagle.com/decision/196427642mtc234_1264/hollywood%20baseball%20association%20v.%20commissioner*
- Justice Samuel A. Alito Jr., Society for American Baseball Research (SABR), "Alito: The Origin of the Baseball Antitrust Exemption," *sabr.org/research/alito-origin-baseball-antitrust-exemption*

Analysis

Scott Boras' *The Arm* Claim Is All Bark, No Bite

by Jeff Zimmerman

The holy grail in baseball right now is finding a way to keep pitchers healthy. Doing that for a full season takes many forms, but most solutions focus on pitching less: pitch counts, skipping starts, moving to the bullpen, shutting him down early. One person who has a vested in the situation is agent Scott Boras. Boras needs to keep his pitching clients healthy to keep getting paid. And when there is money at stake, Boras and his team construct binders.

Usually, the binders are for players entering free agency. But as Yahoo! Sports columnist Jeff Passan explains in his fantastic book *The Arm*, which debuted earlier this year, there was one that was different:

> On the conference table rested a blue binder, the reason I came here in the first place. The title page said: "Strasburg UCL Reconstruction (Tommy John) Timeline." Boras's infamous binders usually teem with data meant to convince teams to drop nine figures on his top-end free agents. This was one was different. It contained dozens of sheets of paper that defended the most controversial, debated decision in recent baseball history: the shutdown of Stephen Strasburg.

Boras commissioned this particular binder after Stephen Strasburg underwent Tommy John surgery during the 2010 season. The report explained his reasoning for shutting Strasburg down during the 2012 season and not letting him pitch in the playoffs. In *The Arm*, Passan gives the down and dirty on the research Boras quotes:

> Boras's binder provided the argument in favor. It looked at pitchers from 1980 to 2003, the first quarter century or so of the five-man-rotation era, and focused on those who logged heavy innings early in their careers. Forty-seven pitchers exceeded four hundred innings prior to turning twenty-four years old, and ten of those threw more than 600 innings. Of the four hundred-inning group, only six went on to throw more than one thousand innings past their thirtieth birthdays. And just one of the six hundred-inning group survived to pass the thousand-inning mark: Greg Maddux, heralded for his clean delivery and ultra efficient innings.

When I first read this, I had several immediate questions. What about pitchers who get to the majors later? Don't minor league and college innings count? How do these numbers compare over different eras?

The biggest question I had is why did he pick 1,000 innings pitched after age 30? The threshold just seems like a high mark to reach and maybe that is why only six of the selected pitchers made it.

With so many possible questions, I wanted to try to recreate Boras' study. Neither myself nor others were able to replicate the study using the above-stated criteria. Simply, nothing would line up exactly. But perfect is the enemy of good, and I wasn't going to let not being perfect shut the idea down entirely. Instead, I created a similar study that gets as close as possible to the inputs and outputs of the Boras study. I kept all the parameters the same, except I moved "30 and older" to "31 and older." With this change, the six pitchers who tossed 400 innings or more before their 24th birthday and over 1,000 after their 30th (31st) stayed the same. Alas, instead of 47 pitchers meeting the early career innings pitched requirement, I got only 40, when researching using both the FanGraphs database and the Baseball-Reference Play Index.

Here are the 40 pitchers, with a breakdown of their innings pitched before the end of their age-23 season (Early IP), from 24-30 years old (Middle IP) and from age 31 on (Late IP).

Selected Pitchers Used in Study							
Pitcher	Early IP	Middle IP	Late IP	Pitcher	Early IP	Middle IP	Late IP
Dwight Gooden	1,172	996	630	Bill Gullickson	534	1,107	915
Fernando Valenzuela	1,012	1,341	573	Tom Gordon	531	1,093	477
Bret Saberhagen	805	1,267	488	**Mark Buehrle**	**511**	**1,548**	**1,221**
Steve Avery	765	771	16	**John Smoltz**	**503**	**1,554**	**1,410**
Alex Fernandez	713	1,045	0	Juan Nieves	489	0	0
Mike Witt	708	1,357	41	**Roger Clemens**	**485**	**1,735**	**2,691**
Storm Davis	700	933	146	Jose Rosado	484	235	0
Greg Maddux	**673**	**1,691**	**2,641**	Andy Benes	481	1,453	568
Ismael Valdez	646	1,128	50	Sid Fernandez	470	1,119	275
Jim Abbott	635	955	82	Pedro Martínez	453	1,436	934
Ramón Martínez	588	1,140	163	Jamey Wright	446	856	730
CC Sabathia	587	1,587	789	**Tom Glavine**	**431**	**1,523**	**2,455**
Jon Garland	570	1,457	122	**Ryan Dempster**	**427**	**789**	**1,168**
Sidney Ponson	567	998	193	Dave Stieb	425	1,695	642
Britt Burns	563	517	0	Jaret Wright	415	544	10
Jose Rijo	563	1,221	94	Kevin Appier	414	1,264	914
Dan Petry	551	1,178	250	Brad Radke	413	1,453	582
Mark Gubicza	546	1,208	466	Dave Fleming	412	197	0
Javier Vazquez	544	1,515	777	Floyd Youmans	412	126	0
Richard Dotson	535	1,268	28	Greg Swindell	405	1,341	483

It is important to understand that these were largely phenom pitchers. That's why teams called them to the majors early in their careers. With that said, only six—or 15 percent—of these pitchers were able to go on and pitch 1,000 innings after age 30. To see how the data stand up, I will start by changing some of the input variables.

I think a lower total of 500 innings is reasonable to expect from a pitcher after age 30. Of the initial group, 17—or 43 percent—reach the 500 inning threshold.

Age Groupings

What are the changes in a pitcher's future if he is established in the majors before his age-24 season, compared to a later age? The 40 pitchers in the survey pitched in the majors an average of 3.4 years before their 24th birthdays. If we go through the data and group all pitchers from 1980-2003 in four-year intervals (round 3.4 up), we can see how the younger group performed compared to those who debuted later.

Percentage of 400, 600 IP Pitchers Who Reached 500, 1,000 IP From Age 31 On, by Four-Year Age Groups						
Time Frame	# 400 IP	% 500 IP, Age 31-	% 1,000 IP, Age 31-	# 600 IP	% 500 IP, Age 31-	% 1,000 IP, Age 31-
23 or younger	40	43%	15%	10	40%	10%
19 to 22	11	36%	9%	2	100%	0%
20 to 23	40	43%	15%	10	30%	10%
21 to 24	99	36%	11%	31	48%	19%
22 to 25	163	35%	12%	70	46%	16%
23 to 26	221	36%	13%	105	47%	16%
24 to 27	278	37%	14%	123	50%	18%
25 to 28	282	39%	16%	143	50%	19%
26 to 29	268	43%	17%	145	58%	22%
27 to 30	256	49%	20%	136	69%	30%

First and foremost, the group of early pitchers is a small group compared to the others. Taking away the notion of a small sample, these pitchers compared decently to the other age groups, especially with the 500 IP group (maybe which is why Boras stayed away from mentioning them). It takes until pitchers are in the 26-to-29 age bracket to start seeing similar results to the 20-to-23 age group. Now the 10 pitchers in the 600 IP group don't measure up, but this is obviously a very small sample.

Time Frame

The time frame is a pretty easy change to mess with without incorporating too much bias. I couldn't go too far past 2003, as the pitchers needed a chance to pitch past the age of 30. When I divide up the time frames, some pitchers don't get included if their early career overlaps the time frames. As such, the combination row is going to have a larger sample than the other groups.

Percentage of 400, 600 IP Pitchers Who Reached 500, 1,000 IP From Age 31 On, by Decade						
Time Frame	# 400 IP	% 500 IP, Age 31-	% 1,000 IP, Age 31-	# 600 IP	% 500 IP, Age 31-	% 1,000 IP, Age 31-
1950 to 1959	20	20%	10%	6	33%	17%
1960 to 1969	40	25%	15%	15	13%	7%
1970 to 1979	29	34%	17%	8	50%	25%
Combination	96	26%	16%	35	26%	11%
1980 to 1991	25	40%	16%	7	43%	14%
1980 to 2003	40	43%	15%	10	40%	10%
1991 to 2003	14	50%	14%	1	0%	0%

Just looking at the pitchers reaching 1,000 innings, we don't see much real change between the prior data and the current samples. On the other hand, the number of pitchers able to throw 500 innings past their 30th birthday has steadily gone up over time. This change is probably because of medical advances and the move from a four-man to a five-man rotation.

After digging around a little, we start to see the flaws in the Boras study.

Young Tommy John Cases

One reason Boras is probably having everyone focus on throwing past 30 years old is because the careers for Tommy John pitchers are historically short. Here is a look at major league pitchers under 25 years old who had Tommy John surgery before 2011:

- In all, 60 pitchers make this list.
- Twelve (20 percent) of the pitchers never threw after their 25th birthday.
- Only 22 (37 percent) made it to their age-30 season.
- The average number of innings pitched after age 25 is 279. The median value is 210.
- The most innings ever thrown by a pitcher after age 30 who had Tommy John surgery is Ryan Vogelsong with 875 innings. Matt Morris is next with 428.2 innings. One of the current pitchers, like Francisco Liriano, may eventually break this number but currently, no one has reached 1,000 innings.

Using the above historic data, the possible outcomes are not encouraging for a young pitcher who had Tommy John surgery. It's easy to see why Boras, having this exact or similar information, might have recommended to Strasburg earlier this year to sign his contract extension while he was still healthy.

Reaching 1,000 innings After 30 Is Hard

The 1,000 innings part of Boras' statement seems innocent, but it is actually not very common for a pitcher to throw 1,000 inning after age 30. Observe:

Debut Age for Pitchers to Reach 1000 IP after 30

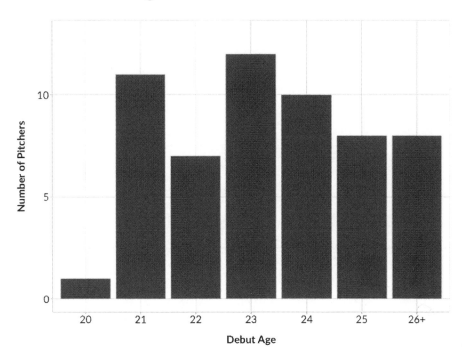

Or, if you prefer, in table form.

Debut Age for Pitchers Who Reached 1,000 IP After Age 30, 1980-2003	
Age	# Reached 1,000 IP
20	1
21	11
22	7
23	12
24	10
25	8
26+	8
Total	57

Boras is looking to limit the innings of young players, but historically pitchers who debut young are more likely to make it to 1,000 innings pitched after 30 than pitchers who debuted later. Additionally, it took some of these pitchers years to reach the 1,000 inning total. On average, the 1,000-inning pitchers were 39 years old when they finally hung up their cleats. For reference, here are the 57 pitchers who turned the trick.

Pitchers With 1,000+ IP After Age 30, 1980-2003									
	Age					Age			
Pitcher	Car IP	Min	Max	31+ IP	Pitcher	Car IP	Min	Max	31+ IP
Jamie Moyer	4,069	23	49	3,218	Bronson Arroyo	2,361	23	37	1,324
Randy Johnson	4,130	24	45	2,887	Hiroki Kuroda	1,318	33	39	1,318
Roger Clemens	4,911	21	44	2,691	Rick Reed	1,542	22	37	1,278
Greg Maddux	5,005	20	42	2,641	Bob Tewksbury	1,804	25	37	1,253
David Wells	3,435	24	44	2,561	Livan Hernández	3,186	21	37	1,237
Tom Glavine	4,409	21	42	2,455	Mark Gardner	1,761	27	39	1,236
Tim Wakefield	3,223	25	44	2,395	Mark Buehrle	3,280	21	36	1,221
Kenny Rogers	3,297	24	43	2,356	Kevin Tapani	2,263	25	37	1,219
Curt Schilling	3,256	21	40	2,016	Roy Halladay	2,746	21	36	1,187
Tom Candiotti	2,722	25	41	1,965	José Contreras	1,171	31	41	1,171
Woody Williams	2,213	26	40	1,810	Ryan Dempster	2,384	21	36	1,168
Kevin Brown	3,253	21	40	1,804	John Lackey	2,663	23	37	1,163
Mike Mussina	3,557	22	39	1,787	Jeremy Guthrie	1,761	25	36	1,160
Bartolo Colón	3,164	24	43	1,775	Kevin Millwood	2,717	22	37	1,159
Derek Lowe	2,668	24	40	1,762	Aaron Harang	2,318	24	37	1,142
Chuck Finley	3,194	23	39	1,746	Paul Byrd	1,695	24	38	1,131
Jeff Fassero	2,030	28	43	1,740	Mark Langston	2,959	23	38	1,117
Andy Pettitte	3,312	23	41	1,730	Jimmy Key	2,588	23	37	1,111
Orel Hershiser	3,126	24	41	1,671	Bud Black	2,050	24	38	1,095
Al Leiter	2,387	21	39	1,652	Jon Lieber	2,195	24	38	1,060
R.A. Dickey	1,879	26	41	1,617	Kyle Lohse	2,528	22	37	1,049
A.J. Burnett	2,728	22	38	1,575	Randy Wolf	2,323	22	38	1,048
Terry Mulholland	2,572	23	43	1,524	Ted Lilly	1,979	23	37	1,045
Tim Hudson	3,123	23	39	1,474	Dave Burba	1,774	23	37	1,030
John Burkett	2,645	22	38	1,461	Steve Sparks	1,318	29	38	1,028
Miguel Batista	1,952	21	41	1,429	Greg Harris	1,463	25	39	1,025
John Smoltz	3,467	21	42	1,410	Hideo Nomo	1,974	26	39	1,015
Tim Belcher	2,439	25	38	1,407	Doug Jones	1,125	25	43	1,013
David Cone	2,894	23	40	1,376					

In a 2014 report I wrote for MLB Trade Rumors (also about a Boras quote), I found that the more pitches a pitcher has previously thrown, the less likely he is to get hurt in the future.

> *Just because a pitcher has a ton of mileage on his arm doesn't mean he is about to break down. He could continue to throw for years to come. The more pitches a pitcher has thrown, the better the chances he continues to throw.*

Boras' focus should be looking at how to prevent the injuries in the first place or how pitchers performed when they returned from injury. That however, is outside the scope of this article.

Why Are Only Major League Innings Counted?

Another issue with the Boras study is it looks just at major league innings. It is not like these pitchers who debuted later in their careers weren't throwing before they reached the majors. I looked at minor league innings going back to the 2005 season. Looking at kids drafted out of high school, 47 starters (who started at least 50 percent of their games in both the minors and majors) debuted in the majors before 2011. Of this group of pitchers, 33 (or 70 percent) went on to throw over 600 innings before their 25th birthday. And 45 of 47 (96 percent) threw over 400 innings combined between the minors and majors. Of course, that isn't the largest sample, but I doubt the story would be much different if we went further back in time.

The story is much the same for college pitchers. For those who pitched in college, I used 200 innings as a general catch-all number. Most drafted pitchers are starters, who could be expected to toss 70 to 100 innings each college season. Most probably started their sophomore and junior seasons, putting them in the 140 to 200 IP range. With a few mid-week starts and bullpen appearances as a freshman, they will be at or above the 200 IP range. That's a fair number of innings on their arm before they get drafted.

Looking again at just starters, 138 made a major league debut over the 2005-present time frame. Counting in the likely 200 college innings, 96 (or 70 percent) had over 600 innings before they turned 25. Adding in the college innings makes it 131 (96 percent) with over 400 innings.

There is just no reason to choose the 400-inning or 600-inning limit, because almost all pitchers will reach that amount when combining their college, minor league, and major league workload. There was no reason to limit the study to the selection of pitchers who debuted young like he did.

Conclusions

The only useful part of the Boras study is it shows us how not to do a study.

Boras used the data from the study for a reason. It probably wasn't for general managers and their staffs. They would have looked at their own data and come to conclusions similar to mine. The study isn't going to influence them. It resonates with the informed and casual data observer. It caught my attention. It seems like a big deal when it is first read, but lacks any comparison data or context. Also, the team likely doesn't care about the player's production eight to 10 years from now. In a game that just grinds through pitchers, why should it?

The study is seemingly aimed at two groups of people. The first group is team owners. Scott Boras is notorious for going around general managers to get deals done. The shock-and-awe hits them and the owners feel a little guilty about ruining the player's career.

But the more I think about it, the more I think this study targets his pitchers. Pitchers want to pitch and make money as long as possible. If he shows his pitchers that they need to take it easy (which the data do not show) and then they can then throw into their 30s, the pitchers aren't going to check to see if their agent is wrong. They are paying the agent good money to treat them right.

Instead of looking at how many innings a younger pitcher might throw later in his career, Boras or others should be having a legitimate conversation on what is the best method to return from Tommy John (or even to prevent it in the first place). What works and what doesn't? To Passan's credit, he explores much of this in his book. Each year, the data become richer and richer as more data points are added as more pitchers go on and off the disabled list. If any future research should be done on the preceding subject, it should be on the conditions and time frame for Tommy John surgery rehabilitation.

Scott Boras is a smart man and makes sure only the information he wants the public to see is the information that the public sees. With the study he used to justify limiting Strasburg's early career innings, he tried to give most people a reason to go along. The problem was that once context was added to the story, almost the opposite conclusion could be drawn. Pitchers who threw more innings earlier in their major league career continue to keep throwing more innings compared to pitchers who debut later.

I don't blame Boras for saying what he did. It obviously worked, as the Nationals did limit Strasburg's innings, and Strasburg eventually signed a bountiful contract extension with the team. However, the study misses the mark once it is put into context, and it is a great example of why we always need to examine the finer details of people's claims.

References & Resources
- Baseball-Reference
- FanGraphs
- Jeff Passan, *The Arm*, 2016
- Jeff Zimmerman, MLB Trade Rumors, "Scherzer, Lester, Shields And Career Pitch Counts," *mlbtraderumors.com/2014/11/scherzer-lester-shields-and-career-pitch-counts. html*

Solving the Defensive Quandary with Statcast: Introducing LARS

by Rob Arthur

Defense isn't like hitting or pitching. In hitting or pitching, there are individual attributes that are largely up to one participant or another. We can say with confidence that a pitcher who throws 95 mph fastballs does so because of his own arm; nobody else plays a greater role. And while there may be slight adjustments (the stadium gun might be hot, or the weather cold), we can feel confident in assigning the vast majority of the credit for the fastball to the pitcher himself.

Defense is different. A shortstop can work only with the balls hit into his vicinity. Those might be screaming line drives or they might be weak pop-ups, but whatever they are, the shortstop has nothing to do with it. He fields them as best he can, given only the opportunities that he has.

What's more, defense inherently involves a large number of participants. For a battle at the plate, there are only two participants—batter and pitcher (with the newly-realized importance of catcher framing, we might add the catcher as a third, albeit less consequential, actor). Defenders are working with the batted ball that is a product of the hitter and the pitcher, but their job is even more complicated than that. Often, they are throwing to another defender, whose position and performance may affect their own. Sometimes, they must factor in a runner on base, and his behavior. Do you throw to home to challenge the speedster coming in from third, or settle for an out at second base? This is a more challenging question than whether a pitch is a ball or a strike, whether to swing or take.

Altogether, quantifying defense is a more complex endeavor than measuring hitting or pitching. As a result, it's probably the weakest spot in our sabermetric understanding of baseball. We do have models to address it—admirable ones like Ultimate Zone Rating, at that—but to truly understand defense, we simply need more information than has been available.

That's where Statcast comes in. In this article, I use data from MLB Advanced Media's latest toy to create a new defensive metric called LARS. Using UZR as a foundation, LARS is both more reliable and precise than prior statistics. More than that, the general approach used within LARS will be applicable to further data that might be released from Statcast, potentially resulting in even better defensive metrics in the future.

Imitating UZR

Crafting a defensive metric is a daunting task. Fortunately, I can stand on the shoulders of giants, patterning the structure of my statistic after Ultimate Zone Rating, Mitchel Lichtman's invention. Before I dive into the details on my new metric, let me thus begin by offering a brief overview of UZR.

UZR relies on determining two pieces of information about each batted ball: how hard it is to field, and how many runs it would be worth if it wasn't fielded. You can calculate a given fielder's worth from those two bits of data.

How does UZR determine whether a given ball is easy or tough to field? It takes into account manually-entered information from stringers, in particular where a batted ball landed, its trajectory, and its speed. To determine where it has landed, every batted ball is assigned a zone on the baseball field (for this reason it is called a "zone rating"). Trajectories are assigned to one of several classes, including line drives or ground balls. And finally, speed comes in three flavors for UZR: soft, medium and hard.

From the speed, trajectory and position of each batted ball, it's possible to estimate how likely an average fielder is to successfully convert that batted ball into an out. Furthermore, you can take those same three pieces of information and guess the most likely outcome of the play if the fielder doesn't convert. For example, a hard-hit line drive to the corner of the outfield may be extremely unlikely to be successfully fielded, and will probably go for extra bases if it isn't.

So let's say the fielder does make the play. If so, he gets credit in proportion to whether other fielders would have made the same play (the probability of fielding the ball) multiplied by the damage the batted ball would have done if he hadn't. The same logic applies in reverse to a play the fielder doesn't make. If most fielders would have made it, and the result is costly, he takes a big penalty. Add up all of those credits and debits over a season, and you have a final tally of how many runs a certain fielder has saved or cost his team.

For this initial foray into defense, I'm only going to be computing a rate statistic, so I won't be adding up the credits and debits as UZR does to produce a final run value.

Enter Statcast

That's a good and reasonable scheme to grade defense, so I'm going to steal it for my own statistic. Instead of using the subjective judgments of stringers, however, I turn my attention to Statcast's cold, unfeeling, but objective radar array.

Statcast is the new, hot data in sabermetrics, and for good reason. Using a Doppler radar combined with a camera tracking system, Statcast tracks the velocity and angle off the bat of most of the struck balls in the majors. The result is a more accurate and granular dataset on batted balls than we've ever had before: Instead of three classes of batted ball velocity, we have a quantitative range from zero miles per hour to 120 or so. Instead of vague batted ball classifications—judgments that we know can be affected by the geometry of the park and the location of the stringer—Statcast generates a precise angular measurement.

The information from Statcast is a new and more powerful kind of data. Implicitly, a method like UZR assumes that two balls hit to the same zone, with the same trajectory class and the same speed class are equally difficult to field. That's likely not always the case, however. A ball hit into the edge of the zone on a flatter trajectory with a higher exit speed will be much more difficult than one hit into the center on a higher trajectory with lower exit speed. UZR is necessarily constrained by the data given to it, which is a product of stringers who can't distinguish between a 10 degree launch angle and an 11 degree launch angle. Because Statcast's measurements are quantitative, and not binned, we can parse the difference between any two batted balls with greater resolution.

There is one major issue with Statcast: lost data. The system misses a lot of batted balls, failing to record tracking numbers for about 10 percent of all struck balls in 2016. Furthermore, although we know that Statcast is capable of measuring horizontal angle off the bat, MLBAM has not yet released those data. As a result, there are blind spots in the numbers.

One possibility would be to simply discard these missing data and make do with exit velocity and vertical angle. But there's a better way. To fill in the missing data, I blend the incomplete numbers from Statcast with information from stringers employed by MLB. These observers estimate the location at which every batted ball was fielded, and this data is provided in the same Baseball Savant files that record Statcast numbers. By regressing the batted ball characteristics on the stringer coordinates (in cases where we have both datasets), I can substitute in the best guess about batted ball characteristics on the occasions when the radars lose track of the batted balls (the accuracy of those guesses are about r=.7 for exit velocity and r=.9 for launch angle).

From the stringers' coordinates, I can also calculate horizontal angle, using some geometry and the fact that batted balls generally travel in relatively straight lines from home plate. So, for example, if a right fielder catches a ball pulled straight along the foul line, the location would be recorded by the stringer relative to home plate, and by drawing a line between home and the stringer's coordinates, I can estimate that the ball was hit on a +45 degree horizontal angle.

Combining the stringer information with Statcast's numbers allows me to create a complete dataset on the horizontal direction, launch angle, and exit velocity of every batted ball in the major leagues in 2016. Although the advantage of Statcast data is muted somewhat by needing to rely on stringers to fill in the gaps, I believe this dataset still represents the most accurate and complete compendium of information on batted ball characteristics.

The Guts of a Defensive Metric

So now we've got a general scheme for quantifying defense, and a more powerful dataset to feed into it. In theory, that should be all the necessary ingredients for a more accurate defensive metric. But as usual, there's a long and gory-math-filled road between the data and the final output. I'll cover that here, at a low level of detail. For the math-phobic, you'll be better served by skipping to the next section.

The main task is to determine how difficult each ball is to field. To compute that we need to include a lot of different information: the batted ball characteristics (exit velocity, horizontal and vertical launch angles), but also the ballpark where the ball is being fielded, the team doing the fielding (to account for its defensive positioning tendencies) and the handedness of the batter.

I integrate all of that data into a Generalized Linear Mixed Model. For the statistical aficionados, that's the same kind of model that Deserved Run Average uses to partition runs to pitchers, or Called Strikes Above Average uses to determine how good catchers are at framing. Here, it's repurposed to determine how much better each fielder is above an average player at his position.

I run the model on the set of all batted balls that were in play in 2016 (i.e. excluding home runs and foul balls that weren't caught). That produced more than 100,000 rows of data. Every play is coded as a hit or an out, and the model is a binomial (logit) regression on those two outcomes. Because exit velocity and the angles have complex, nonlinear relationships with each other, I interact all three of those terms together, making each a polynomial (sixth degree for horizontal angle, third for vertical angle, and fourth for exit velocity).

This model has two random effects in it: one for the fielding team, and one for the player. For the uninitiated, random effects are a more flexible way to measure the impact of a given participant on a certain play, and assume that there will be some variation around that participant's true ability. Random effects have another advantage, which is that they are automatically regressed to the mean, unlike fixed effects. The team random effect measures how much better a team's fielders are, on average, relative to other teams. It is a stand-in for whatever sabermetric advantage those teams have, whether it be in terms of shifting, more subtle defensive positioning, or some other kind of technique we don't yet know about.

The player random effect is what we're most interested in. Because it's a random effect, this coefficient measures the skill of each player at fielding a certain position, regressed heavily to the mean. In other words, regression is built into this metric: the more opportunities a player has had, the better we can feel assigning him a large positive or negative coefficient. Meanwhile, players with few opportunities tend to sit close to the average, reflecting our lack of knowledge about them.

Putting it all together, the model achieves an area under the curve (AUC) value of .9235 on out of sample data (in predicting hit or out status). To put that into context, an AUC value of 1 represents perfection, while .5 would be a perfectly random model with no information. Interestingly, the vast majority of the accuracy comes from including Statcast information on the launch characteristics of the batted balls. With only the launch data, the model has an AUC value of .9, barely worse than the full model. That reiterates that defense, while valuable, is a marginal effect relative to the inherent characteristics of each batted ball.

Introducing LARS

With the gory math now complete, it's time to name my creation. I'm calling my new metric LARS, for Launch-Adjusted Runs Saved. It's launch-adjusted because it takes into account the launch metrics—namely exit velocity, as well as horizontal and vertical angle—of every batted ball. Since those launch characteristics can make a big difference to how easily a batted ball is fielded, measuring and including them is LARS' main strength relative to existing methods of measuring defensive value.

Unsurprisingly, LARS correlates quite well with UZR. For 2016, looking at only qualified hitters, LARS matches UZR/150 with an r value of .52 (right now, LARS is available only as a rate statistic, so that's why I'm comparing it with the rate version of UZR). That indicates solid, if not complete agreement. Most importantly, both LARS and UZR agree on the extreme fielders, those who are either very good or very bad. Of the top 10 in UZR, for example, nine out of 10 are accorded positive defensive value by LARS as well. Similarly, of the bottom 10, seven are given negative values.

While there are disagreements between the metrics, I believe that LARS represents a significant step forward from UZR. To be clear, that's no knock on UZR; with Statcast, I have the advantage of better, more granular and reliable data than Lichtman ever had in crafting UZR. It's no surprise that a metric patterned after his, but using more powerful data and a statistical model, would produce better results.

There are two main advantages to LARS. One is that it better isolates the performance of the fielder from the batted balls that he fields. The second is that it's more reliable.

As I mentioned above, UZR is constrained by the data it has. Because those data is less granular than Statcast, it assumes that two balls hit in the same way to the same part of the field have the same probability of being successfully fielded as each other. In point of fact, two balls hit into the same zone can be of radically different fielding difficulties, depending on fine gradations in their speed and angle. Because LARS has those data and UZR doesn't, LARS should be better able to measure the difficulty of balls that players are fielding.

To see whether UZR was missing on players with harder-to-field batted balls, I looked at the average probability of making an out for each player in baseball. I found that there was a significant divergence between infielders and outfielders. As you might expect, once a ball gets into the outfield, it's already much more difficult to field. What's more, outfielders tend to get fewer opportunities to make plays than infielders.

The consequence of this difference is that outfielders vary significantly from one another in terms of their difficulty of fielded balls. The average outfielder sees plays with an out probability of around 49 percent. But two qualified outfielders—each with more than 900 innings in the field—could differ in terms of their batted ball difficulty by up to 15 percent. For example, Melky Cabrera had the hardest to field batted balls in the majors in 2016 among outfielders—his average batted ball had only a 40 percent chance of turning into an out. By UZR, he was rated the eighth-worst outfielder in baseball. By LARS, he was only 11th. On the other end of the spectrum, Ender Inciarte had some of the easiest balls to catch in baseball, with 53 percent of them expected to become outs. He was rated the sixth-best outfielder in baseball by UZR, while LARS had him at a more modest ninth. These are small differences, but they likely stem from the batted balls that were hit to each fielder, and not the fielders themselves.

In contrast, you don't see the same problems with infielders. The standard deviation in difficulty for the batted balls directed to infielders is about half as much as for outfielders. Because there's so little difference, UZR doesn't seem to show any preference for infielders with easier-to-field batted balls.

So the first advantage of LARS is that it zeroes in on the fielding abilities of outfielders, regardless of the difficulty of the batted balls they've faced. That also has implications for LARS' reliability, or the rate with which it converges on a fielder's true defensive talent. Reliability is traditionally measured with split-half correlations, in which you divide each fielder's plays into two halves, compute the fielding metric of interest in each, and then compare the two to each other. The closer together the statistics are from each half, the more you can trust that metric in a smaller sample.

Lichtman has noted that UZR takes three full years to stabilize, or reach a correlation of .7 between split halves. One of the broader weaknesses of defensive metrics is that they are unreliable: a fielder can be +15 runs in one year and -15 the next, implausibly oscillating in ways that don't seem to correspond to real shifts in ability.

Because we have full Statcast data for only one year (2015 Statcast data had a much more severe missing data problem), I can't run a year-to-year reliability test for LARS. But I can compare LARS' reliability *within* one year, by repeatedly splitting the data into halves and comparing those halves against each other. When I do that, I find that LARS correlates between halves of the same year at about r=.26, which is a solid, if unspectacular, performance.

How does that compare to UZR? UZR isn't available in short-term increments, being computed for only a year at a time. However, we know from extensive work by sabermetricians like Colin Wyers and Russell Carleton that the correlation between two consecutive years of UZR is about .29. That number is very close to what LARS achieves in half the data, suggesting that LARS is more reliable than UZR. It's impossible to say if that number would extrapolate over longer time periods, that is, whether LARS is always twice as reliable as UZR. But it bodes well for the idea that LARS is zooming in on each fielder's raw ability, independent of the batted balls he sees.

Best and Worst Fielders By LARS

Hopefully, by this point I've convinced you that LARS is a reasonable way to grade defense using a new kind of data. Although it's not as all-encompassing or well-tested as older defensive metrics, I wanted to provide a preview of the LARS metric on 2016 fielders. What follows are LARS scores (expressed as coefficients from the mixed model) for the 10 best and worst fielders in baseball of 2016. Higher scores are better, indicating that a fielder's presence is more likely than average to turn a batted ball into an out; lower, negative scores have the opposite meaning.

2016 LARS Leaders	
Fielder	LARS
Mookie Betts	0.27
Adrián Beltré	0.21
Billy Hamilton	0.19
Jose Iglesias	0.18
Jose Altuve	0.17
Kyle Seager	0.15
Mallex Smith	0.15
Nick Markakis	0.15
Brett Eibner	0.14
Jean Segura	0.14

The best fielders by LARS are, unsurprisingly, some of the best fielders by UZR as well. The top four are uncontroversial: Billy Hamilton and Mookie Betts are both in the top 10 of UZR/150, and Adrián Beltré is correctly regarded as one of the best fielders of all time. Jose Iglesias is a well-known defensive specialist with a talent for fielding wizardry, although UZR hasn't always been kind to him.

However, there are significant disagreements further down the list. By UZR and DRS, Jose Altuve and Jean Segura have actually been below average in their careers on defense; LARS has them among the best. Tom Tango's Fan Scouting Report had them about average for 2016, so in between the extremes of LARS and UZR. In theory, infield defense should represent a strength for UZR in comparison to LARS. As I noted above, sample sizes are larger for infield defenders and as a result, UZR tends to be much more reliable within the diamond. Meanwhile, Statcast struggles to track bouncing ground balls, which means that LARS leans more heavily on stringers for infield data. Combining UZR's strength in the infield with LARS' weakness,

I wouldn't be surprised if the truth about Altuve, Segura and other infielders was a little closer to UZR than to LARS.

In the outfield, Nick Markakis represents perhaps the largest and most interesting potential dispute between conventional fielding metrics and LARS. Over a long and extensive sample, UZR insists that Markakis has been a poor defender at nearly every position he's played. Nevertheless, Markakis was signed to a rich contract by the Braves in part for his defensive acumen, much to the chagrin of sabermetric-savvy observers. Still, Markakis has been lauded by the fans for his glovework, and this past season, UZR ranked him slightly above average. Just as UZR may perform better in the infield, I suspect that LARS has an advantage in the outfield, where contact quality of batted balls varies much more.

2016 LARS Laggards	
Fielder	LARS
Yasmany Tomás	-0.23
Jonathan Villar	-0.20
Carlos Gomez	-0.19
Rougned Odor	-0.17
Mark Trumbo	-0.16
Scooter Gennett	-0.15
Wilmer Flores	-0.15
Erick Aybar	-0.15
Jose Reyes	-0.14
Gregor Blanco	-0.14

There was broad agreement about the best fielders in baseball, and the worst are concordant as well. Nobody who's watched Yasmany Tomás "defend" has had anything good to say about it, at least relative to other major league ballplayers. Jonathan Villar is rated fourth-worst by UZR/150, Scooter Gennett seventh, Rougned Odor eighth from the bottom.

Generally, the worst fielders in baseball are easier to identify than the best—even something as simple as looking at fielding percentage would often recognize problematic defense. Even though errors are a problematic stat for a whole host of reasons, it's hard to be a valuable defender if you throw away dozens of otherwise-certain outs. On the other hand, given that the top fielders in baseball make relatively few mistakes per year, determining who within that group has been most valuable is a much more challenging task.

Most of the players on this list whose LARS score diverges most dramatically from UZR were part-time players in 2016 with low, but not extreme scores. For example, Wilmer Flores got limited action across the infield for the Mets, and was rated consistently poorly at every position except first base. Even so, his UZR/150 marks wouldn't have been worst in the league, even combining his positions. LARS—despite being regressed to the mean, just like UZR—is more aggressive about labeling his defense inferior, even in limited action. We see similar stories with Jose Reyes and Gregor Blanco.

Staring at both the best and worst fielders, you may have noticed that there isn't much spread between them. It's important to note that this is a rate statistic based on the number of fielded balls—not innings, as UZR/150 is—so that difference can be deceiving. Nevertheless, it appears preliminarily as though LARS believes the gap in value between the best and worst fielders is smaller than in UZR or other defensive metrics. Whether this will hold up after transforming LARS into a cumulative run value statistic remains to be seen.

Beyond LARS

While LARS is generally consistent with the consensus defensive metrics, I've argued that LARS is a step forward due to its superior underlying data and statistical model. With that said, let me be clear: At this stage, LARS is decidedly imperfect. Unlike UZR, I can't easily break LARS down into components like Arm and Range. Furthermore, LARS has no mechanism to cope with more complex defensive plays, like fielders' choice situations and possible double plays.

All of those capabilities can and will be developed and integrated into LARS in the future. Alongside more granular defensive breakdowns, another area for improvement might be additional data from Statcast, both in terms of batted balls and fielders. Fortunately, LARS is easily extendable to include those data, if and when it becomes available.

For example, we know that batted balls have significant spin, which causes their trajectories to bend and potentially creates odd bounces. Similarly, wind can change the direction and distance of a batted ball, making an easy fly ball impossible to field if a gust hits it at the right moment. These factors can significantly alter the difficulty of fielding, and while they probably mostly average out over the course of a season, it's possible that they distort some players' numbers every year.

To even more completely measure the difficulty of fielding each batted ball, we would therefore like to have the full path of every batted ball. Unfortunately, that information has not yet made its way into the public sphere. But when spin and wind can be factored into fielding, I can update the metric to include them by adding them into the model. (I'll call it TARS—trajectory-adjusted runs saved.)

The biggest missing piece in the fielding puzzle is undoubtedly starting position. In the age of the shift, we know that teams are providing explicit instructions to fielders about where to stand on the field to best make defensive plays. Although we're most familiar with the infield shift, this past season has shown that outfielders are moving to match their opponents' spray tendencies just as much. As a result, formerly incredible catches are becoming routine, since players have a few extra steps to get to the ball.

Without knowing where a fielder is standing at the beginning of a play, all we can do is look at the final result—whether an out was made or not. We don't know whether that out was made due to keen strategy on the part of the player or team versus an incredible athletic effort. As a result, most of the value in fielding position in LARS is going to the players, and only a little to the team (in the form of the team random effect in the statistical model). If we had player positioning information, we could better divide the credit, calculating how difficult a catch was depending on the player's location relative to the batted ball. For now, we'll leave position-adjusted runs saved as a hypothetical, with the hopes that Statcast eventually opens up enough to allow us to calculate it.

Even without all of this information, LARS appears to be more precise and reliable than existing defensive metrics. The basic idea of LARS—patterned after UZR—is to better calculate the difficulty of fielding each batted ball, and in so doing more completely isolate the fielder's abilities from his surroundings. Drawing on the richer and more powerful data now available to us, LARS represents a first step in that direction, but is certainly not the last word on fielding.

References & Resources

- Colin Wyers, The Hardball Times, "How Reliable Is UZR?," *hardballtimes.com/tht-live/how-reliable-is-uzr*
- Russell Carleton, Statistically Speaking, "On the reliability of defensive abilities, part 1," *statspeakmvn.wordpress.com/2008/07/21/on-the-reliability-of-defensive-abilities-part-1*
- Dave Cameron, FanGraphs, "On Nick Markakis and Defensive Metrics," *fangraphs.com/blogs/on-nick-markakis-and-defensive-metrics*
- Mitchel Lichtman, FanGraphs, "The FanGraphs UZR Primer," *fangraphs.com/blogs/the-fangraphs-uzr-primer*
- Jonathan Judge, Baseball Prospectus, "DRA 2016: Challenging the Citadel of DIPS," *baseballprospectus.com/article.php?articleid=29898*
- Rob Arthur, FiveThirtyEight, "MLB's Hit-Tracking Tool Misses A Lot Of Hits," *fivethirtyeight.com/features/mlbs-hit-tracking-tool-misses-a-lot-of-hits*
- Rob Arthur, Make No Little Plans, "Imputing Statcast's Missing Data," *makeno-littleplans.net/imputing-statcasts-missing-data*
- Colin Wyers, The Hardball Times, "When is a fly ball a line drive?" *hardballtimes.com/when-is-a-fly-ball-a-line-drive*

The Rise of Positional Offensive Parity

by Corinne Landrey

Baseball is constantly evolving. Although there are times when the sport as a whole has been criticized for being slow to adopt change, there's no denying change is a constant in the sport. Revolutionary changes such as the designated hitter rule or the Wild Card are landmarks in its history, but more subtle changes are also an unavoidable component of the game. We've watched the average size and strength of players gradually increase over time and industry norms for equipment—bats, gloves, balls, etc.—progress to modern standards. Baseball is history and tradition, but it is also progress and change.

During the 2016 season, one such subtle evolution began to move into the spotlight as statistical realities challenged one component of baseball conventional wisdom. Baseball 101 informs us acceptable levels of offensive production exist on a sliding scale and decline in direct relation to the difficulty of one's defensive position. And what's more, the reason for this is perfectly logical.

Almost every professional ball player possesses the athleticism to play first base and, as a result, the only way to provide true value out of that position is to distinguish oneself offensively. Whereas, for up-the-middle positions such as catcher or shortstop, the pool of capable defenders is dramatically diminished, the potential defensive value contributed is significant, and, consequently, the offensive bar is much lower.

This basic understanding of roster expectations is backed up by decades of actual statistical performance. Using Baseball-Reference, I pulled the OPS+ for each positional split since 1973. (wRC+ is a more precise measurement, but given we are looking at broad overarching offensive trends, OPS+ capably does the trick.) Why 1973? Starting points are often part necessity and part arbitrary. In this case, 1973 was chosen partly because we had to start somewhere and partly because of the fact that it was the year the Designated Hitter Rule first took effect makes it the natural starting point of the modern configuration of defensive positions.

For a crude measurement of how each position has stacked up against the others offensively since 1973, I took the each season's positional OPS+ split, found the mean for each position, and sorted from lowest to highest.

Mean OPS+ by Position, 1973-Present	
Position	Mean OPS+
SS	86.8
C	92.5
2B	95.0
CF	104.0
3B	104.8
DH	108.9
LF	111.4
RF	113.4
1B	118.8

That looks perfectly normal. Up-the-middle positions (shortstop, catcher, second base, center field) are the weakest offensively, and corner positions (third base, left field, right field, first base) are the strongest. The shortstop position historically has been the most egregious underperformer—nearly 14 percentage points worse than league average—while first base has lived up to its billing as the biggest offensive force in the lineup, with production nearly 19 percentage points above league average. Designated hitter isn't quite living up to its role as a vessel for elite offensive players who can't stick at a position, but that's a topic for another time. Beyond that anomaly, this order essentially aligns with our expectations.

Now let's take a look at the OPS+ splits from this season:

2016 OPS+ by Position	
Position	Mean OPS+
C	90
SS	96
LF	100
CF	102
RF	106
2B	108
DH	109
3B	110
1B	114

Well, that's not quite as comfortable a fit for our expectations. There was more offensive production out of second base than any outfield position? Shortstops were just a few notches below league average? Left field was among the weakest positions by offensive performance? These are all glaring departures from typical trends.

As it turns out, this was a record-setting season for the majority of positions. The 2016 campaign saw the highest OPS+ from the second base and shortstop positions in the DH era, and it tied with the strike-shortened 1981 season for the highest OPS+ from the third base position. Meanwhile, it was the lowest mark from left field and tied six other seasons for the lowest first base OPS+. Right field narrowly missed out on its own record low mark of 105, set in 1983. Only catcher, center field and designated hitter finished the season with reasonably typical numbers.

We're going to take a look at four of the most glaring expectation-defying positions—shortstop, second base, third base and left field—and try to determine what happened. Is baseball in the midst of a significant offensive transition, or was 2016 just an anomaly?

The Shortstop Power Surge

The first thing to note about offensive production out of the shortstop position is that it's been on a steady incline for decades.

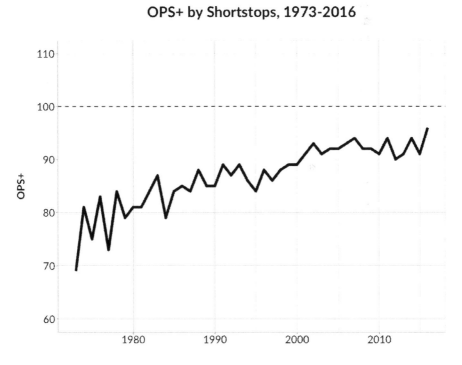

OPS+ by Shortstops, 1973-2016

In the 1970s and early '80s, shortstop offense hovered about 20 percent below league average, but in 2001 it crossed the 90 OPS+ threshold for the first time, and it's yet to fall back below that mark. Although we still talk about all-glove, no-bat shortstops, it describes a type of major leaguer that is nowhere near as ubiquitous as it once was.

Of the 21 shortstops to qualify for the batting title in 2016, 11—or 52.4 percent—posted a league average or better OPS+ (100 or higher). It marked just the fourth time in our sample that at least half of shortstops were league average or better with the stick.

Percentage of Qualified SS w/OPS+ >= 100, 1973-2016

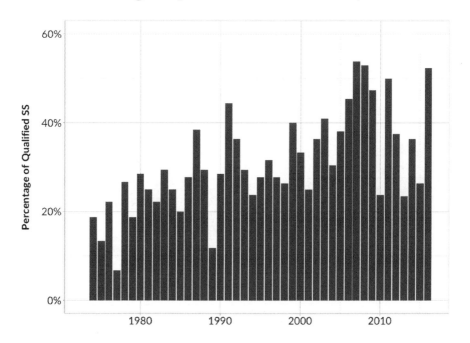

On the flip side, five qualifying shortstops—or 23.8 percent—posted an 80 OPS+ or lower. Since 2005, that figure has largely been between 20 and 30 percent, but in the '70s and '80s, it was common for more than half of qualified shortstops to display that level of offensive ineptitude.

Percentage of Qualified SS w/OPS+ <= 80, 1973-2016

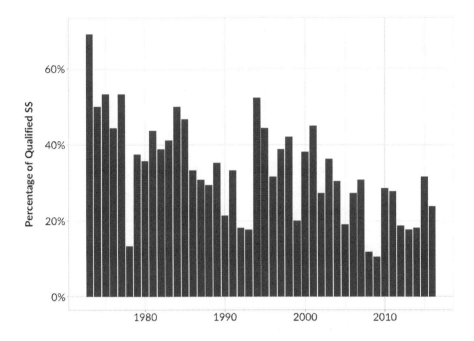

Where shortstop performance this past season distinguishes itself above and beyond recent trends, however, is in power. The league as a whole hit home runs at the second-highest rate in history, so it's not tremendously surprising the number of home runs hit by shortstops was the highest in history.

What is eye-opening, however, is the degree to which 2016 shattered previous records for home runs by shortstops. Before 2016, shortstops had averaged fewer than 50 plate appearances per home run only four times. It's likely not a surprise to learn those four years were consecutive and occurred right in the heart of the most recent power era (as well as the apex of the Derek Jeter/Alex Rodriguez/Nomar Garciaparra shortstop triumvirate):

- 2000: 49.5 PA/HR
- 2001: 49.5
- 2002: 49.2
- 2003: 48.8

This year, shortstops absolutely obliterated that 2003 record and averaged just 41.2 plate appearances per home run!

Home runs were up for most everyone, but the rate at which they increased from the shortstop position outpaced the increase across the rest of the league. The 5,610 total home runs hit by shortstops accounted for 8.8 percent of all home runs hit in the majors—surpassing 2007 and 2002 (8.4 percent) as the highest percentage in our modern sample.

These aren't your daddy's shortstops. Offense has been steadily trending upward for years from the shortstop position, and this year they built upon that trend with home run power we've never seen previously from the position.

The Corresponding Decline of Left Fielder Offense

In recent years, left field offensive production has been on the opposite trajectory as that of shortstops, although the decline hasn't been quite as smooth.

OPS+ by Left Fielders, 1973-2016

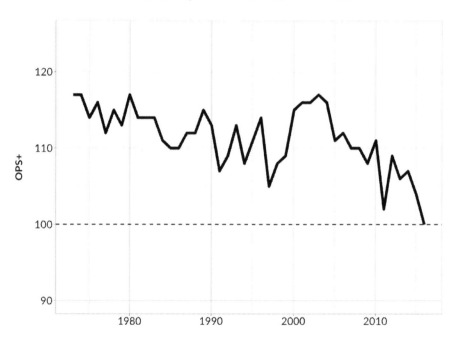

From 2000 to 2004, there was a big boost in production from left field, but, as you may recall, those were also the five seasons during which left fielder Barry Bonds won four Most Valuable Player awards and posted the following slash line over 3,050 plate appearances: .339/.535/.781. Consider the enormous impact of Bonds' production and the downward trend in production from left field is even more evident. Imagine for a moment that Bonds played any position other than left field. The following graph adds an additional line showing what the overall OPS+ would look like during Bonds' career as a left fielder (1987-2007) in that alternate universe where Bonds played another position.

OPS+ by Left Fielders, 1973-2016

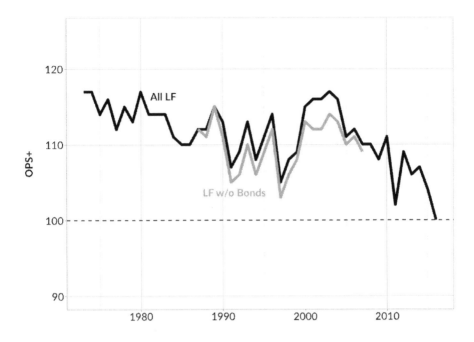

On a fundamental level, if the offensive production of shortstops relative to the league is steadily improving, a corresponding decline from other positions is an inevitable result—that's simply how league averages work. The league-average OPS+ always will be 100, so the shortstops' increased chunk of the league offense pie must come at the expense of other positions. Consider that offensive surges also have been demonstrated by second basemen and third basemen, and clearly something had to give—and it looks like left field offensive dominance was one of those things.

While shortstops are accounting for a larger percentage of league home run production than ever before, the percentage from left fielders is reaching new lows. Of the 44 seasons of this DH era, the three with the lowest chunk of the league home run pie being accounted for by left fielders are: 2014 (11.73 percent), 2015 (11.77 percent), and 2016 (10.61 percent). At the plate, left fielders as a collective group are steadily falling back toward the pack.

Of the eight (non-pitching) defensive positions, left field should be the second lowest on the defensive spectrum—ahead of only first base in terms of difficulty. It's the position where, historically, you stick guys who no longer can play in the infield or have lost the speed necessary for center field, but don't have the arm for right field. Essentially, left field is the final stop before first base or designated hitter. Consequently, it should be among the better offensive positions in the league, but that has not been the case in recent years, and 2016 represented a new low for left fielders.

The Offensive Surge of Second and Third Basemen

The production out of second base in 2016 obliterated the previous highs during the DH Era. Second basemen had produced a precisely league average 100 OPS+ several different times, but in 2016, for the first time, they collectively broke the league-average barrier and out-performed it by a full eight percent. Meanwhile, third basemen reached a milestone of their own as they finished with the second highest OPS+ in the league—outperforming every other position except first base—for the first time during this post-1973 stretch.

The hot corner crew was led by MVP-caliber performances from Kris Bryant, Manny Machado, and Josh Donaldson. Meanwhile, second basemen were headed up by the tremendous breakout of Jose Altuve, the resurgence of Robinson Cano and the Ruthian second half from Brian Dozier. Ultimately, the final stat lines for both positions were reasonably comparable:

- 2B: .277/.334/.436, .159 ISO, 108 OPS+
- 3B: .266/.331/.445, .179 ISO, 110 OPS+

Third basemen held the notable edge in power, but the second basemen maintained a slight advantage in on-base percentage to keep the overall production at comparable levels. It's worth noting at this point that we've been addressing only the hitting component of offense, but of course, offense also includes baserunning. When pulling baserunning into the mix, second basemen actually pull ahead of third basemen by a slim margin. According to FanGraphs' offensive value metric combining batting and baserunning runs, second basemen come out on top by a margin of 168.6 to 162.9 offensive runs.

This year's group of third basemen may further distinguish itself through star power and possible MVP awards, but, of the two positional groups, it's undoubtedly the performance of the second basemen that stands out as most remarkable. Third base is the position of Eddie Mathews, Mike Schmidt and George Brett. It's a corner position, and we expect strong offensive performances from the top-tier third basemen. Second base, on the other hand, more closely resembles the Island of Misfit Toys. It's where shortstops who lack the agility and/or the arm to remain shortstops land. Peruse a prospect list and you'll find plenty of third basemen, but second basemen will be few and far between. More often than not, the position is a fallback plan, and that's not naturally conducive to fostering star-level talent.

For those reasons, it comes as no surprise that second basemen as a unit had topped off at major league-average offensive production…until this year. The trio mentioned above—Altuve, Canó and Dozier—were among the best in the league, but they were hardly the only second basemen to distinguish themselves. Daniel Murphy and DJ LeMahieu went down to the wire in one of the most anti-climatic batting races to be decided by one one-thousandth of a percentage point. (LeMahieu triumphed over Murphy .348 to .347, but both players sat out the final games of the season, Murphy due to an injury and LeMahieu presumably due to his standing atop the batting average leaderboard.) Additionally, 13 second basemen hit 20 home runs, including surprise power threats such as Jean Segura, Logan Forsythe and a very real baseball player named Ryan Schimpf.

Pull it all together, and we were left with the best collective performance from second basemen in the modern era.

This Is Fun and All, But What Does it Mean?

It's impossible to note this trend in the direction of positional parity without immediately wondering whether it's related to the league-wide power surge. After all, the 2016 league home run rate was the second highest in history. Although it's clear that this recent surge isn't the only or even the primary cause—recall that this trend has been occurring over many years for left fielders and, in particular, shortstops—it would be disingenuous to say the two trends are completely unrelated.

We've been primarily using OPS+ as a proxy for overall offensive trends. As you know, there are two components to OPS: on-base percentage and slugging percentage. In the next graph, I isolated the impact of OBP by comparing it to league average in order to develop a basic OBP+ formula: 100*(OBP/lgOBP). I then charted the season totals for each of the four positions we have focused on in this article—second base, shortstop, third base and left field—over time since 1973:

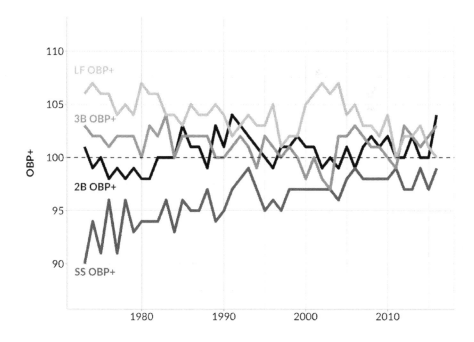

OBP+ by Position, 1973-2016

Then, I repeated the same process to look at power. Instead of crediting batting average through the use of slugging percentage, I opted to use isolated power (ISO=SLG-BA). Once again, I compared the positional splits to league average—this time using a ISO+ metric with the formula 100*(ISO/lgISO).

ISO+ by Position, 1973-2016

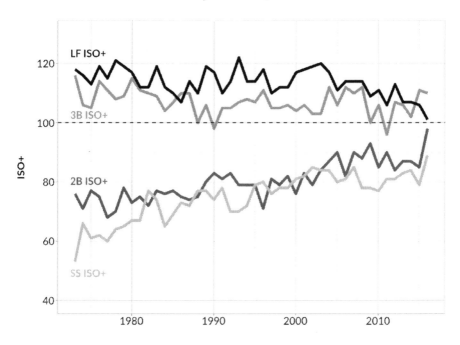

Note that the tightening of the offensive gap among these positions in 2016 is much more notable in the power metric than the on-base percentage metric. Keep in mind that these two graphs are showing production *relative to league average*. As a result the big increase this year in ISO+ for second basemen and shortstops doesn't mean that they are benefiting from the league-wide trend, but that the trend is showing up in their stats disproportionately.

We still don't know exactly what's causing the league-wide power uptick, but it's clear that one way in which it manifested itself this year was traditionally weak power positions—second base and shortstop—pulling nearer to league average power rates.

Fundamentally, it's difficult to imagine positional value as we know it is in the midst of a massive shift. It does seem safe to conclude the offensive bar for short-stops has risen over the past few decades from bloody awful to below average, but that's not enough to negate the validity of the defensive spectrum. There's no logical reason to believe that moving forward, the population of elite hitters who are subpar fielders will wane. As a result, the high defensive standards at up-the-middle positions should continue to serve to deflate the offensive production relative to that of corner positions. With that said, I'd like to posit that this current trend is more than a mere statistical anomaly, and that it tells us something positive about the immediate future of baseball: Players are getting better.

This is hardly a revolutionary theory. For years now, people have been discussing the recent impact of young talent on the game. In a July 2015 piece at FiveThirtyEight, titled "Baseball's Kids are All Right," Rob Arthur presented his findings that the youngest players in the league are accounting for a larger chunk of league production than we've seen in decades. Dave Cameron followed up those findings with his own about the influx of young baseball talent in his article titled "The Coming Fight: Why the Next CBA Won't Be Easy," in *The Hardball Times Baseball Annual 2016*. The extreme success of young players debuting in the majors in their early 20s combined with the drop-off in production of players in their 30s has skewed the productive talent in the league younger. What I contend now is that this shift has had a direct impact on positional splits.

Anecdotally, it certainly feels as though baseball is in the midst of a transition. For me, it's a feeling brought on by a confluence of recent events including, but not limited to, the Hall of Fame enshrinement of Ken Griffey Jr., the retirement of David Ortiz, the "retirement" of Álex Rodríguez, and the aforementioned emergence of young stars.

You, dear reader, are in possession of information I do not have regarding the identity of this year's award winners. Regardless of how the Most Valuable Player vote totals stack up, however, there is a fair and reasonable case to be made that the best position player in the American League in 2016 was (once again) Mike Trout and the best position player in the National League was either Kris Bryant or Corey Seager. Those three players range from the ages of 22 to 25! And, not coincidentally, two of the three play up-the-middle positions.

This personal sense that a changing of the guard is afoot is backed up by the work of Arthur and Cameron cited above as well as the following graph showing that young position players are accounting for a higher percentage of overall production than they have in the recent past.

Percentage of MLB Position Player WAR by Age Group

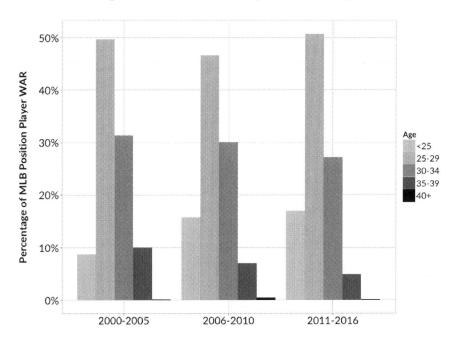

Trout, Mookie Betts and Bryce Harper aside, much of the young talent currently emerging in the major leagues consists of players at the positions exhibiting offensive surges. It is common for young players to begin their careers high up the defensive spectrum and then work their way down as they age. Consequently, the average age by position increases in a reasonably predictable manner—from up-the-middle positions to corner positions and, lastly, to the designated hitter. To calculate the average age by position, I pulled the age of every player to play a position 50 percent of the time or more, weighted it by games played, and then calculated the mean.

2016 Average Age by Position	
Position	Average Age
SS	26.2
CF	27.5
RF	28.1
3B	28.2
2B	28.4
C	29.1
LF	29.1
1B	29.6
DH	33.0

As the talent turnover at the major league level continues, a new normal inevitably will emerge. But for the time being, the young talent is outperforming colleagues while playing premium defensive positions and it is my contention that these atypical positional offensive splits are a natural byproduct. As the league continues to receive its youth infusion, and the young talent already occupying elite defensive positions is forced to slide down the defensive spectrum due to aging or organizational needs, the new normal will establish itself and a new balance of offensive production across defensive positions will form. Time will tell how well that new balance will resemble the old balance.

References & Resources

- Baseball-Reference
- FanGraphs
- Rob Arthur, FiveThirtyEight, "Baseball's Kids Are All Right," *fivethirtyeight.com/features/baseballs-kids-are-all-right*

The Year in Back Picks

by Neil Weinberg

Even in an era of increasingly detailed statistics, there are still some plays during the course of a game that aren't logged for posterity. You see these plays unfold if you're watching, but they don't get written down on scorecards or captured by any of the primary statistical sites. I'm not talking about details of specific plays, like whether the third baseman was hugging the line, but rather entire events that don't make it into the official record.

Technologies such as Statcast and companies like Baseball Info Solutions have made it easier to find these lost plays, but even when someone tracks the play, the data are not always available to the general public. Somewhere down the line, a fully implemented and integrated Statcast system could allow a user to query any set of possible circumstances and events, but we're not terribly close to that day. We have pretty good data on the official outcomes of each pitch, but there's a rich thread of baseball that happens in the background and doesn't make it into baseball's official record.

One of these baseball blind spots happens to be my favorite play, so I set out to fill in the gap for the 2016 season. It's entirely possible that teams or private statistical services track this information, but it's not something the public can find at a granular or summary level. The play is simple, but it's easy to miss. With a runner on first, how often does a catcher receive a pitch and attempt to pick off the runner by throwing behind him? How often do catchers attempt to execute what is known as a back pick?

The idea that you can be removed from the bases even when you're not trying to advance is exciting. The rules grant you safe haven while standing on one of the three bases, but as soon as you venture off you're vulnerable. Yet the farther you venture the more likely you are to make it to the next base safely. Runners are always balancing this risk and reward, while defenders attempt to keep them as close to the bag as possible.

Watching outfielders hold runners with great throws is also something I enjoy, but you can see an outfielder's throw coming from two towns over. Outfielders have a difficult time surprising runners given the distance their throws have to cover, so as long as the runner is paying the slightest bit of attention, an outfielder won't get a throw in behind him. That is not the case with catchers.

First base is just 90 feet from home and baserunners are supposed to take a primary and secondary lead to get in position to advance if a ball is put in play. Runners start about 10 feet from the bag and then take a couple more steps as the pitch is delivered. When the ball gets to the plate, they can see if it's been struck or if it's in the catcher's glove. When that happens, the runner may now be almost 20 feet from safety. There's no excuse to get picked off by the catcher because by definition you're not stealing and the ball isn't in play, but it still happens. It happened 38 times during the 2016 season, according to the data gathered for this analysis.

A conscientious runner might scamper back to the bag as soon as the ball pops the glove, but major league players spend a lot of time standing near bases, and hurrying back can be tiresome and wasteful. There are over 200,000 pitches every year with a runner on first base, but catchers try the back pick only a few hundred times. You can forgive runners for getting a little complacent.

The back pick is an exciting play because it happens so quickly and unexpectedly. It's a display of planning, awareness and talent. The entire thing usually takes fewer than three seconds, but it has the power to change the feel of an inning and a game. Even when the runner isn't picked off, he's likely not going to get as good a jump on the next batted ball.

The problem, as I noted, is that the practice has seemingly been to record these plays only when the pickoff is successful, so we don't have a thorough understanding of their occurrence. You can find successful catcher pickoffs on Baseball-Reference, but there's no public record anywhere on attempted back picks. Until now.

At the start of the season, I asked my Twitter followers for help identifying back picks as they occurred throughout the year. I also asked them to share the request with their followers so that I would have multiple fans of every team on the lookout for these plays and I followed up the request multiple times throughout the season to ensure it stayed fresh in people's minds. I have no way of knowing exactly who saw the request and how many people internalized it, but the response was significant.

Over the course of the 183-day season, I received tweets from baseball fans alerting me to back picks, totalling 218 data points in all. MLB Advanced Media also agreed to share data with me that pointed me to another 150 back picks that I didn't find via the crowd. While the two methods complemented each other, Statcast didn't capture every back pick, leaving open the possibility that the combined data set is incomplete. Finally, Baseball-Reference was kind enough to provide the play-by-play data for its catcher pickoff statistic, which pointed to five successful back picks I didn't find using the other two methods.

When comparing the Baseball-Reference list to the list I developed using the crowd and MLBAM, I discovered that whether something is coded as a pickoff, caught stealing, or "out on advancement" is not an exact science. In reviewing the play-by-play data from Baseball-Reference, I learned that official scorers are not always consistent on these kinds of plays. For this reason, I cannot say for sure that I have every successful pickoff from 2016. In total, we have a sample of 373 back pick attempts for this analysis. As with any potentially incomplete data set, please take all of the following numbers as estimates of the truth rather than a perfect accounting of the 2016 season.

When I was alerted to a back pick, I set out to watch it and record everything I could about the play. The data set includes the date, teams, inning, number of outs, count, ball/strike, pitch location, pitch type, catcher, pitcher, batter, runner, first baseman, if runners were on the other bases, and whether the runner was safe or out. Thanks to Statcast, I also have the pop time and initial lead length for about three-quarters of the observations.

In addition to logging the data, I graded the accuracy of each throw. I was at the mercy of the camera angle, but in order to avoid biasing my judgement as much as possible, I froze the video before the tag was applied to prevent myself from issuing a grade based on the outcome of the play.

Each throw received a grade of 0, 1, or 2 as follows. Throws were "on the money" if they were within a couple feet of the base and no higher than the fielder's waist. These throws were given a rating of "2." If the throw was easily corralled by the first baseman without having to move away from the play, but didn't meet the previous standard, it was a "good" throw and got a "1" rating. Anything where the throw pulled the first baseman from the bag or forced him to do something that made a successful tag essentially infeasible was a "bad" throw, receiving a "0."

I also began gathering data on a number of other factors, but abandoned those efforts after initial tests showed there wasn't much useful information. For example, home/away and score differential didn't produce interesting results, and while I initially thought it might be worthwhile to track what ended up happening to baserunners after a catcher attempted to back pick them earlier in an inning, it didn't turn into anything interesting given the sample size relative to the total number of runners who reach first base.

This data set allows us, for the first time, to study how catchers deploy the back pick. Historically, a lot of our focus on catchers' arms has been on their ability to throw out would-be base stealers, typically considering a statistic like caught stealing rate. Baseball Prospectus has recently improved upon caught stealing rate by utilizing a mixed model approach that allows it to control for pitcher and runner to develop a more isolated look at the catcher's role. The advent of Statcast has allowed us to expand that analysis into more complete measures such as pop time and arm strength, as I did in last year's edition of this publication (MLBAM's Mike Petriello advances us even further in this respect later in this very book). Now we have real data on catchers' attempts to pick off runners at first base, and can see if these data impact stolen base outcomes.

Of the 373 back pick attempts in the data set, there are 38 successful pickoffs. This first table provides a look at teams that attempted back picks most frequently and how many times they were successful. The Cubs led the way by a sizable margin and have three different catchers who utilize the back pick regularly. They were also the only club to have more than three successful pickoffs. The Red Sox, who rank second in attempts, also have multiple catchers near the top of the individual attempts leaderboard. The Royals, Brewers and Angels, who round out the top five, all relied on primarily one catcher for their attempted back picks.

		Back Pick Attempts and Successes By Team						
Rank	Team	Back Pick Attempts	Successful Pickoffs	Rank	Team	Back Pick Attempts	Successful Pickoffs
1	Cubs	48	8	16	Rangers	9	0
2	Red Sox	36	3	18	Astros	9	1
3	Royals	31	1	17	Yankees	8	1
4	Brewers	23	0	19	Padres	8	0
5	Angels	21	1	20	Nationals	7	2
6	Cleveland	19	5	21	Rays	7	1
7	Tigers	17	3	24	White Sox	7	3
8	Orioles	15	3	22	Athletics	6	1
9	Reds	14	0	23	Blue Jays	6	0
10	Rockies	13	1	25	Dodgers	5	1
11	Cardinals	12	0	26	Phillies	4	0
12	Giants	11	2	27	Braves	2	0
13	Mariners	10	0	28	Marlins	2	0
14	Twins	10	0	29	Pirates	2	0
15	D-backs	10	1	30	Mets	1	0

Sixty-four different catchers made at least one back pick attempt in 2016. Thirteen of them tried it at least 10 times. Those catchers are summarized in the following table, while the nine catchers who were successful more than once are listed in the table after that.

Back Pick Attempts and Successes By Catcher (Min. 10 Attempts)			
Name	Team	Back Pick Attempts	Successful Pickoffs
Salvador Perez	Royals	31	1
Christian Vazquez	Red Sox	22	1
Martin Maldonado	Brewers	21	0
Carlos Perez	Angels	19	1
Willson Contreras	Cubs	18	3
David Ross	Cubs	15	4
James McCann	Tigers	15	3
Miguel Montero	Cubs	14	1
Sandy Leon	Red Sox	13	2
Tony Wolters	Rockies	12	1
Yadier Molina	Cardinals	12	0
Matt Wieters	Orioles	11	2
Tucker Barnhart	Reds	11	0

Back Pick Attempts and Successes By Catcher (Min. Two Pickoffs)			
Name	Team	Back Pick Attempts	Successful Pickoffs
David Ross	Cubs	15	4
Willson Contreras	Cubs	18	3
James McCann	Tigers	15	3
Sandy Leon	Red Sox	13	2
Matt Wieters	Orioles	11	2
Yan Gomes	Cleveland	9	2
Wilson Ramos	Nationals	4	2
Dioner Navarro	Blue Jays/ White Sox	3	2
Roberto Perez	Cleveland	3	2

After learning who is responsible for back picks, we can move on to when back picks occur. The distribution by inning is quite consistent, with two notable exceptions. The number of back-pick attempts that occurred in the third inning was much higher than any other inning and the number of back-pick attempts that occurred in the ninth inning was much lower than any other inning. Presumably, the ninth inning effect can be explained by the fact that the bottom of the ninth is not always played. There is no obvious reason why the third inning would have more attempts than any other inning, but the spike exists in both the crowdsourced and MLBAM data.

Back Pick Attempts By Inning	
Inning	Back Pick Attempts
1	43
2	39
3	64
4	45
5	50
6	35
7	41
8	40
9	12
10+	4

Catchers didn't go for the back pick as often with no one out, and their attempts were most successful with one out.

Back Pick Attempts By Number of Outs			
Outs	Back Pick Attempts	Successful Pickoffs	Pickoffs Per Attempt
0	87	8	9.2%
1	156	20	12.8%
2	130	10	7.7%

One of the most striking patterns is that catchers tried to execute the back pick only when no one else was on base. Of the 373 attempts, 339 took place with only a man on first (90.9 percent). There were 17 attempts with runners on first and second, 13 with runners on the corners, and four with the bases loaded. This is somewhat interesting, given that catchers overthrew the first baseman extremely rarely and no runner attempted to advance from second or third when one of those bases was occupied. Presumably, the positioning of the first baseman is a deciding factor, but that shouldn't have impacted situations when runners are on first and third.

Roughly 32 percent of back-pick attempts were thrown to left-handed first basemen. During the course of the season, left-handed first basemen played about 25 percent of all innings at the position. This might appear interesting given that left-handed first basemen have an easier time receiving a throw of this nature, but most of this can be explained by Anthony Rizzo and Eric Hosmer, who caught more than 20 percent of the attempted back picks but only played roughly six percent of the first base innings in 2016. Catchers probably need to trust their first basemen to execute the play, but the numbers don't provide much evidence that attempts are a function of first baseman handedness.

You might also imagine that back picks would be more frequent with right-handed batters at the plate because the catcher has a better view and a more open throwing lane, but 57 percent of back-pick attempts occurred with a right-handed batter in the box relative to about 59 percent of overall plate appearances. Given that we have a sample of 373 back pick attempts and over 180,000 plate appearances, it seems likely the difference is mostly statistical noise.

Catchers also preferred to attempt a back pick on fastballs (four-seam, two-seam, sinker, cutter) as opposed to breaking balls and offspeed pitches. Roughly 72 percent of attempts came on fastballs, with about 21 percent on breaking balls and seven percent on offspeed pitches. During the entire season, pitchers threw fastballs about 63 percent of the time.

The next table shows that catchers typically prefer to attempt a back pick when they were ahead in the count. Almost 41 percent of back-pick attempts happened when the pitcher was ahead, but pitchers were ahead in the count for only about 29 percent of pitches in 2016.

Back Pick Attempts By Count		
Count	Back Pick Attempts	Entire Season
0-0	22.7%	25.8%
1-0	13.2%	10.3%
2-0	2.4%	3.6%
3-0	0.3%	1.2%
0-1	19.2%	12.8%
1-1	10.8%	10.2%
2-1	5.4%	5.3%
3-1	0.5%	2.2%
0-2	10.0%	6.4%
1-2	11.6%	9.4%
2-2	4.3%	8.1%
3-2	0.3%	4.8%
Pitcher Ahead	40.8%	28.6%
Batter Ahead	22.2%	27.3%
Even	37.8%	44.1%

Rather than using PITCHf/x coordinates for location, I decided to categorize each pitch horizontally and vertically. I opted for this strategy partly for simplicity in data collection, but also because I wanted to factor in the location of the batter and where the catcher set up. The next table shows the results of that process. You can see that catchers generally prefer to attempt back picks on pitches that are lower in the zone and away from the hitter, but it's by no means a certainty.

Back Pick Attempts By Pitch Location			
Location	Inside	Middle	Outside
High	17	34	28
Middle	39	53	74
Low	36	47	45

One thing that does seem clear is that catchers targeted base-stealing threats. According to Baseball-Reference, there were stolen-base attempts in roughly five percent of stolen-base opportunities in 2016. However, if you create an expected stolen-base attempt rate using 2016 data for runners who were on first during a back-pick attempt, weighted by the number of attempts made against them, the expected stolen-base attempt rate rises to about eight percent. This isn't a perfect proxy, because some runners like to get big secondary leads even if they don't attempt to steal bases, but it definitely shows the runners don't seem to be targeted at random.

Additionally, BP's Jonathan Judge was kind enough to share their Takeoff Rate Above Average (TRAA) metric, which tracks the propensity of base runners to attempt a stolen base, controlling for factors like the pitcher and catcher. Using the same weighting method as I did for the expected stolen-base rate, I found that runners who were targeted for a back pick had a TRAA about two percent higher than league average, indicating that base-stealing threats are more likely to be on the receiving end of a back-pick attempt than the average player.

Statcast tracked 279 of the 373 back picks in our data set. The average pop time (the time between the ball reaching the catcher's glove and it reaching the first baseman) was 1.678 seconds. Carlos Perez owns the best *single* pop time of the sample, coming in at 1.417 seconds. Roberto Perez has the worst single pop time at 4.105 seconds. The following table shows the average pop time for the catchers with at least five back picks that Statcast tracked in 2016.

Average Back Pick Attempt Pop Time (Min. 5 Throws Tracked By Statcast)			
Player	Team	Average Pop	Tracked Attempts
Christian Vazquez	Red Sox	1.48	15
Carlos Perez	Angels	1.51	17
Salvador Perez	Royals	1.53	22
Juan Centeno	Twins	1.54	5
David Ross	Cubs	1.54	9
Tucker Barnhart	Reds	1.56	10
Yadier Molina	Cardinals	1.57	9
Martin Maldonado	Brewers	1.58	20
Willson Contreras	Cubs	1.59	12
Sandy Leon	Red Sox	1.60	12
James McCann	Tigers	1.61	7
Robinson Chirinos	Rangers	1.68	6
Miguel Montero	Cubs	1.72	8
Yasmani Grandal	Dodgers	1.73	5
Matt Wieters	Orioles	1.80	10
Tony Wolters	Rockies	1.83	9
Stephen Vogt	Athletics	1.88	5
Chris Gimenez	Cleveland	1.89	5
Welington Castillo	Diamondbacks	1.99	6
Buster Posey	Giants	2.30	6

It's worth noting that pop times for back picks shouldn't be viewed like pop times to second base. While they are measured the same, glove to glove, the back pick is about opportunity and there can often be some deception or decision making on the front end. For example, there were many occasions when the catcher scooped the ball out of the dirt and threw to first because the runner extended his lead when he read that the pitch was going to be in the dirt. This takes longer than catching the ball cleanly and firing it to first, but the actual exchange and delivery might have been just as quick. Other times, the catcher froze for a second and then unleashed a throw as if he was lulling the runner into a false sense of security. This is quite different from pop times on steal attempts where there is no element of surprise -- it's all about catch and release.

Statcast tracked the initial lead length for the same 279 back picks, with an average lead length of 10.76 feet. The average initial lead at first base is 10.2 feet, meaning that back-pick targets did start a touch farther off the bag than average. Secondary lead length would further help to flesh this out, but that information is not yet available.

Using my 0-2 accuracy grading system, 58 throws were "bad," 145 were "good" and 161 were "on the money." The next table provides the average accuracy rating for the catchers who made at least 10 back-pick attempts.

Average Back Pick Attempt Accuracy Rating (Min. 10 Attempts)			
Player	Team	Average Throw Accuracy	Back Pick Attempts
Yadier Molina	Cardinals	1.92	12
Carlos Perez	Angels	1.47	19
Miguel Montero	Cubs	1.43	14
Salvador Perez	Royals	1.42	31
Christian Vazquez	Red Sox	1.41	22
Sandy Leon	Red Sox	1.38	13
Tucker Barnhart	Reds	1.36	11
Willson Contreras	Cubs	1.33	18
David Ross	Cubs	1.33	15
Tony Wolters	Rockies	1.25	12
James McCann	Tigers	1.13	15
Matt Wieters	Orioles	1.09	11
Martin Maldonado	Brewers	1.05	21

Put this all together and the typical back-pick attempt looks something like this. A potential base-stealing threat is on first base and the other bases are empty. There are one or two outs and the pitcher is ahead in the count. The pitch will likely be a fastball and it will probably be somewhat low and away. The runner will have started with a lead of around 11 feet and it will take the catcher about 1.7 seconds to get the ball from his glove to the first baseman. The throw will very likely be either on the money or good, but the runner will be safe nine times out of 10. There's also probably a decent chance you're watching a Cubs, Red Sox, Royals, Brewers or Angels game.

We don't have a huge sample size, and the number of successes are particularly limited, so creating a complex model to predict when a back pick will be successful isn't going to be a fruitful endeavor. However, we can compare the outs and the non-outs along a couple of key variables. Here are the 279 back picks tracked by Statcast with the average pop time, accuracy rating, and initial lead length. You can see that it's accuracy and lead length that seem to more closely relate to successful pick-offs, while pop time goes in the opposite direction.

Comparison Between Successful and Unsuccessful Back Pick Attempts			
Outcome	Average Accuracy	Average Pop Time	Average Initial Lead
Safe	1.22	1.668	10.6
Out	1.67	1.805	12.2

This generally squares with my impressions after having watched 373 of these attempts over the course of the 2016 season. The key isn't so much the extra 0.05 seconds. It's recognizing when the runner is too far off the bag and getting the throw to the first baseman in a location where he can get the tag on the runner as efficiently as possible.

As you can see from the data set, there are a lot of catchers who are pretty great at this, but the success rate is still extremely low. The most successful catcher in 2016 picked off only four runners. It seems much more likely that catchers use this tool to police the kinds of leads and jumps runners get at first base. Actually picking the runner off is a nice bonus, but the real intent is making sure he doesn't go first to third on a single or score on a double.

There are plenty more questions I would like to be able to answer, particularly how do runner leads and jumps change given the presence of a good back-picking catcher and in the immediate aftermath of a back-pick attempt. We can't answer those questions with the data we currently have, but hopefully this is a good start that offers a solid foundation for future work.

Back picks aren't anywhere close to the most important catcher skill, but given the rise of new catcher defense metrics, filling in the gap makes sense. We know more than ever about pitch framing, stolen-base prevention, and game calling, but we've never really taken a close look at when and how catchers throw behind the runner at first. Now, thanks to the help of many curious readers, we have such a data set—that can be made available for anyone to use in further studies—and in the future it'll hopefully become more robust.

References & Resources

- Special thanks to Daren Willman at MLB Advanced Media, Jonathan Judge at Baseball Prospectus and Hans Van Slooten at Baseball-Reference for providing data used in this essay.
- Special thanks also to the dozens of individuals on Twitter who helped identify attempted back picks throughout the year.
- Jonathan Judge, Harry Pavlidis, and Dan Turkenkopf, Baseball Prospectus, "Introducing Deserved Run Average (DRA)—And All Its Friends," *baseballprospectus.com/article.php?articleid=26195*
- Neil Weinberg, *The Hardball Times Baseball Annual 2016*, "Analyzing Catcher Pop Time," 2015
- Baseball-Reference, 2016 MLB Catcher Statistics, *baseball-reference.com/leagues/MLB/2016-specialpos_c-fielding.shtml*
- Baseball-Reference, 2016 MLB Baserunning/Misc. Statistics, *baseball-reference.com/leagues/MLB/2016-baserunning-batting.shtml*

The Effect of the Marine Layer on Fly Balls

by David Kagan and Chris Mitchell

It is simply baseball lore. Garrett Anderson warned Torii Hunter when he joined the Angels in 2007. Hunter alerted Albert Pujols when he joined the team in 2012. No doubt, Hunter or Pujols shared the word with Mike Trout, and given Trout's enthusiasm for all things weather-related, there's no telling how many people he's told. It has been handed down from generation to generation: The marine layer will turn homers into lazy fly balls.

On the face of it, this seems reasonable. The marine layer is the moist, humid, foggy air that flows from the ocean to West Coast ballparks at night. It sure feels thicker than the warm air of the afternoon—perhaps thick enough to obstruct the flight of a deep fly ball. Torii Hunter estimated the marine layer hacks 15 feet off of fly balls during night games at Angel Stadium.

What is the Marine Layer?

The marine layer is a complex weather phenomenon that happens only along the West Coast. In the United States, weather patterns generally flow from west to east. As air flows eastward across the Pacific Ocean, the water keeps the air cool and moist year-round, resulting in a temperate climate on the West Coast. Further east, the air flows across land that is warmer than the ocean in the summer and cooler in the winter. This explains the hot summers and cold winters in the Midwest and the East.

However, California's temperate climate has a downside: the marine layer. It rears its ugly head from time to time—particularly in June and July—to drag down what would otherwise be warm temperatures. As Mark Twain once remarked, "The coldest winter I ever spent was a summer in San Francisco." Twain was undoubtedly experiencing the marine layer.

As warm air moves across the ocean, the air near the surface of the water is cooled and, therefore, becomes denser. Since denser air sinks, it becomes trapped below the warmer air. The trapped air also becomes more humid due to evaporation from the water. Under the right conditions, fog can form. That fog is the marine layer.

What Does Physics Tell Us?

If you ever took physics or chemistry, you might remember something called the Ideal Gas Law (don't worry, there won't be a quiz). The law tells us that the density of a gas grows with increasing atmospheric pressure and it drops with increasing temperature. In addition, the density of a gas grows as the average mass of the gas molecules increases.

The density of the air will determine the distance of fly balls because less dense air is thinner air. Think Coors Field. A physicist would say something more wonky like, "The higher the air density, the higher the drag force on a ball in flight."

Things are getting complicated now. The marine layer's low temperatures should increase the density of the air and reduce the distance of fly balls. However, the marine layer's high humidity level has the opposite effect. Humidity is the result of water molecules replacing the nitrogen and oxygen molecules in the air. Water molecules are 35 to 45 percent lighter, which reduces the air density. This causes the distance to *increase*. This seems counterintuitive, but it's true: Although it *feels* "thicker," humid air is less dense than dry air.

In Alan Nathan's Hardball Times article, "Going Deep on Goin' Deep," he found that a 10-degree decrease in temperature will shorten the distance of a fly ball by about three feet, while a 50 percent increase in relative humidity will increase the distance by roughly one foot. According to physics, then, there should be little effect due to the marine layer. Both the "temperature effect" and the "humidity effect" are relatively small, and they work to counteract each other.

What Does Statcast Tell Us?

Alan Nathan found that four of the six West Coast parks were below average in terms of average flyball distance. Of these six, only Seattle was not within a standard deviation of the league average. Anaheim is the only West Coast park that falls more than one standard deviation above the average. This provides a little evidence the ball doesn't travel as far on the West Coast, which might explain the lack of run scoring out there. But it's less clear whether this is a result of the marine layer cropping up every so often to knock down fly balls.

Our first thought to test for the Marine Layer Effect was to compare the average distance of fly balls hit during the day with those hit at night. In our experience, the marine layer is more likely to occur at night than during the day, as the layer has a tendency to break down in the morning and reassert itself in the late afternoon. The afternoon heat causes air to rise, and it is often replaced by ocean air that drags the marine layer with it.

We collected all plate appearances that resulted in a fly ball at each of the six parks, ignoring all events where there was no distance measurement recorded. The results are below.

Flyball Distance by Time of Game, Ballpark						
Day/Night	SDP	LAA	LAD	OAK	SFG	SEA
Night	320'	325'	317'	310'	310'	320'
Day	321'	315'	311'	312'	307'	321'

Three of the six parks have slightly longer flyball distances at night, while three do not. By no means does this debunk the Marine Layer Effect, but the lack of compelling evidence is telling. The ball does not seem to travel any further during the day.

Of course, it is possible factors other than game-time conditions could be at play here. For example, the day sample might be skewed by backups filling in during day games after night games, specifically glove-first backup catchers. This might artificially lower the daytime distance, making the nighttime distances appear too long.

So in addition to slicing the data by team, we looked at individual players who hit at least 10 fly balls during day and night games. The plot below shows the average night distance minus the average day distance for each player.

Night Distance - Day Distance

Players who hit balls further at night than during the day have bars to the right of the axis, while players who hit further during the day have bars to the left. Again, there is no clear evidence that the ball travels further during the day. If anything, these data hint that the reverse may be true.

We also tried splitting the data by ballpark. We selected three power hitters from each of the West Coast teams and compared their average flyball distances at the six coastal parks to their average distance at parks not on the Pacific Coast. Here are the results.

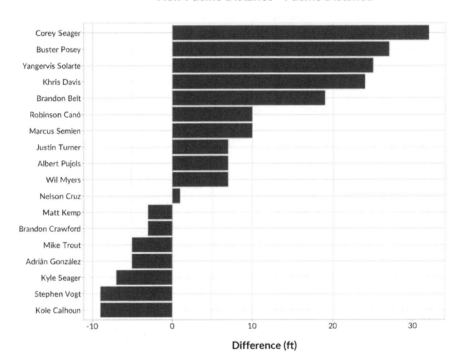

Non-Pacific Distance - Pacific Distance

Of the 18 players, 11 hit the ball farther when removed from their home coast, with some doing so by a huge margin. However, it isn't immediately clear whether this is a direct result of the marine layer. This, along with the fact that seven players actually hit the ball further on the West Coast, keeps this one in the inconclusive category.

What Do Weather Data Tell Us?

The methods we have used to this point don't provide conclusive answers to the Marine Layer Effect. They suggest it's somewhere between minimal and non-existent, but our analyses were admittedly back-of-the-envelope. Carl Sagan once said, "Extraordinary claims require extraordinary evidence." If we are to completely debunk something so ensconced in baseball lore, we'll need to dig deeper.

For a more rigorous analysis, we used the time stamps from Statcast to link to historical weather data from Weather Underground. These weather data are available roughly every 20 to 60 minutes, which is just what we needed, given how quickly the weather can change. On the downside, these fine-grained weather data are available only from airports. We chose the airport closest to the ballpark in each case, but not all ballparks are particularly close to an airport.

There was an additional problem. As Supreme Court Justice Potter Stewart once remarked about pornography during a case, "I can't define it, but I know it when I see it." The same holds true for the marine layer. There is no standard threshold for temperature, humidity or anything else at which fog forms, and therefore no purely objective way to define the marine layer. To settle on a definition, we sought help from several weather professionals, including a TV weatherman. Using their input, we settled on the following definition:

- Temperature less than or equal to 70° F
- Relative Humidity greater than or equal to 80 percent
- Conditions: Partly Cloudy (Scattered Clouds), Mostly Cloudy (Broken Clouds), or Overcast

Here are the average fly ball distances from each ballpark split by this definition.

Flyball Distances, By Marine Layer Definition			
Ballpark	No Marine Layer	Marine Layer	Difference
OAK	312'	291'	-21'
SEA	321'	314'	-7'
SD	318'	322'	4'
LAD	315'	321'	7'
SF	307'	316'	9'
LAA	322'	333'	11'

None of these discrepancies seem overly compelling, except for maybe Oakland's. But we can do better than simple raw averages. For each stadium, we built a regression model to predict flyball distance. This allowed us to control for exit speed, vertical (launch) angle, horizontal (spray) angle, and pitch speed. By controlling for all of these factors, we can be reasonably sure our "Marine Layer" variable isn't picking up anything that isn't weather-related. Here are the results.

Change in Distance Due To Marine Layer					
Ballpark	Marine Layer Effect	Standard Error (+/-)	P-value	R-squared	Miles from Ballpark
SD	-6.1'	3.0'	0.04	0.91	3
OAK	-5.6'	3.2'	0.07	0.89	3
SEA	-1.2'	2.3'	0.53	0.96	4
LAA	-1.1'	2.8'	0.69	0.94	7
LAD	-0.1'	2.4'	0.96	0.93	13
SF	2.8'	2.0'	0.16	0.89	14

We have evidence!…Sort of. Our marine layer variable has a negative coefficient in five of the six parks, though only two of them—San Diego and Oakland—are statistically significant (denoted by P-values below 0.10). However, those two parks also happen to be the two that are closest to the airport weather stations. The further the weather reading from the ballpark, the more the signal fades. This suggests the lack of evidence in Seattle, Los Angeles and San Francisco might be a direct result of sub-optimal weather data. Given how much weather can vary across relatively small geographies, we shouldn't be surprised that anything over a few miles might be enough to sabotage our analysis.

One variable we did not account for was wind. There is no obvious reason to think this skews the results one way more so than the other, but we do know that wind matters a lot. The aforementioned work by Alan Nathan found that a five mph out-blowing wind adds 19 feet to a fly ball's trajectory. Unfortunately, we couldn't do much with the wind data from either Weather Underground or Baseball-Reference. Wind just varies too much over time, across geography and even in different parts of the ballpark for those data to be of much use.

Nonetheless, the R-Squared values tell us that we're accounting for roughly 92 percent of the variance in flyball distance. That's, like, almost all of it! So it's unlikely there are any important factors we're missing aside from better weather data. This analysis seems pretty trustworthy.

Is There Any Evidence of the Marine Layer Effect?

All of this is to say there's compelling directional evidence of the Marine Layer Effect. The marine layer has a statistically significant effect on flyball distance, and since the data are consistent in the two ballparks with the best weather data, that almost certainly isn't a fluke. The effect size is around six feet, which isn't nothing. Six feet could be the difference between an F8 at the warning track and a wall-scraping home run.

But at the same time, six feet isn't *usually* enough to be a difference-maker. While we've confirmed the existence of the Marine Layer Effect, we've also formed an idea of just how minimal its effect is. Yes, the Marine Layer Effect is real, but that doesn't mean it's large enough to wring our hands over.

There's a good chance you saw the headlines last year stating "Bacon is Just as Likely to Give you Cancer as Cigarettes." To everyone's relief, this wasn't actually the case, as smoking cigarettes is orders of magnitude more risky than eating bacon every day. The bad headlines stemmed from the finding that both bacon and cigarettes certainly increase cancer risk, even though eating bacon only does so ever so slightly. So just as eating bacon every day *definitely slightly* affects cancer risk, the existence of a marine layer *definitely slightly* affects flyball distance.

What Can We Say About the Marine Layer's Effect on Fly Balls?

At the very least, we can say the marine layer shortens flyball distances. But there is no evidence the Marine Layer Effect is anything more than marginal. Even when using the best data, our analysis estimated it shortens flyball distances by only by six feet.

Just how much six feet matters is a bit hard to quantify. We tried using our same models to predict linear weight run values rather than fly ball distance, but didn't have much success. With flyball distance, we were able to explain most of the variance just by looking at how the ball was hit, making it relatively straightforward to isolate the Marine Layer Effect. With actual baseball outcomes, however, it's a bit more complicated, as there is so much else that comes into play. Defensive positioning, fielder quality and ballpark idiosyncrasies are all near-impossible to quantify. They're also bigger deals than the Marine Layer Effect, which makes it difficult to isolate its effect on run scoring. We also tried comparing runs per game and home runs per plate appearance in games where the marine layer was in effect to games where it wasn't, but couldn't find any statistical difference.

It's worth noting that our analyses were not perfect. Ideally, we would have used minute-by-minute weather data taken from the field at every ballpark, but we had to do our best with what we had. It's possible our shoddy radar is picking up only a small, six-foot blip when the actual effect is much larger. We don't know for sure how large the Marine Layer Effect is.

The results from our data crunching are a bit wishy-washy, but they make sense in the context of physics. The two atmospheric symptoms of a marine layer are a lower temperature and a higher humidity. We know both of these symptoms have an effect on flyball distances, but we also know those effects are relatively small. And perhaps more importantly, we know they work in opposite directions. The cold air is dense, but the humidity drags down that density. That suggests a minimal effect, which is exactly what we found.

There's common-sense, anecdotal evidence against the Marine Layer Effect, as well. In Colorado, the thin air creates joy among hitters. Lazy fly balls become homers, while pitchers complain their breaking pitches remain stubbornly straight.

On the West Coast, hitters complain they lose homers to the marine layer, yet you never hear that West Coast curveballs snap with extra bite. This disconnect is yet another strike against the Marine Layer Effect.

Every time a ball doesn't travel as far as the fans, players or coaches would have liked, they blame the marine layer. That's human nature. We all like to blame our shortcomings on external factors. Their blame isn't necessarily misplaced, either, as our analysis tells us the marine layer knocks six feet or so off of the average fly ball. Surely, that's enough to turn the occasional home run into an out. But the claim that the occasional presence of a marine layer explains low run scoring on the West Coast? That seems to be—if you'll pardon the pun—a bunch of hot air.

References & Resources

- Special thanks to meteorologists Clay Davenport of the National Oceanic and Atmospheric Administration (NOAA), Kris Kuyper, Chief Meteorologist of Action News Now, and Shane Mayor, Professor of Geosciences at California State University Chico.
- Statcast data from Baseball Savant
- Weather data from Weatherunderground.com
- Alan Nathan, The Hardball Times, "Going Deep on Goin' Deep," *hardballtimes.com/going-deep-on-goin-deep*
- MLB.com, "Hunter warned Pujols about marine-layer effect," *m.mlb.com/news/article/29323982*

The Shape of Talent: Historical WAR Distribution in MLB

by Shane Tourtellotte

Talent in baseball has a distribution, or shape, that we're familiar with even if we don't think about it much. A rare few superstars, players like Mike Trout and Clayton Kershaw, inhabit the top; the shape broadens below to the stars, the good players, the average players, the role players. It ends, not with the mass of replacement-level players, but with a narrower band of sub-replacement figures, sticking around despite performance that merits getting shuffled out.

The shape of talent in the major leagues is not quite a pyramid; it's more like a squat pear. Include minor leaguers, college players and semi-pro players, and it would be a pyramid, at least for a lot longer.

But this shape is not fixed. The evolution of talent evaluation and recruitment over the decades has shifted the dimensions. So have league expansion and the rise of other professional sports drawing away athletes who could have made the majors. Analytics has placed a number value on the minimum production a player must create if he's not to be considered expendable.

So how has the shape changed? Is the top echelon more crowded with players able to perform at the highest level? Is the bottom level thinning out? Is the middle stuffed with a glut of pretty good players? Are position players and pitchers changing their talent distributions in different ways?

To answer questions like these, I looked at player WAR in many season samples, going back just over a century, to see how the distributions have evolved. Along with other relevant statistics, they revealed many interesting trends and surprises.

Methodology

The base of my study was a run of three seasons from every decade from the 1910s to the 2010s. I chose the 'X3 to 'X5 seasons, to stretch from before the Federal League to the present day. To these I added other seasons relating to things I wanted to examine. These years were:

- 1916, for the aftermath of the Federal League folding.
- 1941-42 and 1946-47, for before, during and after World War II.
- Spans completing coverage of the five modern expansions of major league baseball: 1960-62, 1968-70, 1976-78, 1992 and 1997-99.

For each year, I put the players in descending order, according to Baseball-Reference's WAR. I counted down to the points at which the players above constituted 25 percent, 50 percent and 100 percent of total WAR for the majors, usually including a fraction of the final player's performance to make it come out exact.

I then calculated these players as a proportion of the total players in the majors. These percentages would help show how talent in the league was concentrated, top-heavy or more broadly distributed. I also noted the WAR figures where the cutoff points occurred. This would show whether modern methods of bringing talent into baseball really have made it harder to dominate over the average run of ballplayers.

In addition, I determined the proportion of players who accumulated -1.0 WAR or worse over the season. I was interested to see how many players were not just obviously bad but allowed to be that bad for extended periods. Also, as the concept of replacement-level performance has become entrenched during the 21st century, I wanted to see whether teams were altering their playing-time decisions to take sub-replacement players off the field sooner and diminish the ranks of the underachievers.

I did these calculations for all players, then separately for position players and pitchers. Pitchers' WAR did not include their batting, and for position players, it excluded any times they were sent to the mound. My criteria for defining the categories did not always add up exactly to the totals for all players, but the divergence is slight.

I also kept track of the number of active players per team in the majors. This counts them in the majors as a whole, not on specific clubs; someone who played for two teams in a season counts just once. This helps illuminate certain trends and a couple of short-term cases.

As an example of what I'm doing, I'll show my work for the 1913 season. I cannot show all 551 players in the majors that year, but I can show some of the raw numbers.

1913 Season							
All Players	Top 25%	Top 50%	Top 100%	Cut 25 %	Cut 50 %	Cut 100 %	-1 WAR
551	15.6	41.8	138.9	6.0	4.0	1.4	24

Top25 shows the number of players above the 25 percent WAR cutoff point, and so on for 50 and 100. The Cut columns show what the cutoff WAR values were.

With 15.6 players above the 25 percent cutoff out of 551 players in the majors, the percentage of players producing 25 percent of league WAR was 2.83 percent in 1913. For 50 percent of league WAR, it was 7.59 percent of players; at 100 percent WAR, it was 25.21 percent.

That last number may have some heads spinning. Yes, the top quarter of the majors in 1913 produced 100 percent of league WAR. The bottom three quarters, more than 400 players, had an aggregate WAR of zero. While this is a low figure for the years studied, it's not an all-time low, and it isn't something confined to the early years of baseball. The corresponding figure in 2013, an even century later, is four-tenths of a percentage point lower.

Players with -1.0 WAR or worse, 24 out of 551, made up 4.36 percent of the league in 1913. That is almost exactly the mean of all the years I observed (excluding the 1994-95 strike seasons), 4.37 percent.

Before going to results, and to avoid confusion, I will briefly note the abbreviations I'll use in the article. "Top" will refer to the top 25 percent through top 100 percent measures; I'll sometimes use "Top25" and so on for specific ones. Likewise "Cut" for the cutoff numbers, and "Minus1" for the percentage of players with season WARs at or below -1.0.

The Long View

With the methodology explained, I'll proceed to showing how things have changed over 100 years or so. I'll go deeper into specific cases later, but to start I'll look at the longer historical trends. First, the Minus1 numbers.

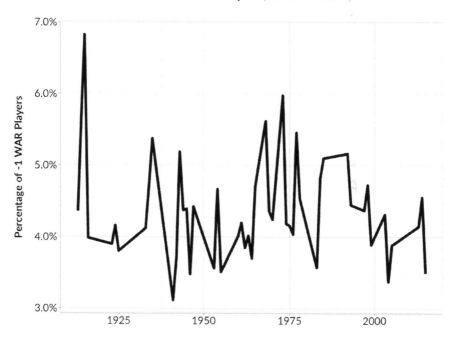

-1 WAR Players, 1913-2015

Note: The 1994-95 strike-affected years are excluded.

The overall trendline for this time frame is downward by about 0.5 percent per 100 years. This is what we'd expect, as talent evaluation improves with time. The problem is that the upward spike in the 1910s distorts the trend. Were we to look at the 1920s through the 2010s, the trend line would be essentially flat. There is reason to consider the 1910s numbers flukish (more on that later).

-1 WAR Position Players and Pitchers, 1913-2015

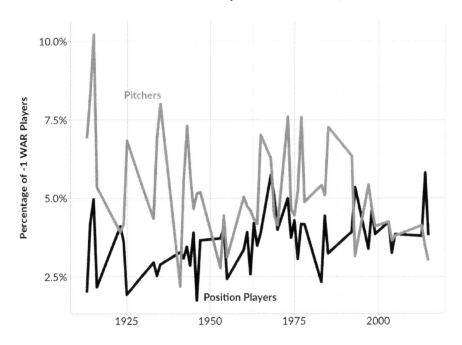

Note: The 1994-95 strike-affected years are excluded.

Separating position players from pitchers, we find contrasting trends. The pitchers are moving down strongly, more than two percentage points per century, while batters are rising by over one percent per century. If we cut out the 1910s again, the batters' trend line keeps its slope, but the pitchers' flattens out by about half.

The cause for the drop in bad pitcher seasons is plain. Their usage has changed massively over time, with starters pitching fewer innings,and back-end bullpen arms becoming much more fungible. There are fewer opportunities for a poor pitcher to keep pitching long enough to accumulate -1.0 WAR or worse.

The commensurate rise for position players is tougher to explain, especially for recent decades and the relief pitching explosion. Their Minus1 rates in the 1990s, 2000s and 2010s are all above the historical mean. One could point to bigger pitching staffs squeezing position players off rosters, forcing worse players to play more, but this doesn't hold water. Total numbers of position players used per season have ticked upward even during the relief explosion, though not nearly as fast as for pitchers.

What caught my attention is that there is no perceptible drop in Minus1 rates since 2000, which is roughly when replacement-level theory came into vogue. I expected that once teams had a statistical measure for when poor players should be removed from regular play, they would use it. There is no such indication.

It might be that the analytics departments of baseball teams have more sophisticated measures, and we on the outside are just mistaken about where the replacement-level line is. With the wide range in capability of those analytics departments, I doubt there's such a league-wide consensus. It is clear that few, if any, teams are using publicly available WAR values as their sole or even primary evaluation tool. What their measures are, and whether they are better or worse than WAR, we can but speculate.

Next, a look at the Cut thresholds.

Cut Thresholds, Position Players, 1913-2015

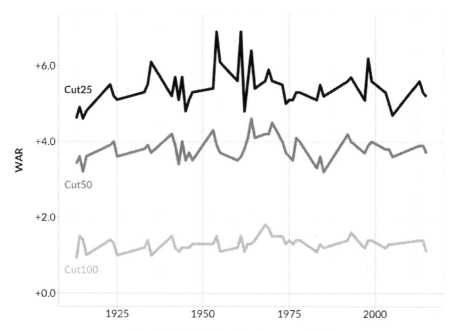

Note: The 1994-95 strike-affected years are excluded.

Cut Thresholds, Pitchers, 1913-2015

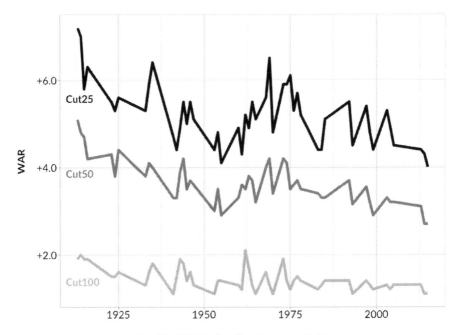

Note: The 1994-95 strike-affected years are excluded.

For all players taken together, the WAR numbers have been trending down for all three thresholds. The drop has been about 0.5 WAR per century for Cut25 and Cut50, and 0.2 WAR for Cut100. Again, there is a serious difference between position players and pitchers.

For the batters, the trend lines instead have been moderately upward, though this comes mainly from the 1980s and earlier. The 1990s onward have tamped down the overall rise, more so for the more elite cutoffs. Great position players have been a bit less great in recent decades.

Do not take that statement too far. While we don't have Ruthian dominance any longer—not without clear and creamy chemical intervention—for a broader, more mortal definition of "great," modern position players are holding their own.

The pitchers are different, and for the same reasons of changed usage observed above. This doesn't pertain just to the recent bullpen explosion, either. Take out everything from 1990 onward, and the trend line slopes are nearly unchanged. Front-line pitchers have seen their innings—and their chances to compile huge WAR scores—taken away from them since the 1880s.

Finally, the Top measures.

Top Figures, Position Players, 1913-2015

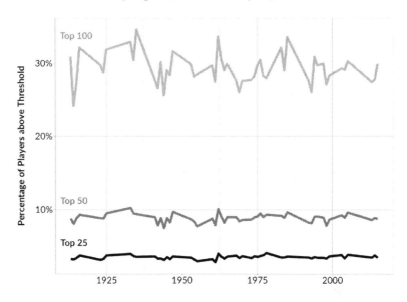

Note: The 1994-95 strike-affected years are excluded.

Top Figures, Pitchers, 1913-2015

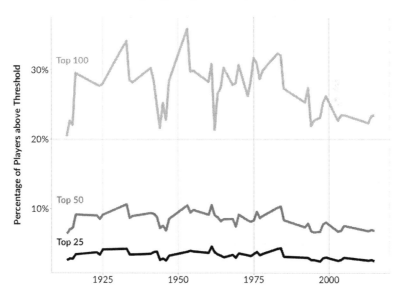

Note: The 1994-95 strike-affected years are excluded.

It can be tough to discern with the naked eye, but pitchers generally have had lower Top values at all three thresholds than position players. As an example, the historical average for Top100 is 27.0 percent for pitchers, compared to 29.2 percent for batters. This means pitching talent has been more narrowly distributed, perhaps what one would expect given the divide between regular starters and all other pitchers.

Movement over the years also has been notably different.

Top 25/50/100 Historical Averages			
Players	Top25	Top50	Top100
Position	0.20	-0.03	-0.80
Pitchers	-0.70	-1.00	-2.00

For position players, the higher two measures have had nearly no change, while Top100 slid downward. Shape for good batters has stayed the same, while for decent players it's become slightly narrower. For pitchers, there's a clear decline across the board, relatively stronger at more elite levels (if looked at by proportions rather than absolute numbers). Modern first-rank pitchers, while not putting up the gaudier WAR figures of decades past, are taking a heftier chunk of league WAR.

I will do my summing up of the wide historical trends at the end of this piece. For now, let's look at specific time periods.

Some Shorter Views

There is one year in the whole study where great changes are obvious, without anything intrinsic to baseball causing them. That year is 1933.

That year, the three Top measures were at their highest levels for all players. Separate ones for pitchers and position players were likewise very high across the board (and for Top50, both their highest). At the same time, the Cut25 and Cut50 values were 0.2 WAR lower than in 1925, the closest previous year. (Cut100 had risen 0.1 WAR, a change too small to be a clear indicator.)

Taken together, these facts show 1933 had the most evenly distributed talent of any year I looked at. The cause is plain enough, once one steps back from baseball itself: 1933 was the nadir of the Great Depression.

With the American economy at rock bottom, baseball teams were cutting their rosters to the bone. Players who used to be depth pieces, playing a little here and there, were gone. If you were on the roster, you were going to pull some weight, not hang around as insurance.

This is reflected in the number of players per team in baseball that year. At 28.81, the ratio is easily the lowest in the whole survey. (1935 comes closest, at 30.25.) It's also the lowest mean seen for position players, though for pitchers it was beaten out by 1914. The long-term trend of more pitchers being used every year may be responsible; even in the early 20th century it had its effect.

The retrenchment, surprisingly, did not reach the worst players. Minus1 figures in 1933 were below average, but not at or near historical lows. Not even in the worst economic times, with the greatest inducement to get rid of bad players, could the teams manage the trick.

Another of the great outside interruptions of baseball came with the Second World War. So many players went into the armed forces, and such scrambling had to be done to find available bodies to fill their places, it seems inevitable the shape of baseball's talent would change.

The reality isn't as neat. There were changes, but few of them clear and unmistakable. The most obvious shift during the era was one that came after the war was over.

Pitchers showed drops in the Top measures, starting in 1943 for Top100 and '44 for the other numbers. Position players also showed some moderate drops during the war years in Top25 and Top 50, but there was no pattern for Top100. The tendency was for the best players to dominate a bit more, but only a bit.

The reason the shape of talent didn't change was, in my opinion, because the war's effects cut evenly across all levels of talent. Even before the war (there was a peacetime draft in 1940), inductees ran the gamut from Hank Greenberg to Hugh "Losing Pitcher" Mulcahy. The case remained similar, on a larger scale, during the war. The lesser talents rising up to fill the vacuum meant remaining first-class players tilted the balance their way, but they weren't good enough to tilt it too far.

Cut numbers behaved oddly. Through much of the war they pinballed around, generally rising for pitchers but with no clear direction for the rest. In 1945, however, the numbers fell across the board, often heavily. This was the end of the war, when teams were scraping the bottom of the barrel for players. To see the spread of performance telescope in on itself at this point is no surprise.

The surprise was 1946, the year after the war ended. Top measures remained somewhat depressed, even though Cut numbers were rebounding. The true eye-opener was the plunge in Minus1 position players, falling by more than half and reaching the lowest level in my survey. There was no such drop among pitchers.

I believe this is the effect of post-war talent re-evaluation. There were nearly 100 more players in the majors in 1946 than in either '45 or '47. The leagues were stuffed with both men returning from the war and those who had taken their places for the duration. Teams had to figure out which returnees no longer could compete effectively (such as Cecil Travis) and which holdovers still could (like Hal Newhouser). This meant failing players could be replaced more quickly and potentially effectively than ever before.

This, I believe, thinned the ranks of -1.0 WAR position players severely. Why the pitchers didn't see a similar plunge is not clear. Their ranks expanded the same way as the position players. I could just say that pitchers are treated differently, but that doesn't actually explain anything.

Had such a wartime disruption happened in modern times, though, the ranks of -1.0 WAR pitchers would have fallen even faster, with coaches not letting starters go from zero back to a full yearly workload. That much certainly wasn't the case in 1946.

The expansion seasons are prime periods for expected changes in the shape of baseball talent. Anecdotally, the toppling of home run records in 1961 and 1998 famously pointed toward the dilution of pitching ability. I looked not only at individual years, but collectively at the six expansion seasons: 1961-62, 1969, 1977, 1993 and 1998.

For pitchers, expansion produces few reliable indicators. None of the Top or Cut measures moved one way or the other more than four times out of six. The Minus1 measure was more consistent, going down in five of six expansion seasons. This was not what one might expect with the influx of new and presumably inferior pitchers. Do recall, though, that sometimes they would be facing new and presumably inferior batters.

Position players show stronger patterns. Top measures fell in 14 of 18 instances, more consistently for Top50 and Top100. Cut measures rose by 13-4, with one showing no change. Minus1 split evenly. So for position players, the echelons of talent grew more elite with higher WAR cutoffs. This falls in with the standard expectation of expansion's effects, which it did not for pitchers.

The years 1961 and 1962 (American League and National League expansion, respectively) provide a strange case. In 1961, the position players' pattern was as I've just given, with pitchers mainly going the opposite ways. In 1962, though, the directions reversed. Top measures for position players soared while their Cut values generally dropped; they did just the opposite for pitchers. The Top100 measures both had huge movements in '62, spreading out talent for position players and narrowing it for pitchers.

The 1961 numbers confirm conventional wisdom about that year. Elite batters feasted on expansion pitching. In 1962, the tables turned dramatically. Pitchers made up all the lost ground, and then some, as batters gave away more than they had gained. The growing dominance of pitching that peaked in 1968 perhaps can be traced back to this swing six years earlier.

The 1961 pattern of sagging pitching and a stronger batting elite did repeat itself in one more expansion season: 1998. It didn't fall out this way in any of the other four expansion years, but those bookend seasons have become received wisdom on the effects of expansion. This is mainly due to the partial coincidence of the Roger Maris and Mark McGwire/Sammy Sosa assaults on the home run record. The truth, I've shown, is somewhat different.

There is one other expansion I have not covered because it's so different it deserves a fully separate look. That is the arrival of the Federal League for the 1914-15 seasons. Creating eight new major-league teams at once, without the planning of the established teams and league structure, is a different animal. Contracting from 24 back to 16 teams in 1916 is even more so.

In 1913, before the FL made its challenge, elite pitchers had an apparent advantage over elite hitters. The WAR cutoffs for pitchers were 7.2/5.1/1.9, compared to 4.6/3.4/0.9 for position players. Likewise, all Top measures were lower for pitchers, indicating superiority of regular and elite players alike. The hitch was that this produced a larger pitching underclass, with almost seven percent of them at -1.0 WAR or worse.

During the FL's existence, those Cut numbers for pitchers fell, especially for the highest rank, while Top numbers rose. Pitching talent was getting flattened, even though the ranks of bad pitchers swelled. By 1915, more than 10 percent of pitchers put up -1.0 WAR or lower. The figures for position players had no clear pattern, except that their Minus1 ranks also grew strongly.

Once the Federals folded, cutting roster spots by a third, Top numbers jumped and Minus1 numbers plunged for both types of player. From 1913 to 1916, talent was more spread out in the leagues, especially at the 100 percent level. While Cut numbers for position players didn't move decisively, they did fall strongly at the 25 and 50 percent levels for pitchers, while their Minus1 ranks ended up smaller. Post-Federal contraction produced a league less top-heavy in overall talent than before the Feds, less dominated by elite pitchers, and less burdened by bad pitchers.

Summary and Conclusions

I had expected the greater reach of modern talent recruitment to produce a flattening of talent shapes, with leading players accounting for less of the total WAR and less extreme peaks and valleys. That hasn't really happened. The absolute best players are less dominant, but much else has gone in different directions.

I had avoided economic terms and metaphors almost until the end of this piece, mainly because doing so raises an inevitable and undesirable connection to politics, especially when a presidential campaign is raging as I write. But there is a parallel, and one can view baseball as a fixed-sum game, with only so much WAR to go around. So with mild trepidation, I'll engage in a touch of economics-speak for my conclusions.

Position players are concentrating the wealth of performance in about the same number of hands. The WAR levels reached by the strata of players has only recently begun falling after many decades of inching upward. Maybe most surprisingly, more position players are compiling clearly sub-replacement seasons and not being pulled from active duty before reaching negative milestones.

Pitchers have seen the wealth of performance concentrated in fewer hands, even as WAR levels and the ranks of sub-replacement pitchers have dropped. The divergence from the pattern of position players is clearly because of the long-term and ongoing changes in how pitchers are used. After seeing these massive differences,

I'm persuaded the evolution of pitcher usage is the greatest force in the history of baseball on the field, greater even than the power surge symbolized by Babe Ruth.

The persistence of sub-replacement players who get extended playing time is another surprise. Only seismic shifts in baseball, like the folding of the Federal League or post-WWII readjustment (at least for position players), have managed to seriously trim their ranks, and only temporarily. Not even today's advanced analytics has kept negative-WAR players off of rosters. It appears the poor (player) we will always have with us.

Changes in the economy of baseball talent are historically gradual, with a few momentous events like wars and rival leagues shaking things up. If you'd like to see things look a lot different, you either need to be very patient, or hope for some calamity. Which is starting to sound like politics again, so I will stop now.

References & Resources
- Baseball-Reference and its estimable Play Index provided the heaps of data I required for this article.

How Much Hope and Faith Is in Major League Baseball?

by Gerald Schifman

"I was a fan for many years. I ran a club, and one thing I've known, I've been convinced of, is that every fan has to have hope and faith. If you remove hope and faith from the mind of a fan, you destroy the fabric of the sport. It's my job to restore it."

- Bud Selig, in a Q&A from January 2000

In 2000, baseball was in a competitive crisis. Success was increasingly tied to payroll, creating a struggle for many small-market teams. And the money disparity between baseball's bourgeoisie and proletariat was growing, leaving numerous teams chronically uncompetitive. On this course, Commissioner Bud Selig saw the sport drifting towards implosion. But this was a war within that Selig was determined to win, with plans rooted in principle.

As Major League Baseball's newly full-fledged steward, Selig wanted to infuse into baseball his Hope and Faith Theory. That meant inspiring belief in as many fans as possible that their teams could be postseason-bound. It couldn't just be rooters of the dynastic (and at the time, financially robust) Cleveland, Atlanta and New York Yankees franchises who could feel a World Series within reach; fans throughout the country needed to be invited to the season-long party, with as many squeezed into the ballroom as could comfortably fit. A competitive climate, Selig argued, would mean more butts in stadium seats, more eyes fixed to game telecasts, and more profits flowing through the game.

Resoundingly, this monetary endgame was achieved, as MLB has become a financial powerhouse. The league now pulls in $10 billion per year on the strength of swelling attendance, massive television contracts, lucrative new ballparks and a flourishing digital arm in MLB Advanced Media. MLB's standing as a Chris Traeger-like picture of good health seems to warrant Selig's place as one of MLB's greatest-ever commissioners. But the vast revenues don't directly reflect how well Selig accomplished the Hope and Faith target he laid out 16 years ago. No doubt, there is greater competitiveness in baseball today than in 2000, but we don't really know the extent of the upturn. To address how well Hope and Faith have been built and sustained through baseball's six-month season and across multiple years, we need a new tool.

Close Competition, Now in Statistical Form

Quantifying an intangible emotion like optimism seems like a tall order, but we absolutely can design a metric that gauges Selig's Hope and Faith ambition for MLB. In keeping with the mantra, we'll call it the Hope and Faith Index (HFI), and it will measure the average number of wins separating teams from playoff spots. The HFI algorithm uses this fundamental process:

1. For each team leading either a division or Wild Card race, a deficit of zero is appended.

2. For each team chasing a playoff slot, the algorithm considers whether the club is fewer games back in the division or, when applicable, Wild Card race. The smaller figure gets recorded as that team's playoff deficit.

3. All deficit figures are summed and then divided by the count of the number of deficits included. And, voila! That's the HFI.

Previous studies have evaluated competitiveness via the spread of full-season win-loss records, but that method has its limits. It examines the standings at only a single point: the last day of the season, following Game No. 162. In reality, competitiveness within the baseball season is fluid across all 162 games, making the HFI a novel way to create a *continuous* index of competition. The HFI is totally time-flexible; it can be built to reflect any span of games that suits our needs.

When it comes to tallying up deficits, I specifically avoid using the standings as of actual dates. They just don't make for good comparison within years (since teams have differing numbers of games played on each given date) and between years (since seasons start on different dates between March and April). To sidestep these inconsistencies, I record the standings at each given game number. Ask me what competitiveness looked like at the halfway point of a season, and I'll give you the HFI as of Game No. 81 instead of June 30. This construction more tidily facilitates HFI comparisons across all years of my dataset.

I omit all data from the strike-disrupted 1981, 1994 and 1995 seasons, as the many canceled games make for biased HFIs. I include all other seasons dating back to 1974, as from that year and onward, Retrosheet has a full accounting of major league games played.

Of course, the postseason format in the '70s was much different than the three-division, one-/two-Wild Card format of the past two decades. With 22 teams in the majors up through 1976, and then 26 teams until 1993, the only playoff slots went to the winners of the two American League and two National League divisions. This highlights another bright spot of the HFI—it adapts to altered playoff-entry formats. That gives way to the initial two questions we'll aim to answer: How much Hope and Faith has there been in baseball since the '70s, and how productive were Selig's playoff format initiatives?

The HFI Across Seasons

Here we'll deploy the Yearly HFI (YHFI), which will include every single deficit piled up by all teams in each season. We'll begin with analysis of the black line in the chart below, which shows the actual YHFI across the entire time frame. When looking at this chart and all HFI figures, remember: the lower the HFI, the better, because smaller deficits mean more of Selig's Hope and Faith flows through baseball.

Yearly HFI by Season

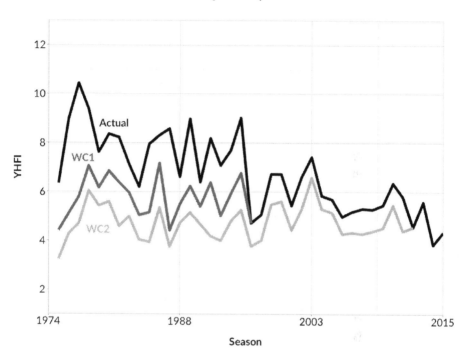

This chart has some seriously jagged lines. The YHFI typically jumps around by one game (either up or down) from year to year. Even with those fluctuations, we can still pick out a trend of poor YHFIs in the earlier two decades. From 1974 to 1993, the YHFI hovered around eight games per season. Think about that: If we had to guess where a given team typically stood in the standings in this 20-year period, our best estimate would be eight games out. As recently as 23 years ago, the average team didn't have a prayer at a playoff berth, and many seasons took the form of a lopsided Charlie Brown baseball hellscape.

But after 1993, competitiveness in baseball was reborn anew. That statement may be surprising; after all, in 1994, Major League Baseball was about to enter its darkest hour—the 1994-1995 strike. But after that season, in Selig's second year as acting commissioner, MLB's playoff structure evolved. Each league's pair of divisions were split into three, giving teams fewer rivals to hop over in a playoff push. And crucially, a Wild Card was added to each league, pitting non-division leaders in a free-for-all for a fourth playoff slot.

The result? The YHFI took a nosedive. In 1993, it was 9.02; in 1996, the next season in which a full slate of major league games was played, it plummeted to 4.71. It swung up and down after that but eventually settled in at a new normal (5.84) in 2003. Fully aggregated across the two-division era (1974-1993), the HFI was 7.91; in the first Wild Card era (1996-2011), it was 5.79. That was a 26.8 percent improvement, representing a very nice boost in Hope and Faith.

More change was still to come, as a second Wild Card was introduced in each league in 2012. Now it's the top two non-division winners who are granted the opportunity to collect a shiny, flag-laden World Series trophy. The second Wild Card rankles purists (and the 2014-15 Pirates) who hate to see a ~90-win season come down to a single sudden-death game. But there's no denying the second Wild Card is good for competition. In the second Wild Card era (2012-2015), the aggregated HFI sank to 4.58, amounting to a 42.1 percent improvement upon the two-division era. It's now typical for teams to be fewer than five games back of a playoff spot and in the thick of the race. This is a remarkable advancement of Hope and Faith.

Beyond the actual HFI figures, showing what baseball's competitive state actually was, we should consider what *could have been*. The medium-dark gray line shows what the YHFIs would have been if, in the two-division format, one Wild Card existed in both the American and National Leagues. Similarly, the light gray line shows the prospective YHFIs had there been two Wild Cards up for grabs in each league. Both curves assume the season would have unfolded in exactly the same manner but with additional playoff spots available at the end. And what we see in these gray curves are big downward shifts and flattened, horizontal trends across the length of the chart. This means there were massive gains to Hope and Faith that could have been netted in these hypothetical scenarios. The addition of a Wild Card in both the AL and NL would have dropped the 1974-1993 aggregated HFI to 5.82. And, if the second Wild Cards were in place, the aggregated HFI over the same 20-year time frame would have been 4.67.

In the two-division era, even when Selig initiatives like revenue sharing and the luxury tax weren't yet in full force, the hypothetical HFIs were just a hair worse than the "actuals" registered later on. Those initiatives may have been good at democratizing major league baseball, giving both big- and small-market clubs a fair chance at contention, but from a purely competitive standpoint, the HFIs are essentially the same. Perhaps the hypothetical HFIs would worsen if historical teams actually worked to attain Wild Card positions, pulling off deadline deals to create greater distance between good and bad teams. But even without identical conditions, we can say the historical implications of this finding are enormous.

Think about all of the revenues owners (and players) of years ago missed out on by not creating more playoff slots and more meaningful races for non-division leaders. We need not shed tears for these millionaires and billionaires, but then again, for a league and union that were in the business of maximizing baseball profits, both sides passed up buckets of money by not making common-sense changes to the playoff format. The very presence of Wild Cards is a huge boon to Hope and Faith.

The HFI within Seasons

The YHFI is great for benchmarking across the 39-year period. But there are more details to explore. Namely, there is a journey through the season the YHFI doesn't capture. So let's look at the HFI in another way. Over the three eras of interest in my dataset—the two-division era (1974-1993), the first Wild Card era (1996-2011) and the second Wild Card era (2012-2015)—let's examine the HFI when the 162-game season is divided into 18-game spans. That partitions the season into nine periods, so we'll call this version of our index the NHFI and chart it in the heat map below.

HFI in 18-Game Intervals

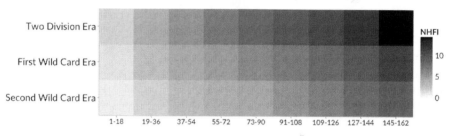

Span of Games, by Number

Here's the Dylan Thomasian guide to reading this chart: The closer that boxes are to black, the deeper baseball's fans are into the depths of despair, when hope for contention is lost upon all but a few fan bases. The nearer that boxes are to bright white, the more optimism brims for fans all across the country, because a greater number of teams are jockeying for playoff slots. With that in mind, what can be gleaned from this chart? Namely this: With each passing era, major league teams have gone less gently into the night of their seasons. Moving downward, darkened gray boxes are pushed out toward the rightward end of the chart, and big NHFI gains are made in the early parts of seasons.

For instance, in the span of games 55-72 (end of May/beginning of June), the 1974-1993 NHFI was 6.80. Teams were still in the earlier stretches of the year, yet it had already become clear that many clubs' postseason chances were quickly evaporating. After the first Wild Card was implemented, the deficit in the corresponding period was chopped to 4.76. With this 30 percent improvement, many more fans could come to the ballpark feeling their club had at least an outside shot at the post-season. And in the modern second Wild Card era, that average 55-72-game deficit has been cut again, now to 3.52. This is nearly a 50 percent improvement from the two-division era.

These are serious upgrades in sustained Hope and Faith, although the gains do shrink as the calendar rolls into the latter stages of the season. In the penultimate period (127-144), for example, improvements on top of the two-division era are a slimmer 24.7 percent in the first Wild Card era and 36.8 percent in the second. That the returns diminish isn't surprising, because even in the hyper-competitive second Wild Card era, teams do sell off and rebuild. But the ample Hope and Faith present in baseball today makes this midseason decision tougher than ever.

Consider this chart of the Daily HFI (DHFI), showing the size of the average deficit at Game No. 108—the generalized two-thirds point of the season for when the trade deadline is set—for every season in the dataset. In addition to the raw line graph, a locally weighted regression (LOESS) smoother runs through the data to iron out the yearly peaks and valleys.

HFI for Game No. 108, by Season

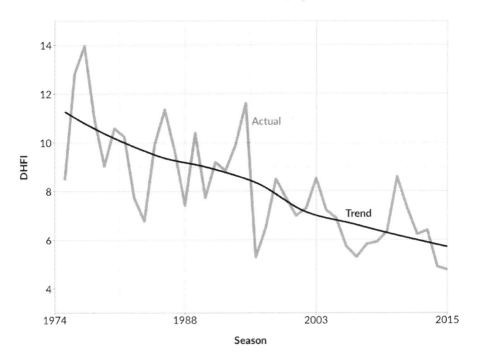

For a general manager, it's easy to justify a pare-down to your owner and fan base when your club is nine games out, which was a typical state of affairs near the trade deadline in the early '90s. But with the sub-six-game HFI seen today, fewer sell-offs are so easily defensible. I've directed this Hope and Faith concept on fans, but it just as easily can manifest itself amongst teams. A five-game deficit feels like an obstacle that can be surpassed with one strong, well-timed run.

In light of this surging Hope and Faith at the two-thirds stage of the season, maybe it makes sense to push the trade deadline back. That shift would give teams extra time for self-assessment ahead of their ultimate buy or sell decision. So, what's an appropriate date? A reasonable choice would be the competitive state that motivated MLB and the union to pin down July 31 as the deadline in 1985's collective bargaining agreement. Perhaps there is a better level of competitiveness for timing a trade deadline, but let's view this as an attempt to modernize, and not optimize, its timing.

The DHFI can guide us here as well. The chart below shows the DHFI across every day of the 1985 and 2015 seasons.

Daily HFI for 1985 and 2015

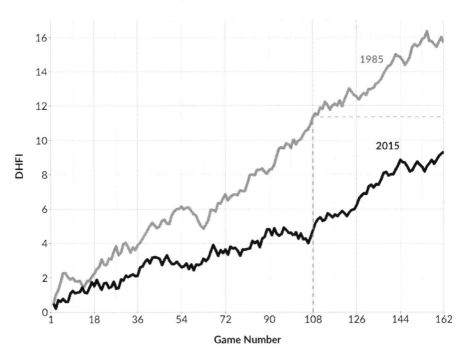

Unlike the across-year charts, these within-year curves are very strongly linear (with R^2 values exceeding 0.94 in both cases). And for these two seasons, there's a clear, huge disparity in Hope and Faith all through each year. The 2015 curve is significantly more gradual than its 1985 counterpart. In 1985, the DHFI worsened by one for every 10.4 games played; in 2015, the DHFI worsened by one for every 19.6 games played.

That 2015 HFI increase rate is great for Hope and Faith. But it has ramifications for an attempted refresh of the trade deadline. Look at the horizontal dotted line, drawn so that it begins with the 11.35 DHFI that teams registered at Game No. 108 in 1985. It never comes close to intersecting with the 2015 curve. The worst DHFI posted in 2015 was 9.30, which is not anywhere close to the same neighborhood. Remarkably, when it comes to the trade deadline, baseball arguably has too much of a good thing: There is so much Hope and Faith that no deadline can be justified by the original 1985 standard.

Selig's Legacy of Hope and Faith

The addition of multiple Wild Card slots looks like a masterstroke from baseball's former commissioner. But before we all jump on eBay to purchase Bud Selig bobbleheads (these do exist), we need to acknowledge one important caveat: The Wild Cards were not an innovation without precedent.

For years, Wild Cards have been used in the other major North American pro sports leagues. The NFL adopted a format of three divisions plus a Wild Card in 1970, over two decades earlier than MLB. The NHL has sent multiple non-division winners to the playoffs in all non-"Original Six" years. So has the NBA, which has done so since that league's inception in 1946. It feels like an expanded MLB postseason should have been a plainly obvious update long before it actually happened.

Yet, I don't think it's fair to say this unoriginality diminishes Selig's achievement. The fact is that because of the toxic situation he inherited—exceptional divisiveness amongst the owners themselves—it took a particular set of skills to accomplish the task, skills that were acquired over a very long career as a baseball fan and owner. Consider this excerpt from Ben Reiter's 2014 *Sports Illustrated* profile of Selig:

> "I understood that if you wanted to get people to cooperate, it may be a slower, evolutionary process, but it was the way to get things done," Selig says. "It would take longer. And it may be more difficult. But my style, which was oft criticized as too slow and too cautious, led to 30-to-nothing votes and led to revenue sharing and the Wild Card and so many other things. There's no way you could have just come in there and say, 'Bang, let's do it.' I was very cautious. And here I am, responsible for most of the changes in baseball over the last 20 years, more changes than ever before. But not without a lot of pain."

In the end, Hope and Faith in baseball was more than restored. The average playoff deficit is 42.1 percent less today than in decades past, and the season's first half is now especially competitive. With more clubs in the playoff hunt, millions of additional baseball fans are engaged deep into the year. And so the fabric of the sport, once a worry for Selig, is now intact and looking better than ever because Hope and Faith is at an all-time high.

References & Resources

- All data come courtesy of Retrosheet
- Phil Rogers, *Chicago Tribune*, "Selig: A Czar Is Born," *articles.chicagotribune. com/2000-01-23/sports/0001230143_1_milwaukee-office-atlanta-braves-owner-bud-selig*
- Ben Reiter, *Sports Illustrated*, "For Love & Money," *si.com/vault/2014/10/20/106650435/ for-love-and-money*
- Associated Press, *Reading Eagle*, "Selig says, 'Time for Changes,'" *news.google.com/ newspapers?nid=1955&dat=20001122&id=pxQyAAAAIBAJ&sjid=u6MFAAAA IBAJ&pg=1291,4722430*
- Mike Bates (under the pseudonym The Common Man), The Platoon Advantage, "The Five Greatest Trade Deadlines in Baseball History," *platoonadvantage. com/2011-articles/the-five-greatest-trade-deadlines-in-baseball-history.html*

Is the Fringe Five Even Worth a Single Damn?

by Carson Cistulli

For four years now, I've produced a weekly, regular-season column at FanGraphs called "The Fringe Five: Baseball's Most Compelling Fringe Prospects." The idea of that column: to identify and/or monitor notable prospects who've nevertheless been omitted from the industry's most popular top-prospect lists. The reason for the column's existence, however flawed, proceeds as follows: first, that there's little substantive difference between the 100th- and 101st-best prospect in baseball and, second that due to the presence of the aforementioned lists, the 100th-best prospect is likely to receive a degree of attention that the 101st-best (and 102nd- and 103rd-best, etc.) is not likely to receive. The Fringe Five is designed, then, to document the exploits of those less-celebrated prospects.

My considerable interest in fringe prospects began in the way that most human endeavors do—namely, from a desire to crush the spirits of those closest to me. Before the late 20th century, the only way to embark upon this sort of Machiavellian campaign of terror was by means of a sustained and very public character attack. With the advent and proliferation of fantasy baseball, however, it's become possible to lord one's superiority over his or her friends from the comfort of the living room.

As a member—in the early part of this century—of a competitive and somewhat Byzantine fantasy league founded by a group of lovable jerks in the Chicago area, I noticed that a number of my leaguemates were abandoning all pretense of victory in certain years to stockpile young players who appeared on the annual lists of outlets such as *Baseball America* and Baseball Prospectus. It wasn't unusual to find that, by the time a talented prospect was promoted to the majors, that he'd been owned in our league for two or three years already. As a result, the possibility of acquiring high-end keeper talent was low.

Too impatient to concede entire seasons, I became keenly interested in identifying minor leaguers who (a) were on the verge of promotion to the majors, (b) lacked the pedigree or physical tools of their more celebrated peers, but who nevertheless (c) exhibited promising statistical indicators—with the idea that said indicators would translate into success at the major-league level.

My actual record of identifying such players in my dumb fantasy league is immaterial here. With the exception of *Beowulf*, perhaps, there's hardly anything more insufferable than other people's accounts of their pretend baseball teams. The point is merely this: I developed an interest in fringe prospects and dedicated some time and energy to understanding what constitutes a promising one. It followed that, when I was accidentally hired by FanGraphs in 2009, I would use that site as a platform for my inquiries into the art and science of the fringe prospects. The result has been four years of this weekly column.

It's not uncommon for readers to ask me, either in the comments section of Fringe Five posts or by way of social-media platform Twitter, about the success rate of players who've appeared among the Five. Others, including even my editor Dave Cameron—who has little patience for me otherwise—will note publicly when a graduate of the Five, like Junior Guerra, holds his own in the majors. Still others have suggested that every case in which a player has appeared both among the Five and then, subsequently, on a major league roster, has been mainly the product of randomness.

My response to all questions regarding the efficacy of the Five has typically been that to determine such a thing as the "success rate" of Fringe Five graduates would require a degree of toil to which I'm generally averse. However. Jerk editor of this publication, Paul Swydan, with his beard and his face, has reminded me once again this autumn that I'm required to perform a degree of toil anyway for the benefit (?) of *The Hardball Times Annual*.

With that in mind, what follows represents an attempt to assess the success of the Fringe Five and the players who've appeared within it.

There's almost no way to perform such an assessment responsibly. But here's the irresponsible way I've chosen. Each weekly edition of the Five is accompanied by a (somewhat arbitrarily calculated) scoreboard. For every appearance among the Five proper, a player receives three points; for every appearance among the Next Five—which recognizes five additional prospects who've made a strong case for inclusion—a player receives one point. By the end of the season, the scoreboard depicts, more or less, the year's most compelling fringe prospects.

What I've decided to do, for the purposes of the present study, is to examine the careers of those players who occupied the top-10 places on the final scoreboard of the inaugural season (2013) of the Five. In theory, these are players who represent the very best of the rest, prospects No. 101 through 110.

Here are those 10 players, in order of finish from 2013. Note that the teams and positions listed are those relevant to the player at the end of the 2013 season. FF and NF denote appearances among Fringe Five and Next Five, respectively.

2013 Fringe Five Leaders						
Rank	Name	Team	Pos	FF	NF	PTS
1	Marcus Semien	White Sox	SS	11	7	40
2	Mike O'Neill	Cardinals	OF	10	7	37
3	Danny Salazar	Cleveland	RHP	8	5	29
4	Wilmer Flores	Mets	2B	8	3	27
5	Mookie Betts	Red Sox	2B	6	1	19
5t	Maikel Franco	Phillies	3B	6	1	19
7	Brian Flynn	Marlins	LHP	4	3	15
8	Rafael Montero	Mets	RHP	3	5	14
8t	Stephen Piscotty	Cardinals	OF	3	5	14
10	Burch Smith	Padres	RHP	4	1	13

Already, you'll find that there are some success stories present here. Other stories are darker and/or shorter. In what follows, I assess the 10 players here in two ways. First, in a more prosaic form. Then, with the help of some objective criteria.

Player Reviews

For each player, I've attempted to address three questions: why he was excluded from multiple top-100 lists, why he was included among the Fringe Five, and what he's done since. I've also included statistics for each player since 2013 for every level at which he recorded at least 100 plate appearances or 25 innings pitched. Note that minor-league index stats (which means wRC+ for hitters and both FIP-/ERA- for pitchers) are adjusted only for league but not park. WAR figures for pitchers are a 50-50 combination of FIP-based and ERA-based WAR.

1. Marcus Semien, SS, Chicago AL

Marcus Semien Statistics, 2013-Present									
Season	Team	Age	PA	AVG	OBP	SLG	wRC+	DEF	WAR
2013	White Sox (AA)	22	483	.290	.420	.483	167	---	---
2013	White Sox (AAA)	22	142	.264	.338	.464	123	---	---
2014	White Sox (AAA)	23	366	.267	.380	.502	142	---	---
2014	White Sox	23	255	.234	.300	.372	91	-1.2	0.5
2015	Athletics	24	601	.257	.310	.405	99	-3.3	1.8
2016	Athletics	25	621	.238	.300	.435	100	3.4	2.5
Totals	- - -	- - -	1,548	.246	.302	.412	97	0.3	4.9

Why He Was Excluded from Prospect Lists

Lack of a standout tool, mostly. Selected in the sixth round out of Cal-Berkeley and given a $130,000 bonus, Semien entered professional baseball as an adequate, but largely unspectacular, player. Reports generally expressed optimism about his ability to remain at shortstop—which might surprise those who observed Semien at short-stop in his first year with Oakland. Generally, however, there was little enthusiasm for the potential of the bat.

Why He Was Included Among the Five

Regardless of the precise position, second or short, the batting indicators recorded by Semien in 2013 suggested he'd likely provide sufficient offensive value for a player who also profiles as a defensive asset. Semien produced a positive walk and strikeout-rate differential for Double-A Birminghan before earning a promotion to Triple-A, where he continued to exhibit a strong approach and power on contact.

What He's Done Since

Developed (incrementally) into an average major leaguer. Semien's first exposure to the majors was unspectacular. Playing second and third base for the White Sox in 2013 and '14, he struck out too often relative to the sort of power he offered. Following a trade to Oakland (for Jeff Samardzija), he became that club's starting shortstop, in which capacity he struggled—although his approach at the plate improved. The 2016 campaign was Semien's most promising, featuring league-average offense and, for the first time, slightly above-average results at short.

2. Mike O'Neill, OF, St. Louis

Mike O'Neill Statistics, 2013-Present									
Season	Team	Age	PA	AVG	OBP	SLG	wRC+	DEF	WAR
2013	Cardinals (AA)	25	434	.320	.431	.384	140	- - -	- - -
2013	Cardinals (AAA)	25	133	.295	.402	.321	105	- - -	- - -
2014	Cardinals (AA)	26	408	.269	.343	.347	101	- - -	- - -
2015	Cardinals (AA)	27	239	.301	.409	.337	119	- - -	- - -
2016	New Jersey (CanAm)	28	472	.338	.426	.438	- - -	- - -	- - -
Totals	- - -		- - -	- - -	- - -	- - -	- - -	- - -	- - -

Why He Was Excluded from Prospect Lists

For nearly every reason. Selected by the Cardinals in the 31st round of the 2010 draft following his senior season at USC, O'Neill received just a $1,000 bonus. Physically, there wasn't—and presumably still isn't—anything impressive about O'Neill. He's short, possesses little power on contact, little speed, and an underwhelming arm. "Tiny, punchless corner outfielder" isn't a type of major leaguer that exists, really—or not one that exists for long, at least.

Why He Was Included Among the Five

Because of the one skill he does possess and the volume in which he possesses it—namely, his control of the strike zone. In 2012, O'Neill recorded the best walk- and strikeout-rate differential (BB-K%) after producing walk and strikeout rates of 14.8 percent and 6.2 percent, respectively. In 2013 (the year of interest here), he actually improved upon that figure while splitting time between Double- and Triple-A, recording walk and strikeout figures of 16.0 percent and 6.5 percent, respectively, for a differential of +9.5 points.

What He's Done Since

As a major leaguer? Nothing, actually. O'Neill remained a member of the St. Louis organization through 2015, continuing to exhibit roughly the same profile but never earning a plate appearance above Triple-A. Selected by the Cubs in the minor-league phase of the Rule 5 in November of '15, he was ultimately released at the end of March. He spent the 2016 season with the New Jersey Jackals of the Can-Am League, with which club he (predictably) posted the league's best BB-K% and one of the highest on-base percentages, as well.

3. Danny Salazar, RHP, Cleveland

Danny Salazar Statistics, 2013-Present									
Season	Team	Age	IP	K/9	BB/9	HR/9	FIP-	ERA-	WAR
2013	Cleveland (AA)	23	33.2	13.6	2.7	0.3	39	67	- - -
2013	Cleveland (AAA)	23	59.1	11.8	2.1	0.6	59	71	- - -
2013	Cleveland	23	52.0	11.3	2.6	1.2	80	78	1.3
2014	Cleveland (AAA)	24	60.2	11.3	4.2	1.0	94	92	- - -
2014	Cleveland	24	110.0	9.8	2.9	1.1	93	110	1.4
2015	Cleveland	25	185.0	9.5	2.6	1.1	89	85	3.4
2016	Cleveland	26	137.1	10.6	4.1	1.1	87	91	2.6
Totals	- - -	- - -	484.1	10.1	3.1	1.1	88	91	8.6

Why He Was Excluded from Prospect Lists

Partly because of performance, partly because of health. As a younger prospect, starting with his first year in the Cleveland system at age 17, Salazar lacked any clearly standout quality. Following a 2010 Tommy John procedure, however—and the subsequent rehab—Salazar began exhibiting plus velocity. That made him a promisng young player. The lack of an established track record, though—and lack of notable secondary pitches—still rendered him something less than a top-100 prospect.

Why He Was Included Among the Five

Because of common sense, largely. Salazar recorded nearly a 40 percent strike-out rate in his first (and only) seven starts at Double-A to begin the 2013 (and his age-23) season. He preserved all the gains in velocity he'd acquired following his elbow surgery while also throwing a change-up which, in itself, served as a sufficient complement to his fastball. A promotion to Triple-A in mid-May was accompanied by hardly any decay in Salazar's rates.

What He's Done Since

Developed into a legitimately above-average starter. In both 2013 and '14 at the major-league level, Salazar recorded run-prevention numbers inferior to his fielding-independent ones—a product, maybe, of some inherent deficiency in his approach or, alternatively, of Cleveland's subpar defense during that same interval. Or just randomness, of course. In either case, the trend has actually been reversed over the last two seasons and, by any standard, Salazar has produced five or six wins above replacement over the last two years, depending on your metric of choice.

4. Wilmer Flores, 2B, New York NL

Wilmer Flores Statistics, 2013-Present									
Season	Team	Age	PA	AVG	OBP	SLG	wRC+	DEF	WAR
2013	Mets (AAA)	21	463	.321	.357	.531	129	- - -	- - -
2013	Mets	21	101	.211	.248	.295	51	1.4	-0.1
2014	Mets (AAA)	22	241	.323	.367	.568	137	- - -	- - -
2014	Mets	22	274	.251	.286	.378	87	7.3	1.3
2015	Mets	23	510	.263	.295	.408	94	4.3	1.8
2016	Mets	24	335	.267	.319	.469	112	-6.0	0.5
Totals	- - -	- - -	1,220	.257	.296	.408	94	7.2	3.5

Why He Was Excluded from Prospect Lists

A combination of prospect fatigue and defensive concerns, it seems. Signed originally out of Venezuela in 2007, Flores actually appeared within the top-100 lists of both *Baseball America* and Baseball Prospectus on multiple occasions as a teenager. Entering 2013, however, there seems to have been less enthusiasm regarding his future—despite the fact that he'd just played the second half of the previous year as a 20-year-old at Double-A. It's possible that lack of enthusiasm was due to his defensive limitations: Flores had moved from shortstop to third base. His body suggested further movement down the defensive spectrum.

Why He Was Included Among the Five

The batting indicators, almost irrespective of the defensive skill. As a 21-year-old in the Pacific Coast League, Flores produced both an isolated-slugging percentage (.210) and strikeout rate (13.6 percent) markedly better than league average (.144 and 19.5 percent, respectively). Those metrics are important for three reasons. One, they directly inform overall batting production. Two, they stabilize more quickly than other batting metrics. And three, they're predictive of future success.

What He's Done Since

Become neither a very impressive nor entirely helpless major leaguer. In about 1,200 plate appearances over parts of four seasons, Flores has recorded 3.5 wins above replacement—which places him somewhere between bench player and regular. The profile remains the same: lots of contact, decent power, some defensive value (even if it doesn't look entirely smooth). Of some note: Flores has produced a .269 BABIP as a major leaguer, which figure sits in just the ninth percentile during that time.

t5. Mookie Betts, 2B, Boston

Mookie Betts Statistics, 2013-Present									
Season	Team	Age	PA	AVG	OBP	SLG	wRC+	DEF	WAR
2013	Red Sox (A)	20	340	.296	.418	.477	160	- - -	- - -
2013	Red Sox (A+)	20	211	.341	.414	.551	166	- - -	- - -
2014	Red Sox (AA)	21	253	.355	.443	.551	177	- - -	- - -
2014	Red Sox (AAA)	21	211	.335	.417	.503	158	- - -	- - -
2014	Red Sox	21	213	.291	.368	.444	129	0.6	1.8
2015	Red Sox	22	654	.291	.341	.479	119	1.3	4.8
2016	Red Sox	23	730	.318	.363	.534	135	10.6	7.8
Totals	- - -	- - -	1,597	.304	.355	.500	127	12.6	14.4

Why He Was Excluded from Prospect Lists

Lack of a plus tool and size. At this point, it's difficult to imagine a time when Mookie Betts wasn't clearly a great talent, but he entered the 2013 campaign as a former fifth-round pick who was only 5-foot-9, had recorded zero home runs in roughly 300 professional plate appearances, and was facing a permanent move to second base. That's not the typical profile of a top prospect. Not only omitted from all the notable top-100 lists, he was ranked only 31st in the Boston system by *Baseball America*.

Why He Was Included Among the Five

The abundance of above-average skills. Whatever Betts lacked—and probably continues to lack—in terms of traditional physical tools, he more than compensated for it with baseball-specific skills. Betts actually wasn't eligible for the Five until early July, when he was promoted to High-A. But over roughly 200 plate appearances at that level, he produced an ISO over .200 and a positive walk- and strikeout-rate differential (BB-K%). And a 20-for-22 stolen-base record. All while playing a position on the plus side of the defensive spectrum.

What He's Done Since

Develop into an MVP candidate. Betts' numbers never really experienced the sort of decay that's typical when a player is promoted from one level to the next. From High-A to Double-A to Triple-A to the majors: in each case, Betts exhibited better-than-average contact and better-than-average power and better-than-average defense and better-than-average baserunning. After a promising debut in 2014 and very strong 2015 campaign, Betts recorded the third-highest WAR in the majors for the Red Sox in 2016.

t5. Maikel Franco, 3B, Philadelphia

Maikel Franco Statistics, 2013-Present									
Season	Team	Age	PA	AVG	OBP	SLG	wRC+	DEF	WAR
2013	Phillies (A+)	20	289	.299	.349	.576	159	- - -	- - -
2013	Phillies (AA)	20	292	.339	.363	.563	153	- - -	- - -
2014	Phillies (AAA)	21	556	.257	.299	.428	97	- - -	- - -
2015	Phillies (AAA)	22	151	.355	.384	.539	166	- - -	- - -
2015	Phillies	22	335	.280	.343	.497	129	-6.3	1.6
2016	Phillies	23	630	.255	.306	.427	92	0.5	1.4
Totals	- - -	- - -	1,023	.258	.312	.437	100	-4.1	2.7

Why He Was Excluded from Prospect Lists

Due to concerns about his foot speed and defense and swing mechanics. Signed out of the Dominican for a relatively modest $100,000, Franco's future has always depended—as it does for many prospects—on the relative strength of his offensive skills relative to his place on the defensive spectrum. The teenage version of Franco didn't overwhelm anyone with his offensive exploits. His body, meanwhile, threatened to confine him to first base exclusively.

Why He Was Included Among the Five

The combination of power and contact at High-A Clearwater. Among all hitters who recorded at least 200 plate appearances in the Florida State League in 2013,

Franco recorded the second-best isolated-power figure (.277, behind only Miguel Sano in that category) and a strikeout rate in the 78th percentile, as well (where a higher percentile equals a lower strikeout rate). He was essentially the José Bautista or Edwin Encarnación of the FSL. Except about three years younger than everyone.

What He's Done Since

Become a top prospect and then serviceable major leaguer. Franco actually appeared on more than one midseason top-prospect list in 2013, rendering him ineligible for the Five starting around July. The next year, he was ranked about 50th or better on most prospect lists. With the Phillies, he's played to type almost perfectly, recording better-than-average contact and power numbers but profiling as merely average due to other shortcomings.

7. Brian Flynn, LHP, Miami

Brian Flynn Statistics, 2013-Present									
Season	Team	Age	IP	K/9	BB/9	HR/9	FIP-	ERA-	WAR
2013	Marlins (AAA)	23	138.0	8.0	2.6	0.5	69	56	- - -
2014	Marlins (AAA)	24	139.2	6.7	3.2	0.8	100	88	- - -
2016	Royals	26	55.1	7.2	3.7	0.8	96	60	0.7
Totals	- - -	- - -	80.1	7.3	4.4	1.0	112	115	0.1

Why He Was Excluded from Prospect Lists

General lack of pedigree and stuff. Selected originally out of Wichita State by the Tigers in the seventh round of the 2011 draft, the left-handed Flynn was traded to Miami as part of a deal that sent Omar Infante and Anibal Sánchez to the Tigers. Despite possessing excellent size (he's listed at alternately at 6-foot-7 and 6-foot-8), he entered 2013 with only average fastball velocity.

Why He Was Included Among the Five

A combination of excellent early-season indicators and promising physicality. Flynn was dominant over his first (and only) four Double-A starts of the 2013 season, recording strikeout and walk rates of 28.7 percent and 3.5 percent, respectively. The rates decayed slightly following a late-April promotion to Triple-A New Orleans, but remained promising nevertheless. Despite Flynn's average velocity, his size suggested that perceived velocities might actually be higher.

What He's Done Since

Become a major league reliever. After failing to earn a spot in the Miami rotation in 2014, he was traded to Kansas City (for Aaron Crow) in November of that year. He then recorded merely 0.2 innings for Triple-A Omaha in April of 2015 before missing the remainder of that season with a torn lat muscle. He passed the majority of the 2016 season as a member of the Royals' bullpen, producing excellent run-prevention, but only adequate fielding-independent numbers.

t8. Rafael Montero, RHP, New York

Rafael Montero Statistics, 2013-Present									
Season	Team	Age	IP	K/9	BB/9	HR/9	FIP-	ERA-	WAR
2013	Mets (AA)	22	66.2	9.7	1.4	0.3	50	61	- - -
2013	Mets (AAA)	22	88.2	7.9	2.5	0.4	73	69	- - -
2014	Mets (AAA)	23	80.0	9.0	3.8	0.5	79	78	- - -
2014	Mets	23	44.1	8.5	4.7	1.6	139	116	0.1
2016	Mets (AA)	25	49.0	7.4	3.5	0.7	106	56	- - -
2016	Mets (AAA)	25	80.0	7.7	4.5	1.4	123	161	- - -
Totals	- - -	- - -	73.1	9.2	5.4	1.5	131	139	-0.2

Why He Was Excluded from Prospect Lists

Lack of pedigree and/or size, it would seem. Unlike most international prospects, who join a major-league organization immediately after turning 16, Montero was signed by the Mets, for just $80,000, as a 20-year-old. His fastball sat at 90-93 mph in 2012—and he also possessed reasonable secondaries—so a lack of stuff doesn't appear to have been a factor in his omission. At just six feet tall, however, Montero's stature was and has remained an issue for talent evaluators.

Why He Was Included Among the Five

An indomitable two months at Binghamton. Over two months in the Double-A Eastern League—his first ever exposure to that level—a 22-year-old Montero recorded a strikeout- and walk-rate differential (K-BB%) of 23.8 points. By way of comparison, that mark would have finished third among qualified major-league starters in 2015, behind only the figures produced by the late, dear José Fernández and Max Scherzer. Montero, meanwhile, was nearly three years younger than the average Eastern League player.

What He's Done Since

Lost his command, surprisingly. Montero didn't sustain the sort of fielding-independent numbers in 2014 that he'd recorded the previous year—and when he earned a series of starts at the major-league level that season, the results weren't particularly impressive. That's mostly been the case for 2015 and '16, as well. There's some possibility that baleful effects of the park in Las Vegas are to blame. It's also possible that Montero's not particularly good.

t8. Stephen Piscotty, OF, St. Louis

Stephen Piscotty Statistics, 2013-Present									
Season	Team	Age	PA	AVG	OBP	SLG	wRC+	DEF	WAR
2013	Cardinals (A+)	22	264	.292	.348	.477	134	- - -	- - -
2013	Cardinals (AA)	22	207	.299	.364	.446	129	- - -	- - -
2014	Cardinals (AAA)	23	556	.288	.355	.406	100	- - -	- - -
2015	Cardinals (AAA)	24	372	.272	.366	.475	125	- - -	- - -
2015	Cardinals	24	256	.305	.359	.494	133	-5.9	1.1
2016	Cardinals	25	649	.273	.343	.457	115	-3.4	2.7
Totals	- - -	- - -	905	.282	.348	.467	120	-9.3	3.8

Why He Was Excluded from Prospect Lists

Lack of power, concern about third-base defense. Unlike many prospects who appear among the Fringe Five, Piscotty actually had some pedigree. He'd won a batting title in the Cape Cod League and received a $1.4 million bonus from the Cardinals, who selected him in the supplemental portion of the first round. Piscotty possessed a slightly awkward skill set as a young professional, however: insufficient skill to remain at third base but less power than is typically associated with a corner outfielder.

Why He Was Included Among the Five

Because the hit tool was sufficient. At some level, concerns regarding Piscotty's offensive ceiling were justified: Corner outfielders need to compensate for their defensive shortcomings with above-average batting numbers. The most expedient way of doing that is by means of extra-base hits. But it's not the only means. Piscotty recorded only 15 homers in 2013, but also produced a strikeout rate below 10 percent. That meant more balls in play. Which meant more opportunities for hits.

What He's Done Since

Developed above-average power, anyway. Between 2015 and '16, Piscotty has received about 900 plate appearances in the majors. The league-average isolated-power figure during that interval is about .160. Piscotty, meanwhile, has recorded a .185 ISO while playing in a park that suppresses power. It's possibly the product of a conscious shift, because the right fielder's contact numbers have declined simultaneously. In either case, the result is fine: Piscotty's accumulated roughly four wins above replacement as a major leaguer, or about 2.6 per 600 plate appearances.

10. Burch Smith, RHP, San Diego

	Burch Smith Statistics, 2013-Present									
Season	Team	Age	IP	K/9	BB/9	HR/9	FIP-	ERA-	WAR
2013	Padres (AA)	23	31.1	10.6	1.7	0.3	50	30	- - -
2013	Padres (AAA)	23	61.0	9.6	2.5	0.6	72	77	- - -
2013	Padres	23	36.1	11.4	5.2	2.2	147	180	-0.5
Totals	- - -	- - -	36.1	11.4	5.2	2.2	147	180	-0.5

Why He Was Excluded from Prospect Lists

Lack of a secondary pitch, maybe? Smith is an interesting case. Both *Baseball America* and MLB.com praised him, during the 2012-13 offseason, for his plus-plus fastball and excellent command. Those outlets also ranked him 22nd and 20th, respectively, in a merely average Padres system. The relative lack of development both of his curve and change-up would appear to be the best explanation—in particular because his numbers were also very strong.

Why He Was Included Among the Five

For his plus-plus fastball and excellent command, and also his promising statistical indicators. Over his first six starts of 2013 at Double-A—which also represented his first six starts ever at that level—Smith produced strikeout and walk rates of 31.4 percent and 5.1 percent, respectively. Those would also represent his last ever starts at Double-A. Smith was promoted to the Pacific Coast League, where he'd record strong numbers, as well.

What He's Done Since

Barely pitch. Smith's promising 2013 season at the minor-league level didn't translate to particularly great run prevention at the major-league one. Despite striking out more than a quarter of the batters he faced, Smith posted an ERA 80 percent worse than average over 36 innings with the Padres. Things went even more poorly after that. Smith missed basically all of 2014 with a forearm injury and then, following a trade to Tampa Bay, missed all of 2015 and '16 after undergoing Tommy John surgery.

Analysis

There's been quite a lot of excellent work performed on the expected value of prospects. Victor Wang, hired by the Cleveland organization in the meantime, published the earliest publicly available research on the matter in 2008 for The Hardball Times. More recently, both Kevin Creagh and Steve DiMiceli have updated Wang's effort with slight changes to methodology where logic dictated. Finally, in last year's edition of this very publication, Jeff Zimmerman utilized several means by which to connect draft number, prospect rankings, wins and surplus value. All that work has been essential for estimating free-market valuations of prospects

For the purposes of this piece, however, I've used another work on expected prospect value—namely, Scott McKinney's "Success and Failure Rates of Top MLB Prospects," which appeared at Royals Review in 2011. McKinney's work has two advantages. First, in it, he establishes a rubric that expressly characterizes prospects as a Success (on the one hand) or Bust (on the other) based on their major league performance (or total absence of it). Because one of the objects of the present work is to determine whether these members of the Fringe Five have succeeded, McKinney's rubric is helpful.

Secondly, McKinney discusses players in terms of average WAR per season over their cost-controlled years—as opposed to total WAR over those years. This might seem like a distinction without a difference, but it makes sense in an evaluation of the 10 players we're considering here. Because those players were all rookie-eligible no earlier than 2013, they haven't produced anything like six years' worth of data. Evaluating their average annual performance, then, is the only sensible means by which to assess their careers to date.

McKinney describes the methodology for his study as follows:

> For the population of top prospects, I used Baseball America's top 100 prospect lists from 1990 to 2003. I stopped at 2003 because that is the last data for which the vast majority of prospects have exhausted their cost controlled years. Many prospects showed up on multiple lists, but I counted each occurrence of the player because my goal is to determine the meaning of various rankings by determining their success and failure.
>
> [...]
>
> For each ranking each year, I calculated that player's average Wins Above Replacement (WAR) from Fangraphs.com over his cost controlled years. If a player totaled fewer than 100 plate appearances or 25 innings pitched in his first major league season, I omitted it from the calculation. If the player also failed to meet those minimums in his second season, I omitted that season as well. I was attempting to account for the fact that many players get very little playing time in their first or second season, and I did not want to give them equal weight in the average WAR calculation. At the same time, I didn't want to omit all short or partial seasons over a player's cost controlled years because they are often due to injury or poor performance.

So, to summarize: McKinney is looking at a player's average WAR per season for every year starting with the one in which he recorded at least 100 plate appearances or 25 innings pitched. I've used the same standard here.

As for what thresholds constitute success and failure, etc., McKinney addresses that, too:

One of the more difficult tasks of analyzing the data was creating an operational definition of "success" and "failure" or what constituted a prospect
"bust." Using the rule of thumb breakdown for WAR, I created the following
groupings.

Here are the groupings in question:

Scott McKinney Groupings		
WAR/Season	Description	Success/Bust
< 0.5	Very Poor	Bust
0.50-1.49	Below Average	Bust
1.50-2.49	Average	Success
2.50-3.49	Good	Superior Success
3.50-4.49	Very Good	Superior Success
4.50+	Great	Superior Success

As McKinney goes on to note, there's always going to be something a bit arbitrary
about establishing a threshold between success and failure—or a Success and a Bust.
Because 2.0 WAR represents a league-average mark, however, and a "successful"
player ought to approach something like a full complement of plate appearances in a
any given season, McKinney uses the 1.5-WAR mark as the standard for success. If a
player's producing one-and-a-half wins per year, he's probably helping his team; less
than that, and he's likely only useful in a bench capacity.

Having established that rubric, McKinney applies it to every prospect who
appeared on *BA's* top-100 list between 1990 and 2003. The results, divided into quin-
tiles, are as follows. (Note that Superior is merely a subset of Success.)

Scott McKinney *BA* Top 100 Prospect Groupings, By Quintile			
BA Rank	Bust	Success	Superior
1-20	47.5%	52.5%	32.9%
21-40	69.6%	30.4%	17.5%
41-60	74.0%	26.1%	13.6%
61-80	77.2%	22.9%	11.1%
81-100	77.9%	22.1%	8.9%

So, what one learns right away is that, all things being equal, a prospect who
doesn't rank among *BA's* top 20 is doomed. Generally speaking, at least 70 percent
of the prospects ranked 20th or worse in any given year are likely to become busts
by McKinney's criteria. And actually, there's a lot more similarity between the group
ranked 21 to 40 and 81 to 100 than there is between the 21-to-40 and 1-to-20 groups.
The curve is steep and unforgiving, as illustrated by this other graph provided by
McKinney:

Average Season WAR by Rank, 1990-2003

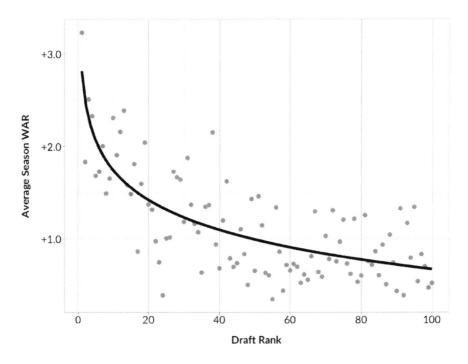

That's average seasonal WAR among all the top-100 prospects over a 14-year stretch—and again, one notes the aggressive slope of the curve between prospects Nos. 1 and 20. Basically, anyone outside out of that group has less than a 50 percent success of developing into a major leaguer.

So what does this say about the 10 graduates considered here? Well, in theory, one would expect them to perform even worse than the 81-100 group above. Which, that would mean something like eight busts (and two successes) out of the 10. It certainly wouldn't be any better than that.

Duplicating McKinney's methodology for the Fringe Five leaders of 2013, one arrives at these results:

	Average Performance and Verdict, 2013 Fringe Five Leaders							
Player	Team	Pos	Yrs	PA	IP	WAR	Performance	Grouping
Marcus Semien	CHW	SS	3	492	0	1.6	Average	Success
Mike O'Neill	STL	OF	0	0	0	- - -	Very Poor	Bust
Danny Salazar	CLE	RHP	4	0	121	2.2	Average	Success
Wilmer Flores	NYM	2B	4	305	0	0.9	Below Avg.	Bust
Mookie Betts	BOS	2B	3	532	0	4.8	Great	Superior Success
Maikel Franco	PHI	3B	2	483	0	1.5	Average	Success
Brian Flynn	MIA	LHP	1	0	55	0.7	Below Avg.	Bust
Rafael Montero	NYM	RHP	3	0	24	0.0	Very Poor	Bust
Stephen Piscotty	STL	OF	2	453	0	1.9	Average	Success
Burch Smith	SD	RHP	1	0	36	-0.5	Very Poor	Bust

Which, that seems pretty great. Where basically any representative sample of prospects ranked somewhere between 20 and 100 by a reputable outlet—where roughly only two of 10 would be expected to succeed, we find that five of the top 10 prospects from 2013's Fringe Five have sustained a level that could be considered "successful" as major leaguers so far.

Conclusion

So the Fringe Five is an unambiguous and unassailable success: is this what we've discovered conclusively? No, almost certainly not. Because this sample is extraordinarily small, is one reason why. And there might very well have been more successes in this particular season than others. And these players could all fall over and become busts still before reaching the end of their cost-controlled years.

What is revealed is a collection of possibilities. The possibility, for example, that a combination of promising statistical indicators—combined with some manner of physical competence—will yield a major leaguer, regardless of whether the player in question has appeared on any preseason top-100 lists. And the possibility, also, that the author won't be fired for the publication of his weekly column, specifically.

References & Resources

* *Baseball America 2013 Prospect Handbook*, 2013
* Carson Cistulli, FanGraphs, "The Fringe Five: Summary and Results and Discussion," *fangraphs.com/blogs/the-fringe-five-summary-and-results-and-discussion*
* Kevin Creagh and Steve DiMiceli, The Point of Pittsburgh, "MLB Prospect Surplus Values—2016 Updated Edition," *thepointofpittsburgh.com/mlb-prospect-surplus-values-2016-updated-edition*
* Jonathan Mayo, MLB.com, "2013 Prospect Watch," *mlb.mlb.com/mlb/prospects/watch/y2013*

- Scott McKinney, Royals Review, "Success and Failure Rates of Top MLB Prospects," *royalsreview.com/2011/2/14/1992424/success-and-failure-rates-of-top-mlb-prospects*
- Jason Parks, Baseball Prospectus, "Top 101 Prospects," *baseballprospectus.com/article.php?articleid=19694*
- Victor Wang, The Hardball Times, "The Bright Side of Losing Santana," *hardball-times.com/the-bright-side-of-losing-santana*
- Jeff Zimmerman, *The Hardball Times Baseball Annual 2016*, "Creating Values for Trading Prospects"

How Much Does Catcher Arm Strength Matter?

by Mike Petriello

On May 9th in Cincinnati, we saw what may have been the least likely caught stealing of the entire season. In the eighth inning of a game the Pirates would go on to lose, 3-2, Pittsburgh catcher Francisco Cervelli accomplished the near-unthinkable: He nailed Billy Hamilton trying to steal second base.

We say that because Hamilton is regarded as baseball's preeminent base stealer, and because Cervelli has been victimized more than any other recent catcher. Since the start of 2015, Hamilton has swiped 115 bags in 131 attempts, making for an outstanding 87.8 percent success rate that's the highest in baseball of the 77 runners with 30 steal attempts in that span. Meanwhile, no catcher in baseball has allowed more stolen bases over the same time than Cervelli's 168, which is a total all the more remarkable because he wasn't even on the field for large chunks of time in 2016 due to a variety of injuries.

To put it far more simply: Hamilton is very good at this! Cervelli is not! On paper, it was just about as big a mismatch as you can get. Dancing off first base with a 1-1 count on Joey Votto, Hamilton took off. The pitch, measured by Statcast as an 87.1 mph slider from Ryan Vogelsong, was slightly inside, and the throw from Cervelli to shortstop Jordy Mercer was on target. "Got him! What a throw by Cervelli… wow!" exclaimed the broadcasters on Cincinnati's Fox Sports Ohio, certainly unaccustomed to seeing Hamilton get thrown out by anyone, much less Cervelli.

The throw's strength was measured as being 79.2 mph. Is that why he caught Hamilton? Is that even *good*?

To answer that question, we need to be able to look at large samples of catcher throws from across the entire major leagues in order to have data to compare that to, and we've never really been able to do that. What we've done, for the most part, is oversimplify things.

Haven't we? Without the ability to measure things like that—and despite the quiet whispers to the contrary from those in the game—fans, media members, and others have insisted on judging a catcher's proficiency at preventing stolen bases by simply looking at stolen base percentage. A low caught stealing percentage makes for a poor catcher; a good one makes for a solid catcher, or so the narrative went. The natural extension to that story is to ascribe a catcher's ability to nail potential base stealers (or not) to having "a strong arm."

Maybe that's true. Sometimes that's definitely true. Of course the strength of a catcher's arm matters to some extent, because it *has* to. For example, while Hank

Conger has his positive attributes, he also has a famously weak arm, and that can't be unrelated to why he's prevented just 19 percent of steal attempts while the league average during his career has been 28 percent. On the other hand, Yankees sensation Gary Sánchez showed a cannon as well as a powerful bat in his rookie season, and he nailed 41 percent of attempted base stealers against a 29 percent league average.

So sure, there's something there, but those are outliers, and either way we know there's so much more that goes into these results. The path to "safe" or "out" on each attempt is really an intersection between a variety of events controlled in part by the pitcher, catcher and runner. Even if the catcher did hold full control over the outcome, arm strength is just a part of the puzzle, because catchers also must release the ball quickly, and he must also place his throw on target. But there are obviously other factors—the pitcher must hold the runner on, and the runner must be quick to the base, and so on. Between the pitcher, catcher and runner—and even the infielder putting the tag on, particularly if we're talking about excellent taggers like Javier Báez or Jonathan Schoop—there are myriad different skills at play, all to get to "safe" or "out."

Arm strength is one of those skills, and now that Statcast is around to track catcher arm strength (as well as just about everything else), it allows us to take a very good first step toward seeing how stolen base success or failure really breaks down. We're only somewhere around the top of the second inning in terms of evaluating all of these new data, as MLB Advanced Media's Tom Tango is fond of saying, so we aren't ready to break out a new fully-formed stolen base metric just yet. What we can do is focus on arm strength and attempt to answer the following questions:

1. Is there a relationship between arm strength and caught stealing percentage, on average?

2. Is there a relationship between arm strength and caught stealing percentage, on individual plays?

3. Is there a wide distribution in arm strength among catchers?

4. What is the distribution between success and failure?

5. And, finally, how in the world did Cervelli actually throw Hamilton out on May 9?

At the end, we should know a bit about how much arm strength "matters," and that's a good first step towards seeing how much it matters compared to everything else that matters.

Using Statcast data, we looked at 1,701 tracked catcher throws to second base on steal attempts from the 2016 season, which broke down into 1,151 successful steals and 550 outs. The number of tracked throws isn't close to being equal to the total number of steal attempts of second base, but it's not expected to be, either, because not every steal attempt draws a throw. Think of how many times a catcher doesn't catch a ball cleanly and doesn't bother with a throw, or throws to third rather than second on a double steal, or doesn't want to risk throwing the ball into center with a man on third base, or never even touches the ball at all because the steal comes on a busted pickoff attempt to the first baseman.

It's more than enough data for a reasonable sample size, so we'll use it and start with our first question above, a relatively simple one: *Is there a relationship between average arm strength and caught stealing percentage?* Above, we briefly discussed Conger and Sánchez, two outliers who seemed to show there was a good relationship between arm strength and caught stealing percentage. How about a relationship across all catchers with at least 10 tracked throws to second on steal attempts? Is there a relationship? Yes. Sort of.

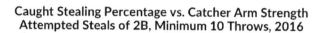

Caught Stealing Percentage vs. Catcher Arm Strength Attempted Steals of 2B, Minimum 10 Throws, 2016

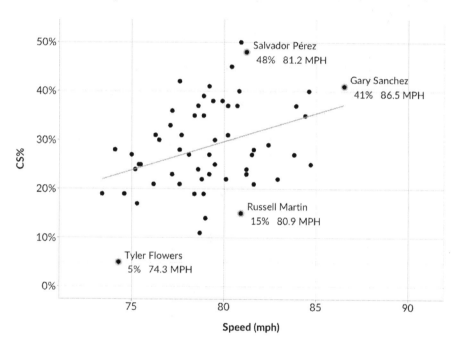

What you see here are the 59 catchers with 10 or more tracked throws to second on steal attempts in 2016, and there's unquestionably some relationship there, though there's a pretty wide distribution around that trend line, too.

Points in favor of "yes, it matters" would be that the lowest caught stealing percentage belongs to Tyler Flowers, who has a weak arm, while one of the highest is Sánchez and his strong arm. Points in opposition would include the fact that Russell Martin and Salvador Perez had similar arm strengths (80.9 mph for Martin,

81.2 mph for Perez), yet had *wildly* differing success rates (15 percent for Martin, 48 percent for Perez).

At the very least we can say it's hard to be very good with a poor arm and you're unlikely to be terrible with a strong arm, but there's still a lot of noise in the middle. Particularly in the 20 percent to 30 percent range of caught stealings, we see arm strength differences of more than 10 miles per hour. Clearly there's more going on here than just hard throws.

So we see somewhat of a relationship, but it's not a satisfying one. Instead of *average*, what does the *distribution* of catcher throws look like? Working in our favor here is that, unlike outfield throws, which include a huge quantity of non-competitive "lobs," all catcher throws to second in theory should be done with strong effort, which helps in our work. So, outliers like Conger and Sánchez aside, is there a huge spread in arm strength of the general population of catchers, in the same way there is between the power of Hamilton and Giancarlo Stanton, or the speed of Hamilton and David Ortiz?

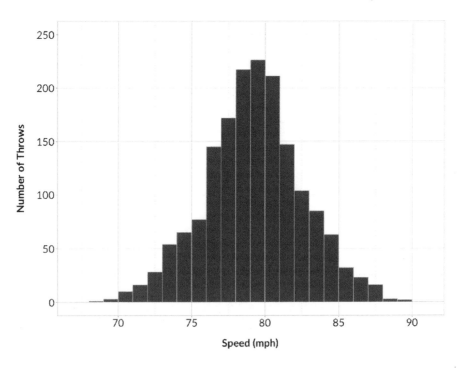

Distribution of Catcher Throws to 2B on Steal Attempts, 2016

As you can see, this is a pretty normal distribution, which isn't unexpected. 65.6 percent (two-thirds, basically) fall in a band between 76 mph and 81 mph, and 48.5 percent (about half) come in the tighter area between 77 mph and 80 mph. When anecdotal evidence started piling up around the Statcast labs this season that most throws always seemed to be between 76 mph and 81 mph, regardless of success, this is what we expected to see. Two-thirds of our sample is about 1,115 throws out of 1,701. It's a huge chunk.

There's a clear "sweet spot" there, and there's obviously some amount of selection bias happening long before the big leagues, where potential catchers who can't make a minimum arm threshold get moved off the position or just don't make it to the majors.

So far, we've seen that it helps to have a stronger arm, but also that it doesn't guarantee success, and the spread between "weak" and "strong," outliers aside, doesn't seem to be that large. In addition, the overall major league average when looking at successes or failures doesn't show much difference:

Average catcher arm strength on stolen bases at second base: 78.8 mph

Average catcher arm strength on caught stealings at second base: 80.1 mph

That's a difference of barely over one mile per hour. Let's convert miles per hour into seconds, and see how long throws take in the air. The average "throw time" (which is the time elapsed from the catcher's release to the time the infielder receives the throw) on stolen bases at second is 1.26 seconds. The average "throw time" for caught stealings is…1.24 seconds. That's two-hundredths of a second, which doesn't seem like all that much.

Maybe, however, this is a failure of "average," where catchers perhaps aren't consistent, or where outliers can skew things. Let's take that same distribution graph and instead of showing strength on *all* throws, we can break it down by "successful steal" and "failed attempt."

Distribution of Catcher Throws to 2B on Steal Attempts
By Outcome, 2016

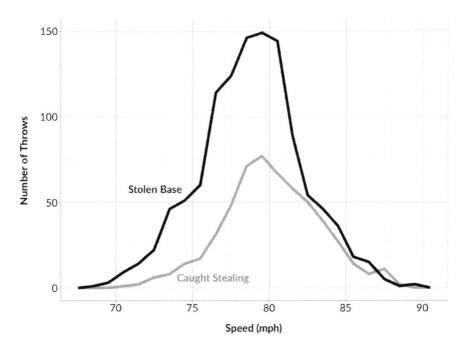

They both follow the same rough distribution pattern of "all throws," though obviously, the raw totals of caught stealings are fewer, since the success rate was around 70 percent. Success or fail, there's a peak around 79 miles per hour, which aligns with our average numbers above. You'll notice, however, that the decline is a lot softer for caught stealings as the velocity increases. Above around 82, the lines nearly intersect. Perhaps it's less about average and more about "percentage of throws above inflection point," where below a certain mph range a bad throw is a bad throw, regardless if it's 70 or 73 or 76—though of course that would affect your "average."

Let's look at it another way. Instead of distribution, what if we look at the success or fail rates for mph buckets, from low to high?

Success Rate for Catcher Throws to 2B on Steal Attempts

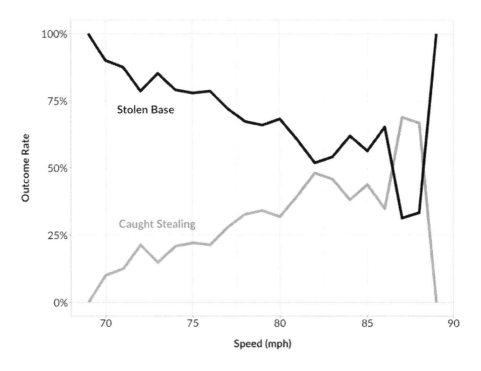

(Don't worry too much about the freakout on the right side, which is all about sample size—there were only five throws at 88 or 89 mph, three by San Diego's Christian Bethancourt, whom the Padres are reportedly considering using as a part-time pitcher in 2017. Sánchez had one, and Drew Butera had the other, though since his throw was tracked at just 102.1 feet of the 124-125 required, baserunner Adam Eaton was easily safe.)

Now we're getting somewhere. We see again that 82 mph is a very important point for success, and maybe that's where it pays to start caring about a catcher's arm strength. To that end, we noted earlier that two-thirds of our throws fell between 76 mph and 81 mph, and separately we're seeing that 82 mph seems to be an important line. What if we broke it down into what happens when throws are in that primary band, as compared to throws above and below?

CS% by MPH, 2016			
MPH	**CS**	**Attempts**	**CS%**
75-	48	257	18.7%
76-81	352	1,118	31.5%
82+	148	328	45.1%

Perhaps this is the purest view. Above, we showed a decent relationship between arm strength and caught stealing success, but looking at the averages for catchers allows for dozens of potential inputs without regard for frequency. This puts the relationship between throwing arm and caught stealing success on an individual basis, and it certainly seems stronger than expected—particularly at 82 mph and above.

Cervelli didn't hit 82, however. His throw was 79.2, remember. But let's go back to the Cervelli play and answer the question we originally posed. The 79.2 mph throw he unleashed was just about at the major league average. So if Cervelli's arm strength wasn't all that notable in the play, what did he do—or, perhaps, what did others do—to help turn the outcome into an out? As you'd expect, it's not that Hamilton wasn't running quickly; he made it from first to second base in 3.68 seconds, better than the average times in our sample both for successful steals (3.78) and failed steals (3.91).

It's not that Hamilton had a poor lead, not really. At the time Vogelsong released the pitch, Hamilton was 21.1 feet off the base, meaning he cut 90 feet down to just under 70 feet. That's better than the usual average for failed steals (20.4 feet), yet below the average for successful steals (23.1 feet), though Hamilton's elite speed should ameliorate that somewhat, and he'd swiped bags with leads as short as 18 feet.

Nor is it that the pitch was so fast that it gave the catcher a head start, either. As we noted above, an 87.1 mph pitch doesn't stand out, and pitch velocity doesn't seem to have any correlation whatsoever between successful steals (89.3 mph) and failed steals (89.2 mph). It wasn't that Vogelsong was particularly quick to the plate, either, with a 1.10 second release time that's right in between the averages for successful steals (1.13) and times caught (1.08).

But there were a few things that stood out. Most notably, while Cervelli's throw wasn't necessarily *strong*, it was *accurate*, nearly perfectly so, as you can see by this frame of the play just a split second before Mercer received the ball. He merely had to drop his hand slightly and allow Hamilton to slide right into the out.

Second, Cervelli did an outstanding job of getting rid of the ball quickly. While we can measure "pop time," which tracks the time from the time the pitch hits the catcher's glove to the time it hits the infielder's glove (i.e., the "pops") that time includes the throw, and we've spent more than enough time on that. So instead let's break it down into just "exchange" time, which measures how quickly Cervelli released the ball after he caught it. Pop time is throw time plus exchange time, so it allows for different measurements.

Overall, Cervelli was a somewhat below-average catcher in terms of exchange time, tying for 35th with a 0.75 second mark, where the range goes from 0.64 (David Ross) to 0.88 (Jarrod Saltalamacchia). The major league average for exchange time on steal attempts at second base was 0.73, so while we're not talking about huge numbers here, every fraction counts.

On this play, however, Cervelli came in at a scorching 0.57 seconds. It was his third-fastest time of the season and best on a successful caught stealing. Interestingly enough, his best two times both came against Milwaukee's Keon Broxton, who stole 23 times in 27 attempts in his rookie season and had speed so elite he had the sixth-fastest home-to-third time measured by a righty hitter on a triple this year, behind four from Byron Buxton and one from Manuel Margot. That triple by Broxton was so blazing that it came on a ball to *left field*, against the strong-armed Starling Marte, with Cervelli right there to see it.

So it seems easily possible, if not probable, that Cervelli was well aware of the speed on the bases and put extra emphasis on getting the ball out quickly. Since he was able to do that with an accurate throw and decent enough velocity, and because nothing Vogelsong did put his catcher at a particular disadvantage, he was able to throw out baseball's reigning base-stealing king.

You can see how much more work remains, of course. Once correlations are run against all of the various inputs that go into "safe" or "out," we'll have a much better idea of how much credit or blame is due to each party. Instead of just how much lead distance a runner had when the pitcher threw the ball, we'll be able to push deeper and see just where he was when the catcher caught and released the ball, too.

It's good to have a strong arm for a catcher, and while that perhaps seemed obvious, it's nice to have some empirical evidence around it. It's just one of a ton of different things that go into it. You probably already knew not to judge a catcher based on "caught stealing percentage" alone. Now, you know where and how arm strength starts to make a difference.

References & Resources

- Special thanks to Jason Bernard and Tom Tango of Major League Baseball Advanced Media for data assistance.

Et Cetera

Glossary

BABIP: Batting Average on Balls in Play. This is a measure of the number of batted balls that safely fall in for hits (not including home runs). The exact formula we use is (H-HR)/(AB-K-HR+SF).

Batted-ball statistics: When a batter hits a ball, he hits either a ground ball, fly ball or line drive. The resulting ground ball, fly ball and line drive percentages make up a player's mix of statistics, with infield fly balls, or pop-ups, being tracked as a percentage of a player's total number of fly balls.

BB%: Walk rate measures how often a position player walks—or how often a pitcher walks a batter—per plate appearance. It is measured in percentage form.

BB/9: Walks allowed per nine innings

ChampAdded: The proportion of a World Series championship contributed by a player or team, based on the impact of a play on a team's winning a game, and the value of that game within the context of winning the World Series. Please refer to "Davis' Dinger, Cubs Team Effort Shine Brightest," for more information.

DRS: Defensive Runs Saved. DRS rates players as above or below average based on "runs," with data from Baseball Info Solutions used as an input. It tracks a number of different aspects of defensive play, including stolen bases, double plays, outfield arms, robbing home runs and range.

ERA: A pitcher's total number of earned runs allowed divided by his total number of innings pitched, multiplied by nine.

ERA-: A pitching version of wRC+: 100 represents a league-average ERA, and a smaller ERA- is better.

ERA+: ERA measured against the league average and adjusted for ballpark factors. An ERA+ over 100 is better than average, less than 100 is below average.

FIP: Fielding Independent Pitching, a measure of all things for which a pitcher is specifically responsible. The formula is (HR*13+(BB+HBP)*3-K*2)/IP, plus a league-specific factor (usually around 3.2) to round out the number to an equivalent ERA number. FIP helps you understand how well a pitcher pitched, regardless of how well his fielders fielded.

FIP-: A pitching version of OPS+ and wRC+: 100 represents a league-average FIP, and a smaller FIP- is better.

Game Score: A metric devised by Bill James to determine the strength of a pitcher in any particular baseball game. An average Game Score is 50, with the range going from 0 to 114. The highest Game Score ever recorded for a nine-inning game was 105, by Kerry Wood in his famous 20-strikeout game on May 6, 1998. FanGraphs uses a newer version of the metric, called Game Score Version 2.0 (GSv2), which was developed by Tom Tango.

GB%: See batted-ball statistics.

ISO: Isolated power. This is a measure of a hitter's raw power, or how good he is at hitting for extra bases. Most simply, the formula is SLG-AVG, but you can also calculate it as such: $((2B)+(2*3B)+(3*HR))/AB$.

K%: Strikeout rate measures how often a position player strikes out—or how often a pitcher strikes out a batter—per plate appearance. It is measured in percentage form.

K/9: Strikeouts per nine innings

K/BB: Strikeout-to-walk ratio

LARS: A new defensive metric introduced in this book. Please refer to "Solving the Defensive Quandary with Statcast: Introducing LARS," for more information.

LI: Leverage Index. LI measures the criticality of a play or plate appearance. It is based on the range of potential WPA outcomes of a play, compared to all other plays. 1.0 is an average Index.

Linear Weights: The historical average runs scored for each event in a baseball game.

OBP: On-base percentage, an essential tool, measures how frequently a batter reaches base safely. The formula is: $(H+BB+HBP)/(AB+BB+HBP+SF)$.

OPS: On Base plus Slugging Percentage, a crude but quick measure of a batter's true contribution to his team's offense. See wOBA for a better approach.

PITCHf/x: Sportvision's pitch tracking system, which has been installed in every major league stadium since at least the start of the 2007 season. It tracks several aspects of every pitch thrown in a major league game, including velocity, movement, release point, spin and pitch location.

Pythagorean Formula: A formula for converting a team's run differential into a projected win-loss record. The formula is $RS^2/(RS^2+RA^2)$. Teams' actual win-loss records tend to mirror their Pythagorean records, and variances usually can be attributed to luck.

You can improve the accuracy of the Pythagorean formula by using a different exponent (the 2 in the formula). The best exponent can be calculated this way: $(RS/G+RA/G)^{.285}$, where RS/G is Runs Scored per Game and RA/G is Runs Allowed per Game. This is called the PythagoPat formula.

Slash Line: At times, writers may refer to a batter's "slash line," or "triple-slash line." They mean something like this: .287/.345/.443. The numbers between those slashes are the batter's batting average, on-base percentage and slugging percentage.

Statcast: A tracking technology capable of gathering and displaying previously immeasurable aspects of the game. Statcast collects the data using a series of high-resolution optical cameras along with radar equipment that has been installed in all 30 major league ballparks. The technology tracks the location and movements of the ball and every player on the field at any given time.

UZR: A fielding system similar to Defensive Runs Saved. Both systems calculate a fielder's range by comparing his plays made in various "vectors" across the baseball diamond to the major league average rate of plays made in those vectors. Both systems also look at other factors such as the effectiveness of outfield throwing, handling bunts and turning double plays.

WAR: Wins Above Replacement. A "win stat" that calculates the number of wins a player contributed to his team above a certain replacement level. WAR is calculated at FanGraphs and Baseball-Reference. Though the two implementations vary a bit, they share a common framework that includes a linear weights approach to runs created, advanced fielding metrics, leverage for relievers and replacement levels that vary by position. In addition, beginning in 2013, both versions unified their definition of replacement level, making the two versions more directly comparable. In this book, it is fair to assume that the version of WAR in question is FanGraphs WAR, or fWAR, unless otherwise noted.

wOBA: A linear weights offensive rating system that is similar to OPS, except that it's set to the scale of on-base percentage.

WPA: Win Probability Added is a system in which each player is given credit toward helping his team win, based on play-by-play data and the impact each specific play has on the team's probability of winning.

wRC+: Like ERA+, wRC+ is scaled so that 100 is average and a higher number is positive. The "RC" stands for Runs Created, but it's not Bill James' Runs Created. It's a "linear weights" version derived from wOBA.

xFIP: Expected Fielding Independent Pitching. This is an experimental stat that adjusts FIP and "normalizes" the home run component according to the number of fly balls a pitcher allowed.

For more information on these and other statistics, visit: *hardballtimes.com/tools/glossary* or *fangraphs.com/library*.

Who Was That?

Rob Arthur is a Chicago-based writer and journalist. His work can be found at FiveThirtyEight, The Athletic, and assorted other destinations both in print and on the internet. After a long and protracted battle, he earned a PhD in evolutionary genetics from the University of Chicago in 2015.

Emma Baccellieri lives in Washington, D.C., where she used to write about both politics and sports and now writes only about the latter. She is a recent graduate of Duke University.

Carson Cistulli lives in Maine with his wife and dog.

Joe Distelheim, a retired newspaper editor, has been part of the Hardball Times staff for approximately 108 years. Having finally willed the Cubs to a World Series championship, he will now turn his attention to promoting peace, justice and the proper use of the apostrophe.

Sean Dolinar is a developer for FanGraphs specializing in data visualization. He lives in Pittsburgh.

Adam Dorhauer grew up a third-generation Cardinals fan in Missouri, and now lives in Ohio. His writing on baseball focuses on the history of the game, as well as statistical concepts as they apply to baseball.

Patrick Dubuque did not make Lookout Landing a thing, but does not still write there about the Mariners. Instead he writes a regular column for Baseball Prospectus, and devises new methods to talk his son and daughter into eating two more pieces of chicken. Okay, one piece of chicken and a spoon of rice. One piece of chicken.

Dan Epstein is the author of *Stars and Strikes: Baseball and America in the Bicentennial Summer of '76* and *Big Hair and Plastic Grass: A Funky Ride Through Baseball and America in the Swinging '70s*. He lives in Chicago with his wife Katie and their cats Oscar and Otis, and he thinks *Tattoo You* was the last great Stones album.

August Fagerstrom used to be a Cleveland-based sports writer who wrote for FanGraphs. Now he works for a major league team. He will always be a graduate of Kent State University.

Stacey Gotsulias enjoys writing about random box scores for The Hardball Times, and also contributes to Beyond the Box Score, FanRagSports and Baseball Prospectus Bronx. She currently lives with two humans and five felines in the suburbs of New York City.

Travis Howell is a marketer and graphic designer who resides in the Denver area. In his spare time, he referees ice hockey games. He killed a bear when he was nine years old.

Brad Johnson is a baseball addict and a statistics junkie who currently resides in Carrboro, N.C. He played four seasons of injury-plagued baseball at Macalester

College from 2006 through 2009, and has since made the transition to a purely off-the-field existence. You can find his work on FanGraphs and RotoWorld.

David Kagan claims to be "The Einstein of the National Pastime." He earned his Ph.D. in physics from the University of California, Berkeley. He has been a physics professor at California State University, Chico since 1981. Dr. Kagan is a regular contributor to *The Physics Teacher*, as well as The Hardball Times.

Corinne Landrey writes for MLB.com's Cut4 site and FanGraphs. At the age of six, she uncovered her passion for baseball analysis by tirelessly complaining about the performance of Kyle Abbott. Everything made sense years later when she discovered Abbott posted an ERA+ of 69 during that fateful season.

Joon Lee is a soon-to-be graduate of Cornell University who has been published in *The Washington Post*, The Ringer, SB Nation, Boston.com, *Boston Herald*, The Hardball Times and WEEI.com.

Jason Linden teaches English and writes stuff (sometimes baseball, sometimes other stuff). Yes, he can give you homework, so be nice. His novel, *When the Sparrow Sings*, is out there knocking around. He digs the folks at The Hardball Times and thinks they are generally decent folk.

Eric Longenhagen is FanGraphs' lead prospect analyst. He hails from Catasauqua, Pa., and currently resides in Tempe, Ariz.

Chris Mitchell created the KATOH projection system and writes about prospects at FanGraphs. In real life, he holds degrees in mathematics and economics from Fordham University and works in economic development. He lives in New York City with his girlfriend, Lexi, who's far too excited to see her name in print.

Jack Moore is a freelance writer based in Minneapolis writing about sports, history, mythology, and the intersection of the trio. He is still waiting for the Twins to tear down their statue of Calvin Griffith.

Dustin Nosler is a writer at Dodgers Digest, co-host of the Dugout Blues podcast, and wears a number of hats for FanGraphs and The Hardball Times.

Sara Nović is a writer and professor who learned most of what she knows about love, loss, and how to curse from watching the Mets with her dad and grandma. She writes about the Mets for Baseball Prospectus, and her first novel, *Girl at War*, is out from Random House.

A former river guide, ranch hand, farm hand, oyster shucker and, most unlikely of all, editor-in-chief of a magazine, **John Paschal** has written sports and opinion for *The Dallas Morning News*, *The (Memphis) Commercial Appeal*, the *Corpus Christi Caller-Times* and other dead-tree publications. Online, he has contributed to The Hardball Times, NotGraphs, Baseball Prospectus, Deadspin and The Good Men Project.

Mike Petriello works for MLB.com, focusing on Statcast. He used to write for FanGraphs & ESPN, and now he does not. He built The Hardball Times website, unless you don't like it, in which case he did not. He lives in New York City with one wife, one toddler and two cats.

Kate Preusser lives in Seattle, where she runs Lookout Landing, the SB Nation site about the Seattle Mariners, and dreams of giving her neighbor's leaf blower the Lou Piniella treatment.

Alex Remington writes for The Hardball Times and manages Braves Journal, and is a product manager at *The Washington Post*. He is still annoyed about Kent Hrbek.

Eno Sarris has ruined beer, sandwiches, pitching, fingers and most of baseball with his nerdery, and is ready to start taking on more inanimate objects like mud, bats and balls. Then one day nothing will be fun for anyone except Eno Sarris.

Gerald Schifman is the lead researcher at *Crain's New York Business* and a writer for The Hardball Times. Previously, he worked in the New York Mets' baseball operations department, Major League Baseball's publishing department and the newsrooms of *Money* and CNN. He graduated from New York University in 2013 with a double major in economics and journalism.

Alexandra Simon first dipped her toe into Detroit Tigers fandom in 1994 as a curious child, but didn't become a full-fledged fan until the disaster that was the Tigers' 119-loss 2003 season. These days you can find her either at Toledo Mudhens games yelling at people to quit trying to start the wave or on Twitter, also yelling at people to quit trying to start the wave. She dedicates her section in this book to retired pitcher Dan Haren.

Greg Simons has been writing about baseball in various formats since the last millennium, and he's been with The Hardball Times since 2010, serving as both an editor and writer. When he's not thinking or writing about baseball, he's playing it, participating in 1860s-era vintage base ball (yep, it was two words back then) matches around the Midwest. While he's an avid St. Louis Cardinals loyalist, he offers heartfelt congratulations to the Cubs and their countless fans.

Jeff Sullivan inarguably continues to write about baseball, here and in other places. Mostly, those other places comprise FanGraphs and previous editions of this very book. He is still alive in Oregon, hopefully.

Paul Swydan is the managing editor of The Hardball Times, and has been writing about baseball for over a decade, somehow. He spends most of his time with his children, Jasmine and Xander.

Shane Tourtellotte is a refugee from the Northeast living in Asheville, N.C. He's published a few hundred thousand words of science fiction, but this didn't strike people as bizarre enough, so he shifted over to baseball. He's attended games at 18 active major-league parks. Once SunTrust Park opens outside Atlanta, he'll be down to 17. Gee, thanks, guys.

Steve Treder contributed a weekly column to The Hardball Times online from its founding in 2004 through 2011, and has been a co-author of many *Hardball Times*

Annual and *Hardball Times Season Preview* books. His work has also been featured in *Nine*, *The National Pastime*, and other publications. He has frequently been a presenter at baseball forums such as the SABR National Convention, the Nine Spring Training Conference, and the Cooperstown Symposium.

In his day job, Steve is senior vice president at Western Management Group, a compensation consulting firm headquartered in Los Gatos, Calif. When Steve grows up, he hopes to play center field for the San Francisco Giants.

Neil Weinberg never successfully executed a back pick during his days as a junior varsity catcher. This failure moved him to take up writing, an avocation for which he is marginally better suited. His work currently appears at FanGraphs, The Hardball Times and New English D.

Sarah Wexler is a Los Angeles native, a Dodgers fan and an aspiring baseball historian. She writes for Dodgers Digest, FanGraphs and The Hardball Times.

Stacie Wheeler, a USC Cinema alumnus, is a writer and video creator for Dodgers Digest, The Hardball Times and her YouTube channel DishingUpTheDodgers. A lifelong fan, she thankfully wasn't banned from Dodger Stadium after her uncle dropped a pen into Raul Mondesi's eye.

Jeff Zimmerman writes for RotoGraphs, FanGraphs, The Hardball Times, RotoWire, *Baseball America* and Baseball HQ. This past year he was nominated for the SABR Analytics Award (for velocity effects on arm injuries) and won the inaugural head-to-head Tout Wars fantasy baseball league. Additionally, he always tries to find a way to include his two lovely kids, Cole and Ruby, in each of his bios.

Made in the USA
Middletown, DE
30 December 2016